Garfield at large

BY: JIM DAVIS

BALLANTINE BOOKS · NEW YORK

PUBLISHED IN THE UNITED STATES BY BALLANTINE BOOKS, A DIVISION OF RANDOM HOUSE, INC., NEW YORK, AND SIMULTANEOUSLY IN CANADA BY RANDOM HOUSE OF CANADA, LIMITED, TORONTO, CANADA.

LIBRARY OF CONGRESS CATALOG CARD NUMBER: 79-93191

ISBN 0-345-28779-7

MANUFACTURED IN THE UNITED STATES OF AMERICA

FIRST EDITION: MARCH 1980

20 19 18 17 16 15 14 13 12 11 10

LOOK INSIDE THIS BOOK
AND SEE THIS CAT...
- EAT LASAGNA
- CHASE DOGS
- DESTROY A MAILMAN
- LAUGH;CRY,FFFT
- SHRED HIS OWNER
- AND MUCH,MUCH MORE!

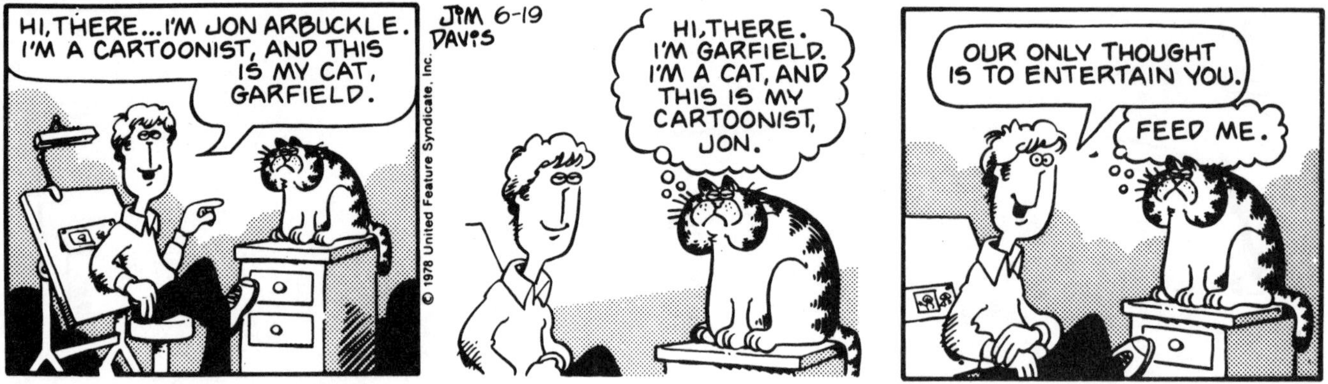
HI, THERE...I'M JON ARBUCKLE. I'M A CARTOONIST, AND THIS IS MY CAT, GARFIELD.
JIM DAVIS 6-19
© 1978 United Feature Syndicate, Inc.
HI, THERE. I'M GARFIELD. I'M A CAT, AND THIS IS MY CARTOONIST, JON.
OUR ONLY THOUGHT IS TO ENTERTAIN YOU.
FEED ME.

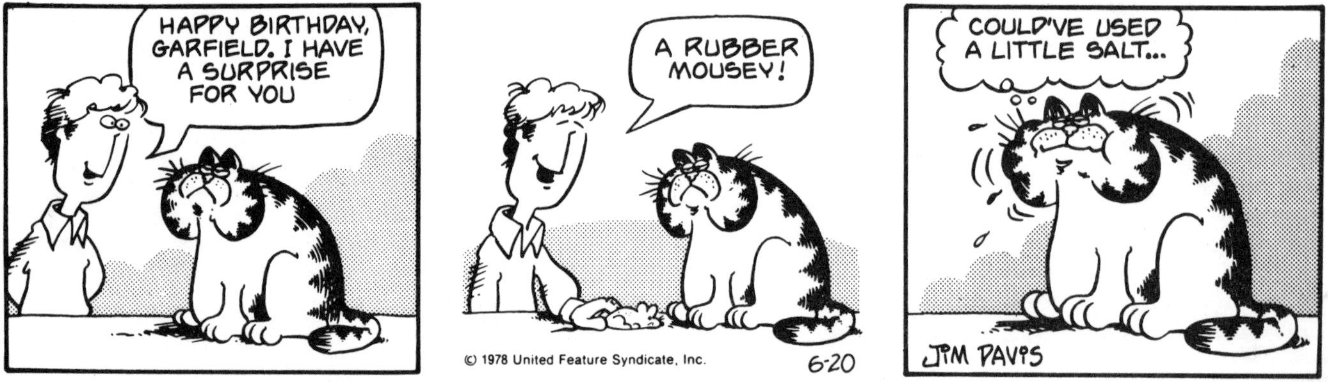
HAPPY BIRTHDAY, GARFIELD. I HAVE A SURPRISE FOR YOU
A RUBBER MOUSEY!
© 1978 United Feature Syndicate, Inc.
6-20
COULD'VE USED A LITTLE SALT...
JIM DAVIS

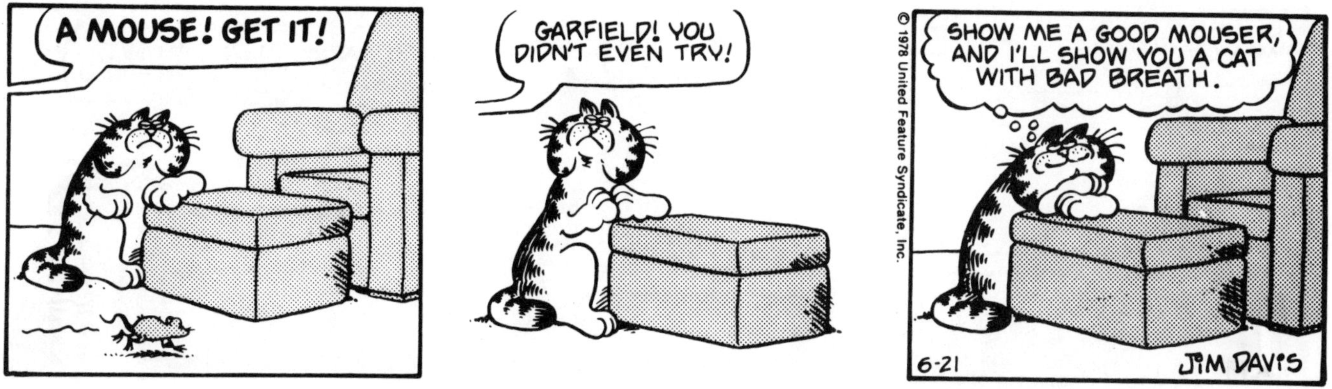
A MOUSE! GET IT!
GARFIELD! YOU DIDN'T EVEN TRY!
SHOW ME A GOOD MOUSER, AND I'LL SHOW YOU A CAT WITH BAD BREATH.
© 1978 United Feature Syndicate, Inc.
6-21
JIM DAVIS

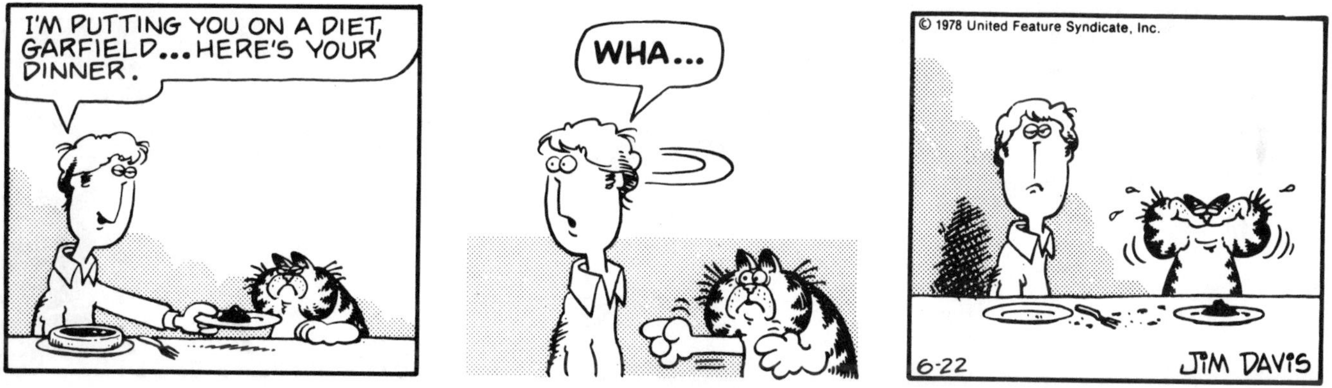
I'M PUTTING YOU ON A DIET, GARFIELD... HERE'S YOUR DINNER.
WHA...
© 1978 United Feature Syndicate, Inc.
6-22
JIM DAVIS

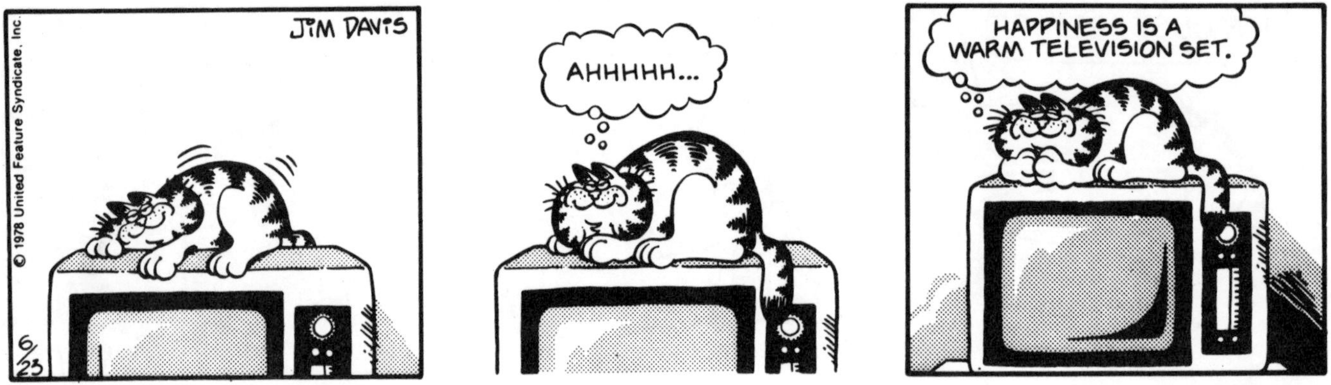

JIM DAVIS
© 1978 United Feature Syndicate, Inc.
6/23
AHHHHH...
HAPPINESS IS A WARM TELEVISION SET.

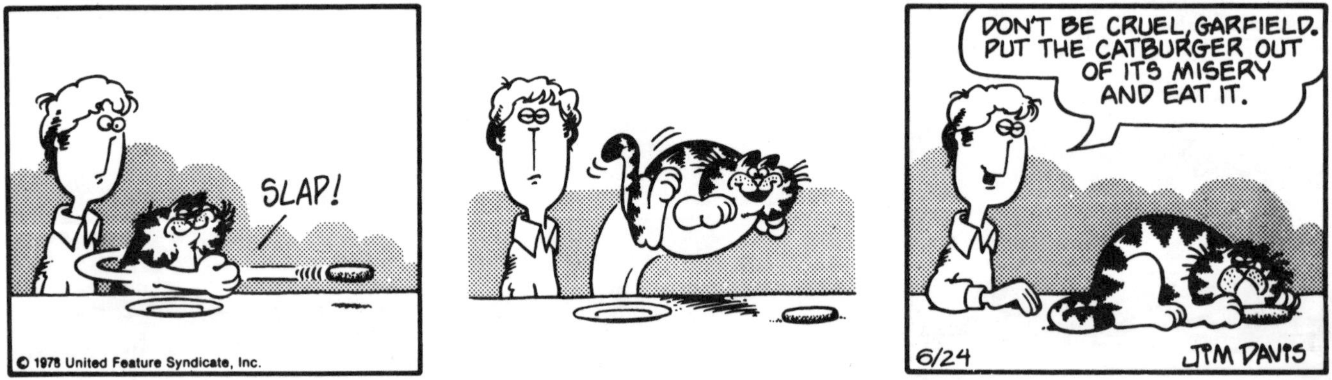

SLAP!
© 1978 United Feature Syndicate, Inc.
DON'T BE CRUEL, GARFIELD. PUT THE CATBURGER OUT OF ITS MISERY AND EAT IT.
6/24
JIM DAVIS

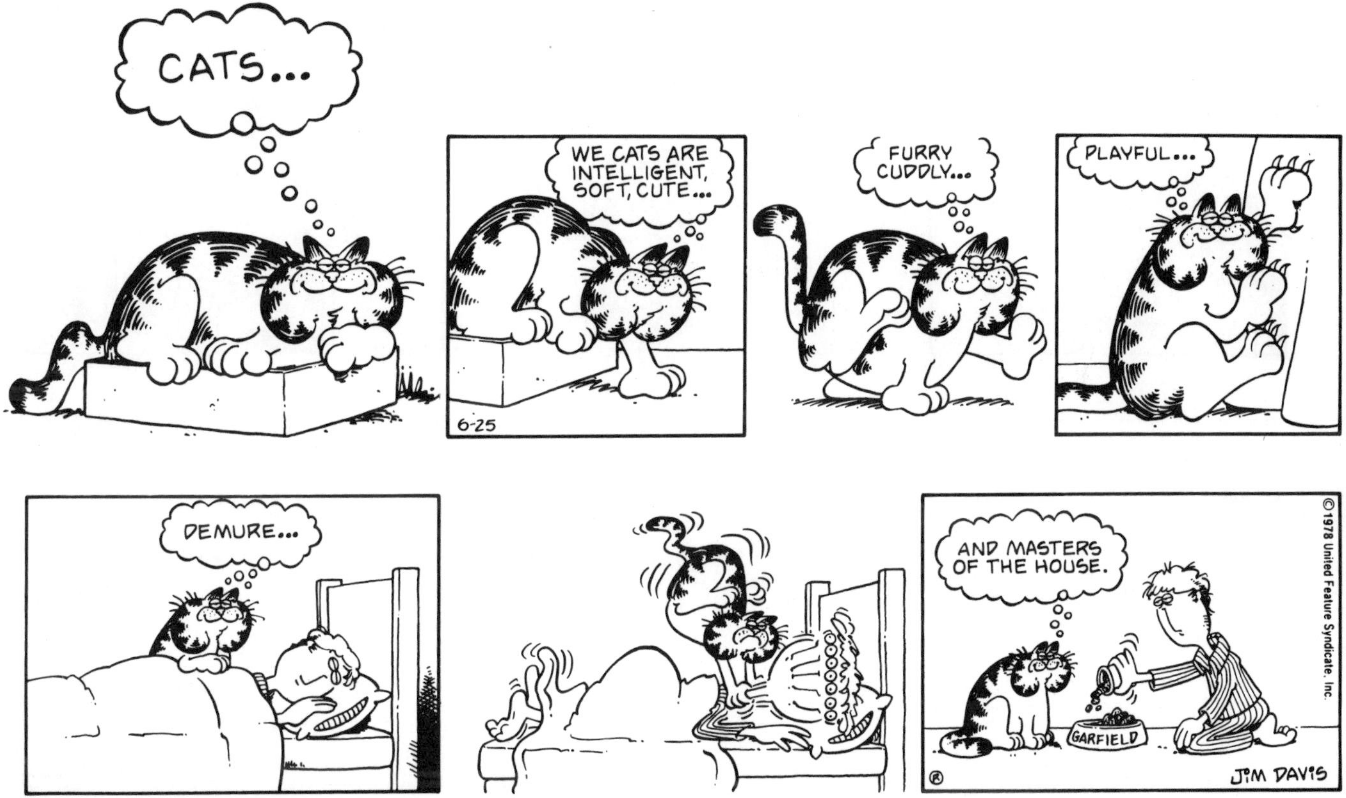
CATS...
WE CATS ARE INTELLIGENT, SOFT, CUTE...
6-25
FURRY CUDDLY...
PLAYFUL...
DEMURE...
AND MASTERS OF THE HOUSE.
GARFIELD
© 1978 United Feature Syndicate, Inc.
JIM DAVIS

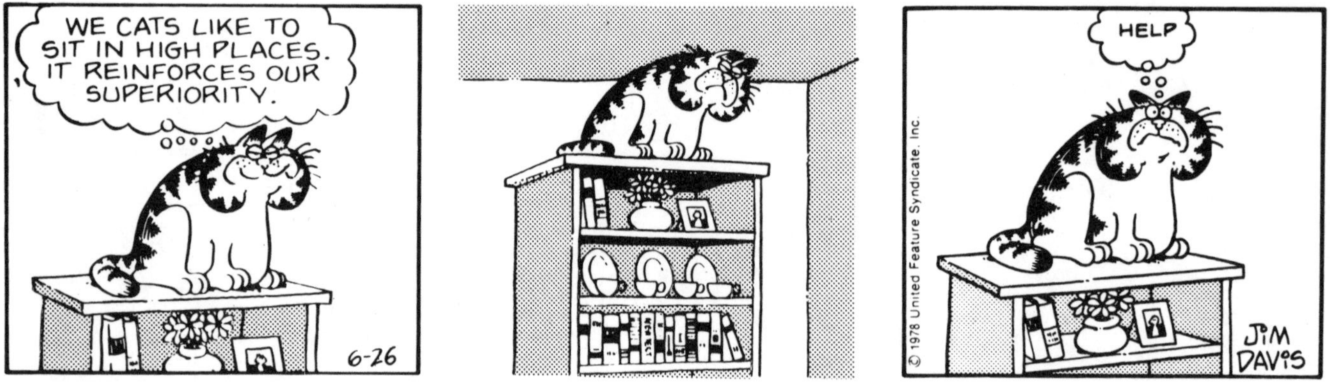
WE CATS LIKE TO SIT IN HIGH PLACES. IT REINFORCES OUR SUPERIORITY.
6-26
HELP
© 1978 United Feature Syndicate, Inc.
JIM DAVIS

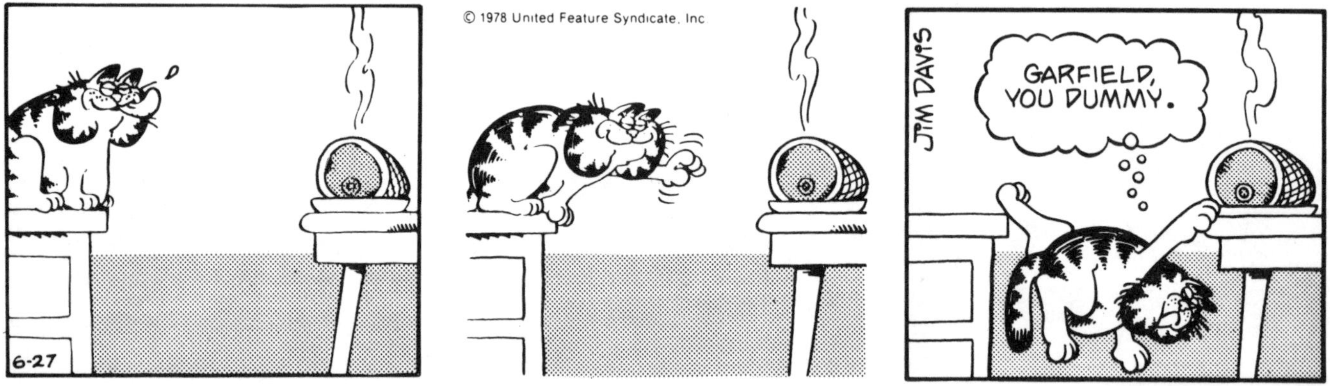
6-27
© 1978 United Feature Syndicate, Inc
JIM DAVIS
GARFIELD, YOU DUMMY.

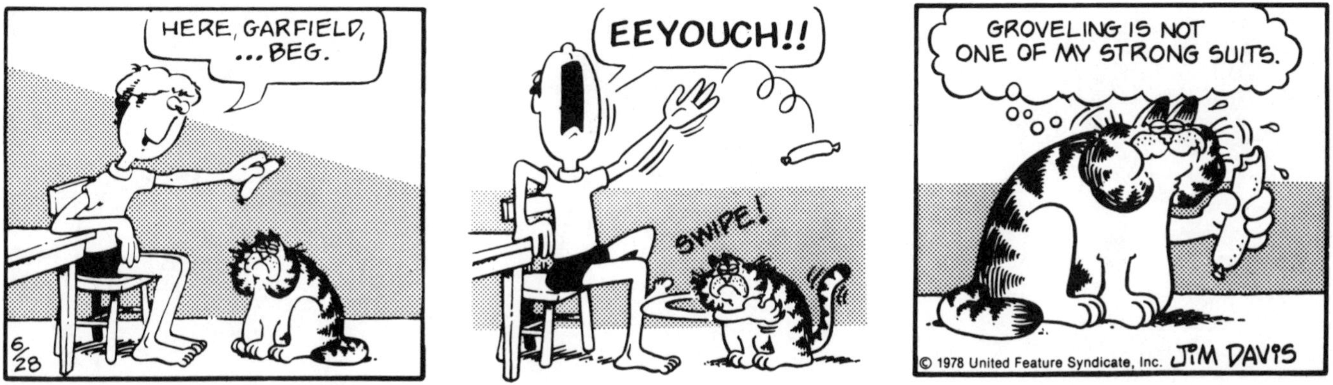
HERE, GARFIELD, ...BEG.
6/28
EEYOUCH!!
SWIPE!
GROVELING IS NOT ONE OF MY STRONG SUITS.
© 1978 United Feature Syndicate, Inc.
JIM DAVIS

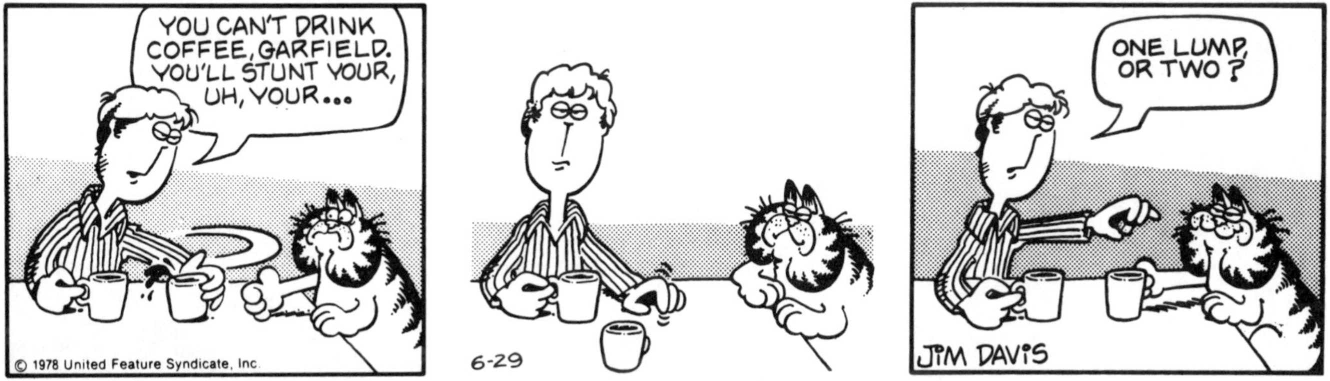
YOU CAN'T DRINK COFFEE, GARFIELD. YOU'LL STUNT YOUR, UH, YOUR...
© 1978 United Feature Syndicate, Inc.
6-29
ONE LUMP, OR TWO?
JIM DAVIS

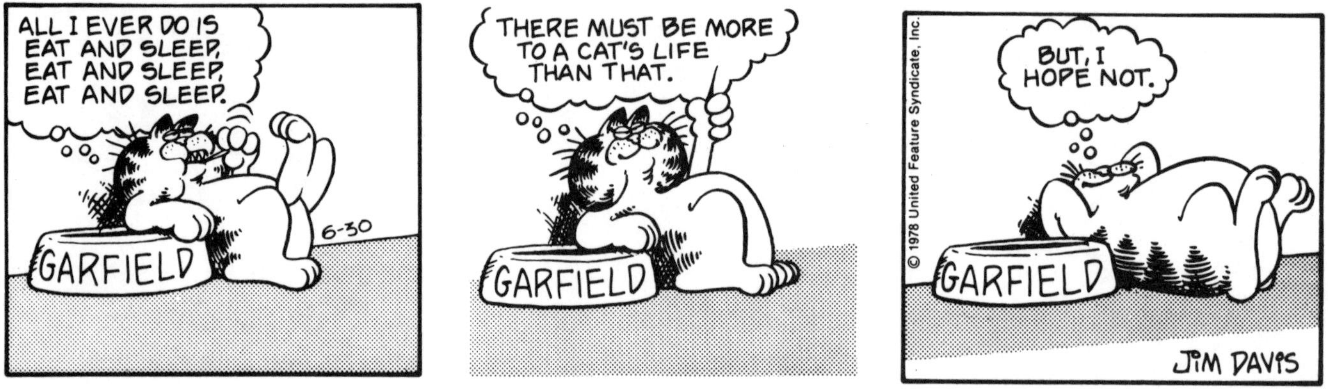
ALL I EVER DO IS EAT AND SLEEP, EAT AND SLEEP, EAT AND SLEEP.
GARFIELD
6-30
THERE MUST BE MORE TO A CAT'S LIFE THAN THAT.
GARFIELD
© 1978 United Feature Syndicate, Inc.
BUT, I HOPE NOT.
GARFIELD
JIM DAVIS

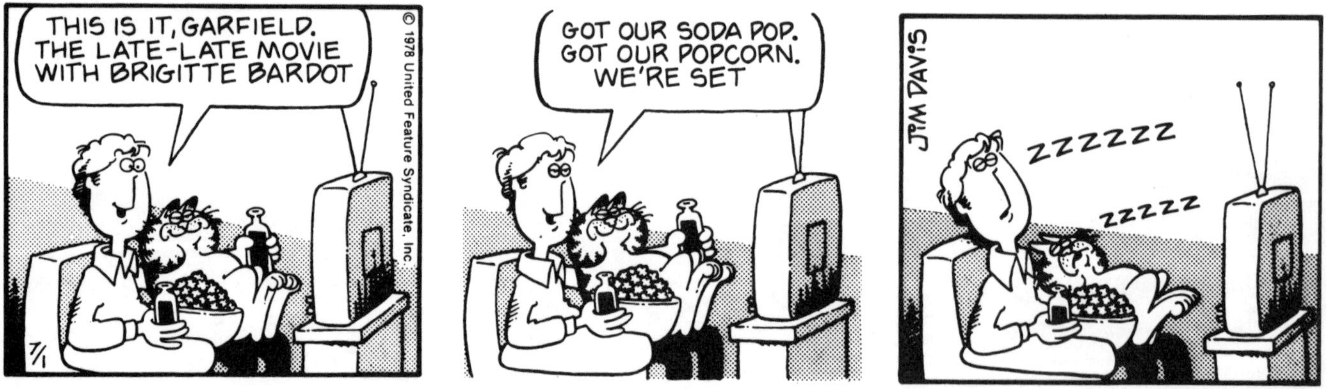
THIS IS IT, GARFIELD. THE LATE-LATE MOVIE WITH BRIGITTE BARDOT
© 1978 United Feature Syndicate, Inc.
7/1
GOT OUR SODA POP. GOT OUR POPCORN. WE'RE SET
JIM DAVIS
ZZZZZZ
ZZZZZ

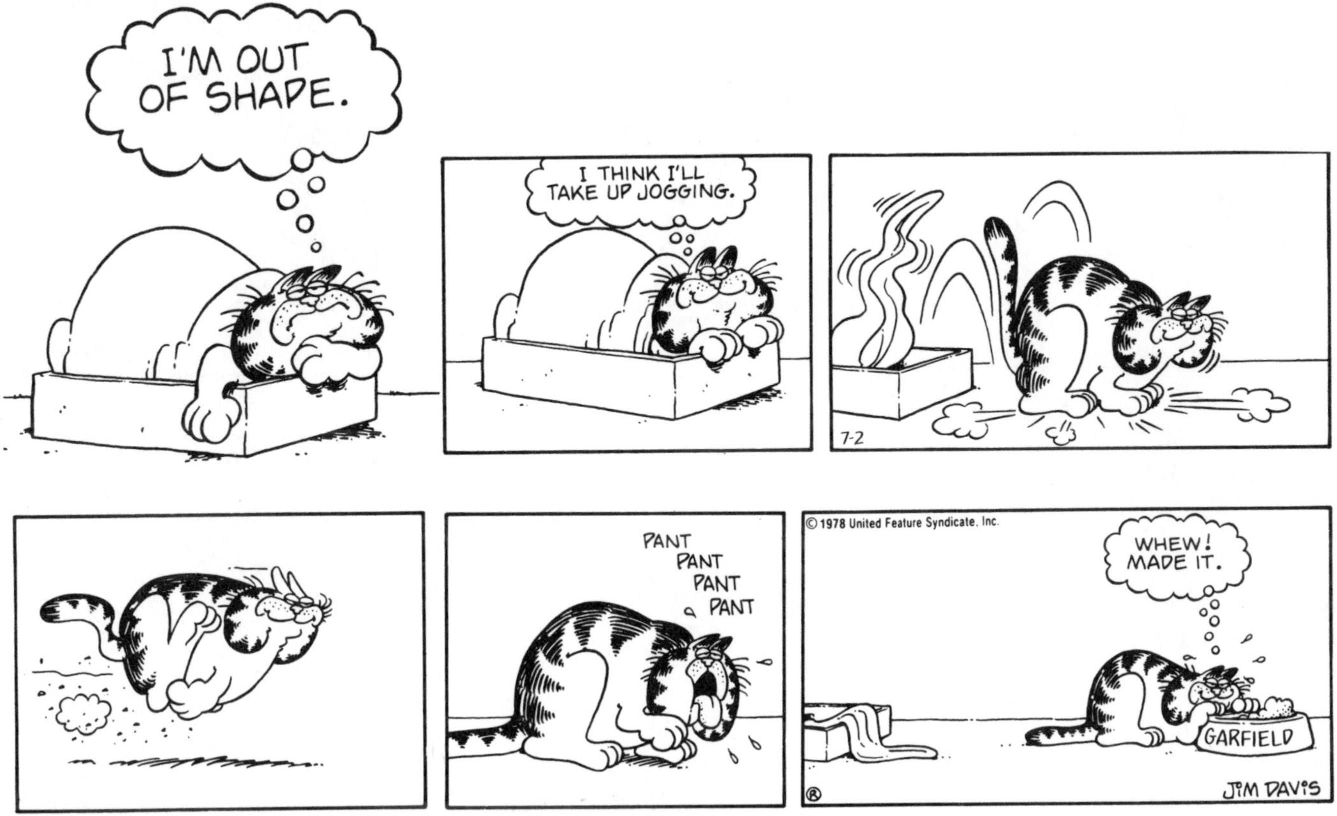
I'M OUT OF SHAPE.
I THINK I'LL TAKE UP JOGGING.
7-2
© 1978 United Feature Syndicate, Inc.
PANT PANT PANT PANT
WHEW! MADE IT.
GARFIELD
JIM DAVIS

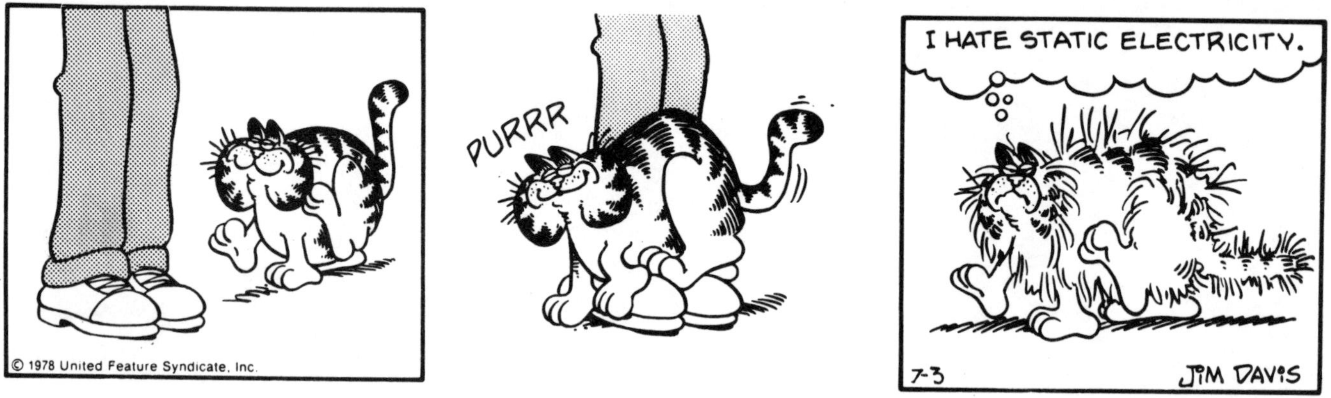
© 1978 United Feature Syndicate, Inc.
PURRR
I HATE STATIC ELECTRICITY.
7-3
JIM DAVIS

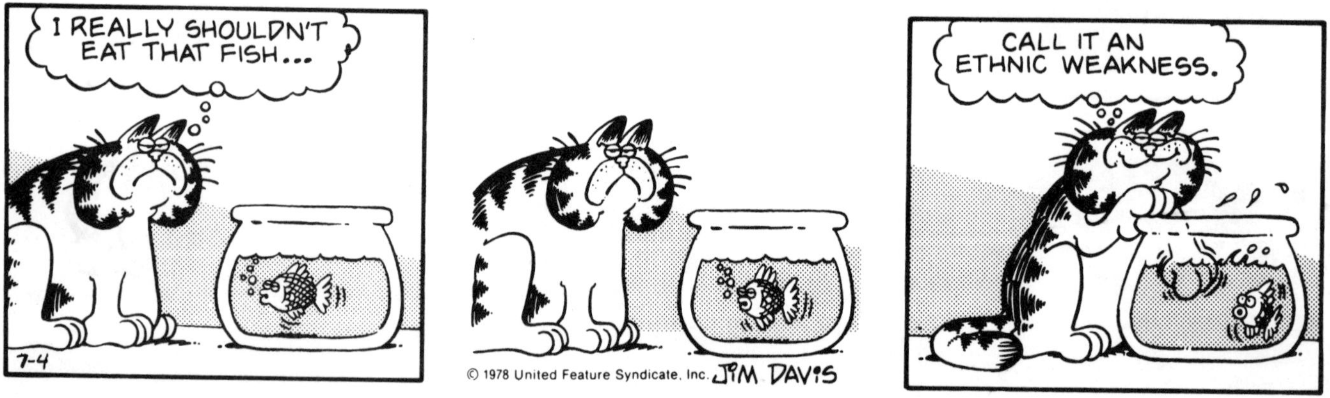
I REALLY SHOULDN'T EAT THAT FISH...
7-4
© 1978 United Feature Syndicate, Inc.
JIM DAVIS
CALL IT AN ETHNIC WEAKNESS.

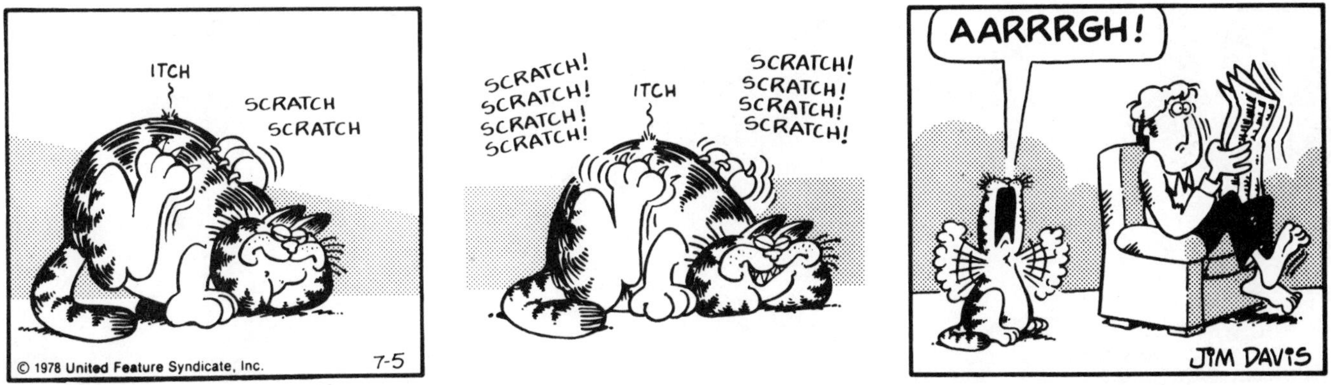
ITCH
SCRATCH
SCRATCH
© 1978 United Feature Syndicate, Inc.
7-5
SCRATCH! SCRATCH! SCRATCH! SCRATCH!
ITCH
SCRATCH! SCRATCH! SCRATCH! SCRATCH!
AARRRGH!
JIM DAVIS

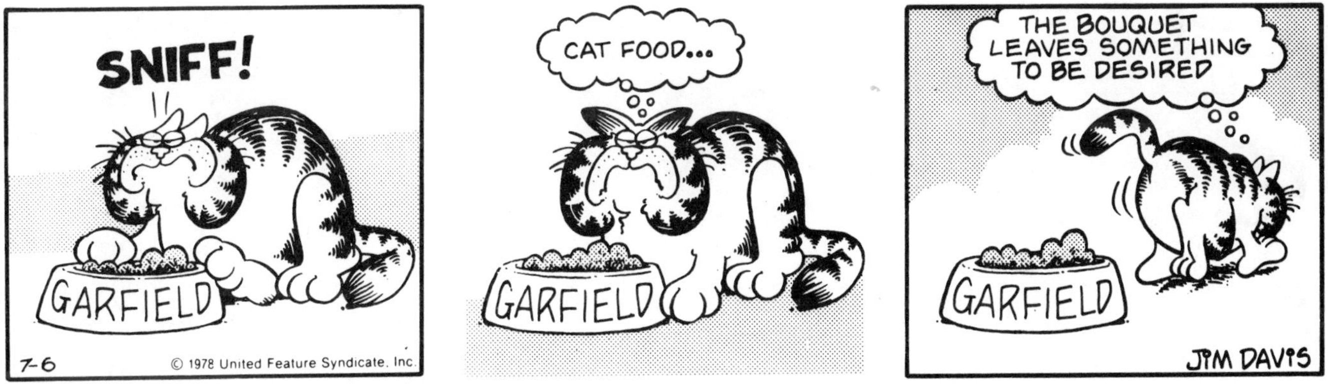
SNIFF!
GARFIELD
7-6
© 1978 United Feature Syndicate, Inc.
CAT FOOD...
GARFIELD
THE BOUQUET LEAVES SOMETHING TO BE DESIRED
GARFIELD
JIM DAVIS

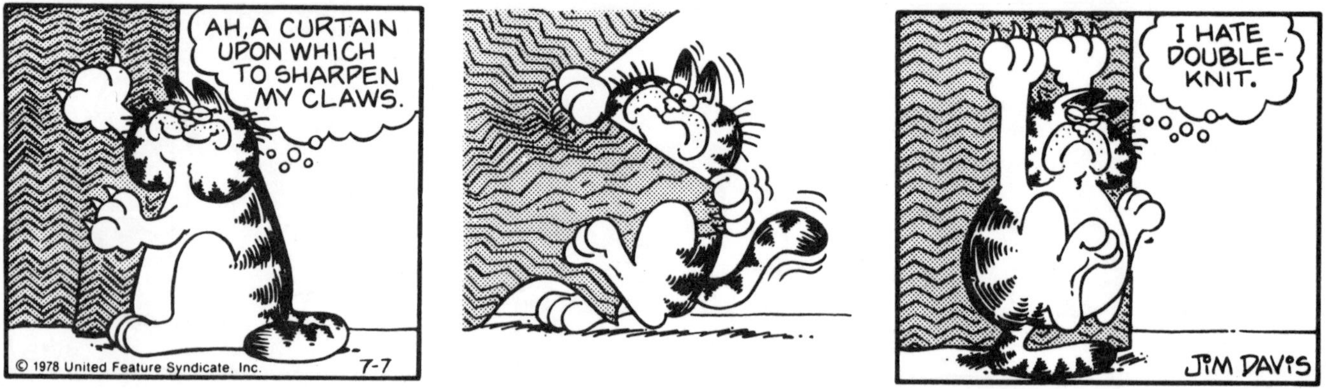
AH, A CURTAIN UPON WHICH TO SHARPEN MY CLAWS.
I HATE DOUBLE-KNIT.
© 1978 United Feature Syndicate, Inc.
7-7
JIM DAVIS

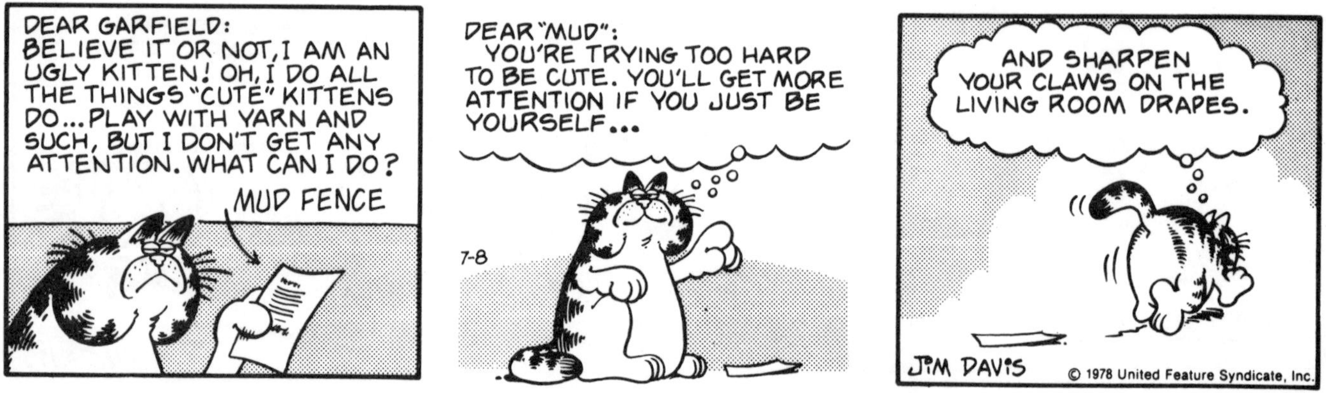
DEAR GARFIELD:
BELIEVE IT OR NOT, I AM AN UGLY KITTEN! OH, I DO ALL THE THINGS "CUTE" KITTENS DO...PLAY WITH YARN AND SUCH, BUT I DON'T GET ANY ATTENTION. WHAT CAN I DO?
MUD FENCE
DEAR "MUD":
YOU'RE TRYING TOO HARD TO BE CUTE. YOU'LL GET MORE ATTENTION IF YOU JUST BE YOURSELF...
7-8
AND SHARPEN YOUR CLAWS ON THE LIVING ROOM DRAPES.
JIM DAVIS
© 1978 United Feature Syndicate, Inc.

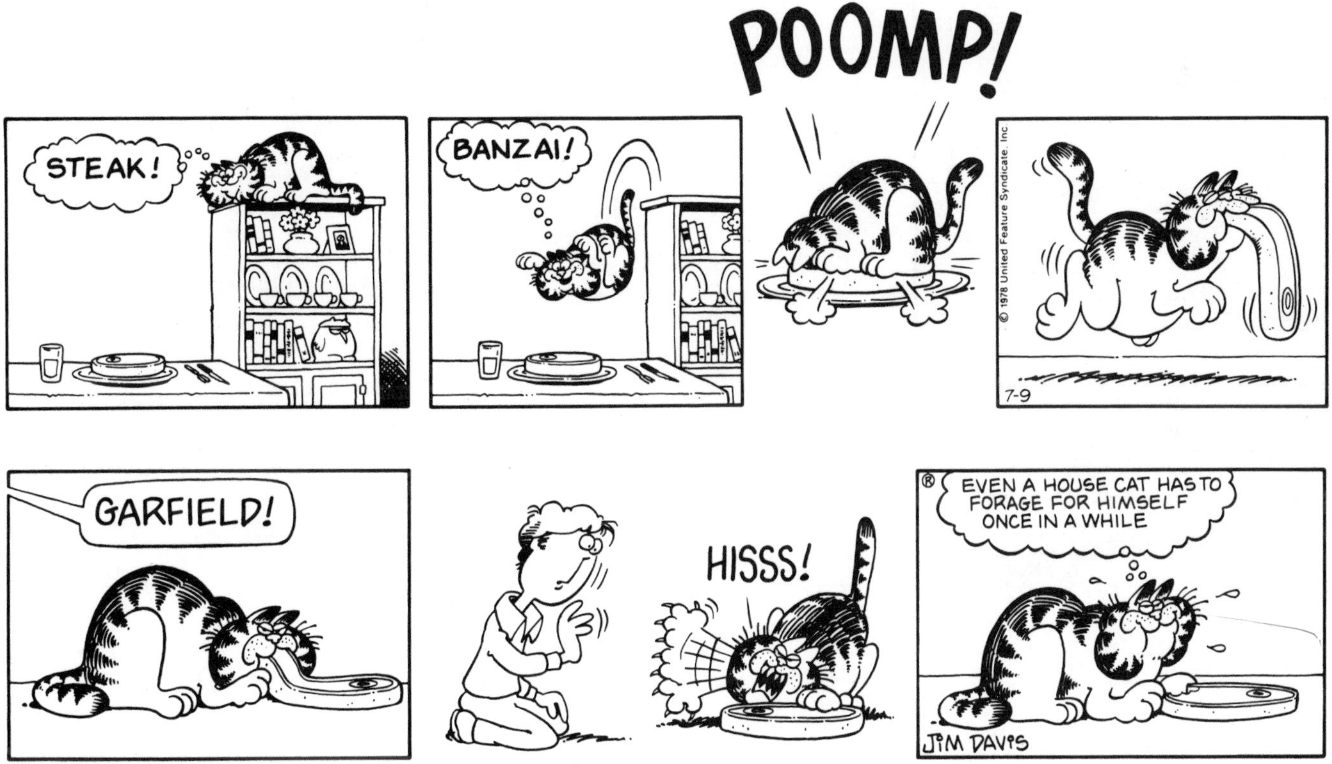
STEAK!
BANZAI!
POOMP!
© 1978 United Feature Syndicate, Inc.
7-9
GARFIELD!
HISSS!
EVEN A HOUSE CAT HAS TO FORAGE FOR HIMSELF ONCE IN A WHILE
JIM DAVIS

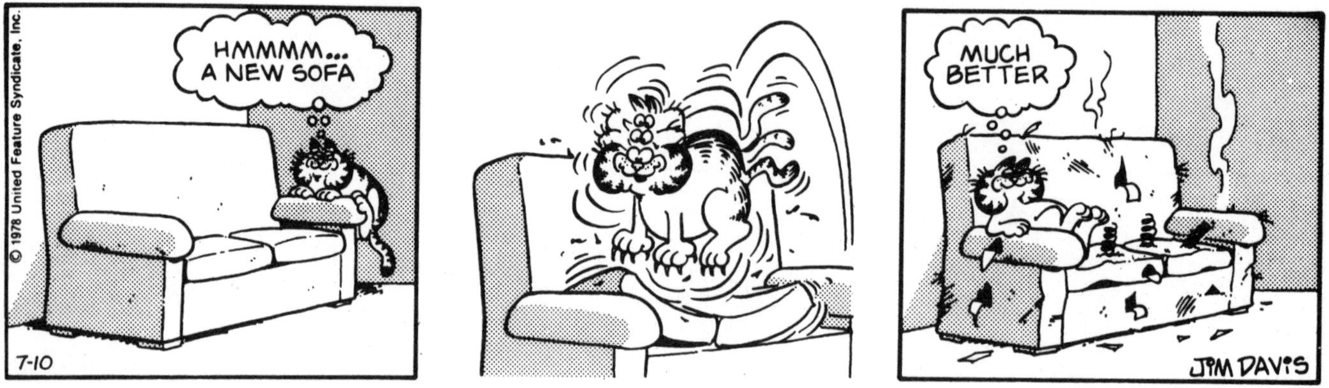
© 1978 United Feature Syndicate, Inc.
HMMMM... A NEW SOFA
7-10
MUCH BETTER
JIM DAVIS

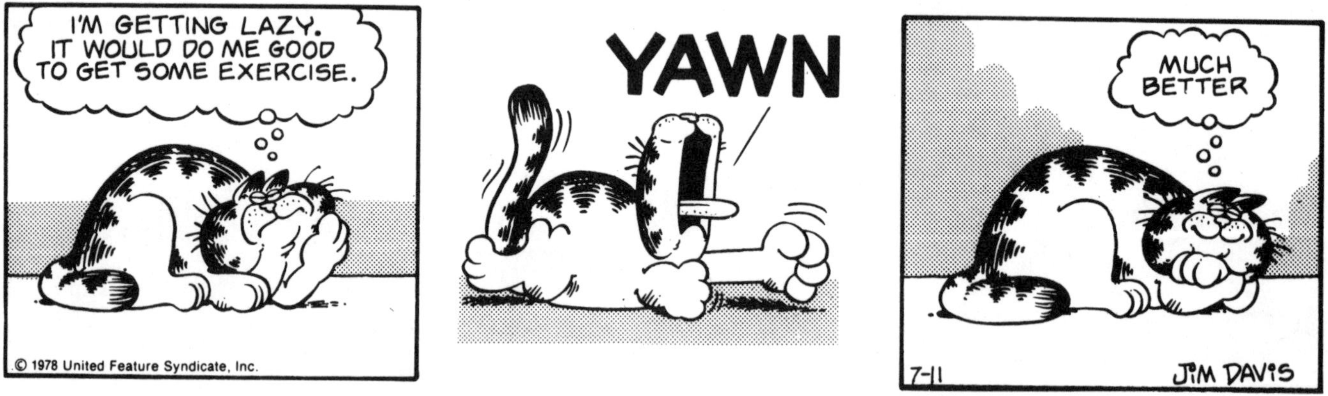
I'M GETTING LAZY. IT WOULD DO ME GOOD TO GET SOME EXERCISE.
© 1978 United Feature Syndicate, Inc.
YAWN
MUCH BETTER
7-11
JIM DAVIS

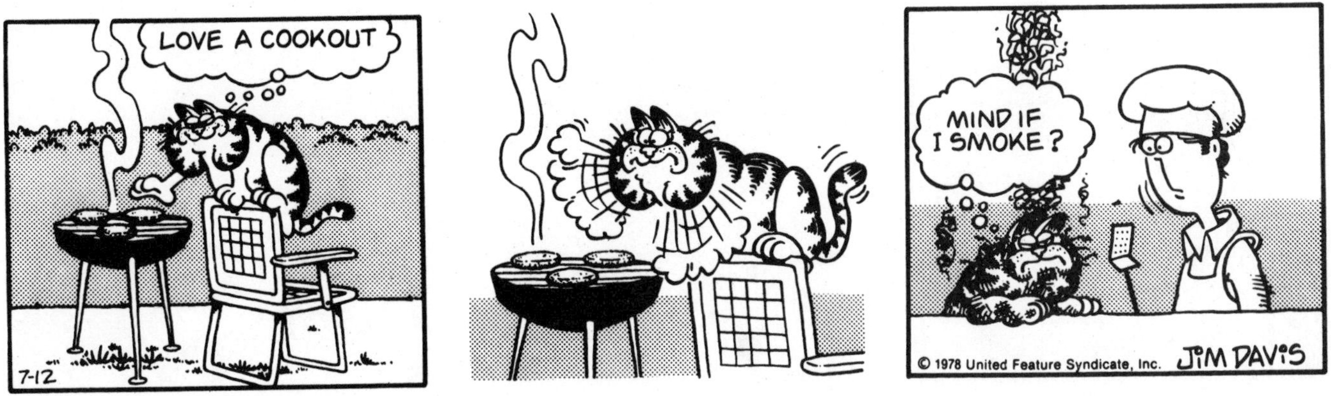
LOVE A COOKOUT
MIND IF I SMOKE?
7-12
© 1978 United Feature Syndicate, Inc.
JIM DAVIS

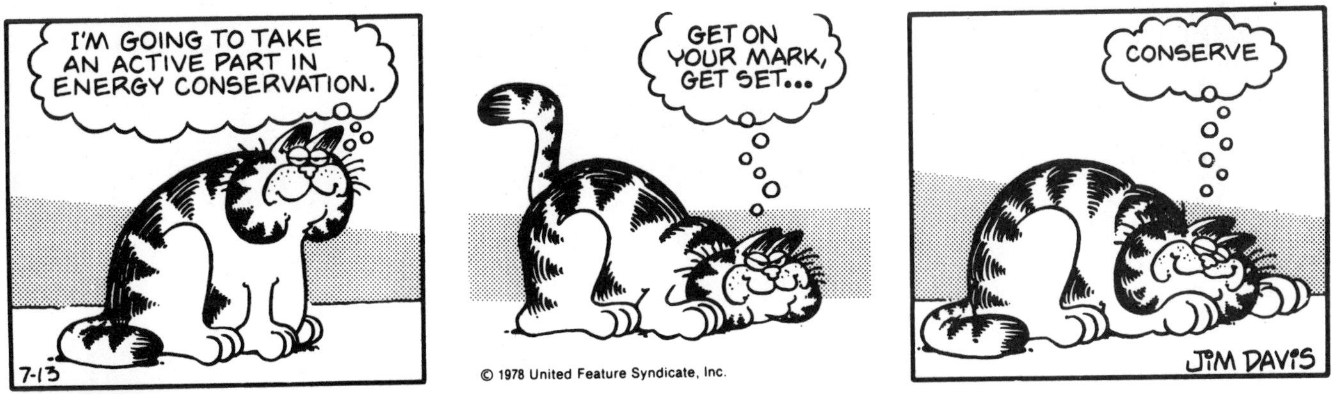
I'M GOING TO TAKE AN ACTIVE PART IN ENERGY CONSERVATION.
GET ON YOUR MARK, GET SET...
CONSERVE
7-13
© 1978 United Feature Syndicate, Inc.
JIM DAVIS

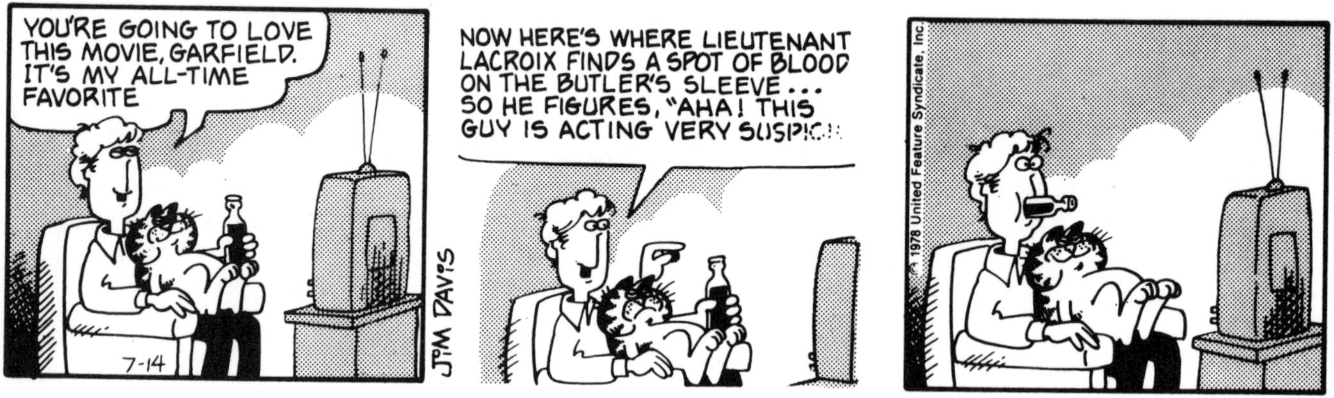
YOU'RE GOING TO LOVE THIS MOVIE, GARFIELD. IT'S MY ALL-TIME FAVORITE
7-14
JIM DAVIS
NOW HERE'S WHERE LIEUTENANT LACROIX FINDS A SPOT OF BLOOD ON THE BUTLER'S SLEEVE ... SO HE FIGURES, "AHA! THIS GUY IS ACTING VERY SUSPIC
© 1978 United Feature Syndicate, Inc.

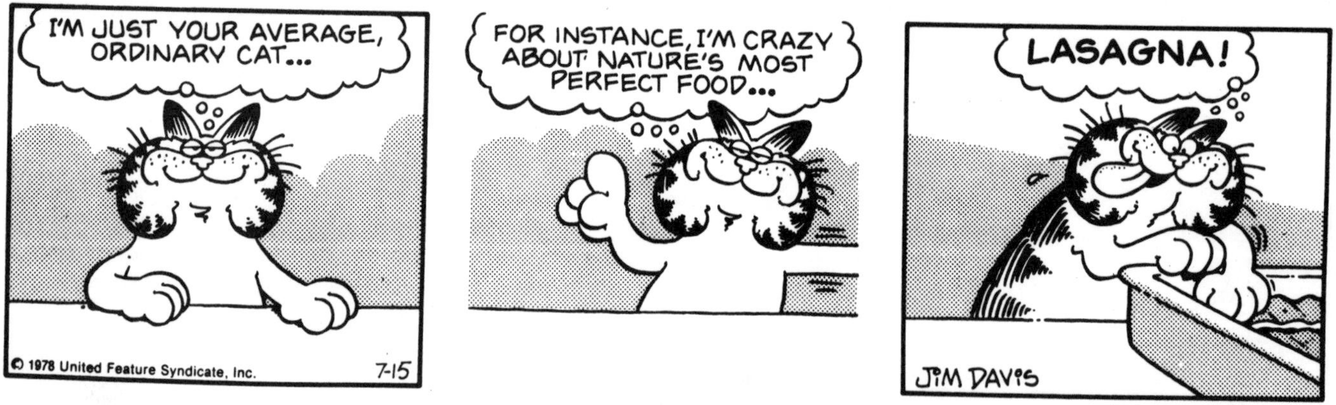
I'M JUST YOUR AVERAGE, ORDINARY CAT...
© 1978 United Feature Syndicate, Inc.
7-15
FOR INSTANCE, I'M CRAZY ABOUT NATURE'S MOST PERFECT FOOD...
LASAGNA!
JIM DAVIS

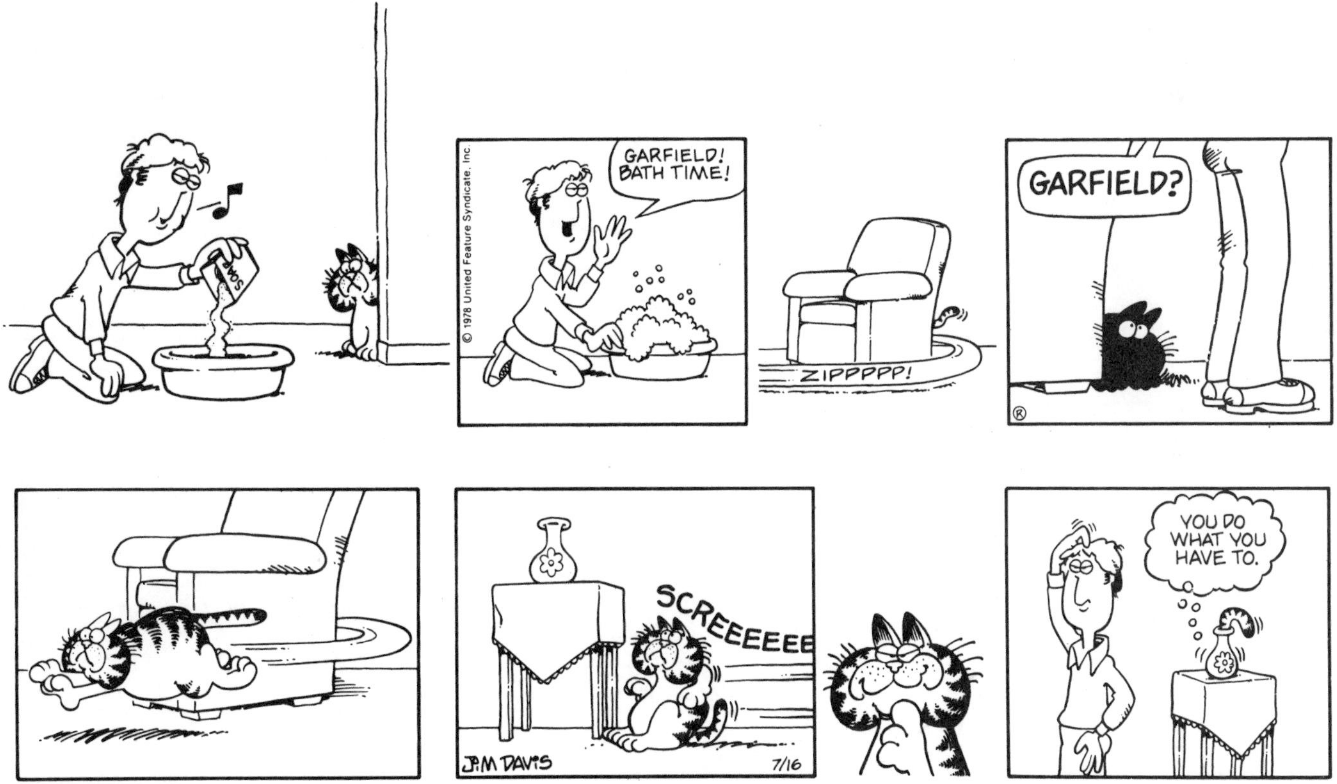
SOAP
GARFIELD! BATH TIME!
© 1978 United Feature Syndicate, Inc.
ZIPPPPPP!
GARFIELD?
®
SCREEEEEEE
JIM DAVIS
7/16
YOU DO WHAT YOU HAVE TO.

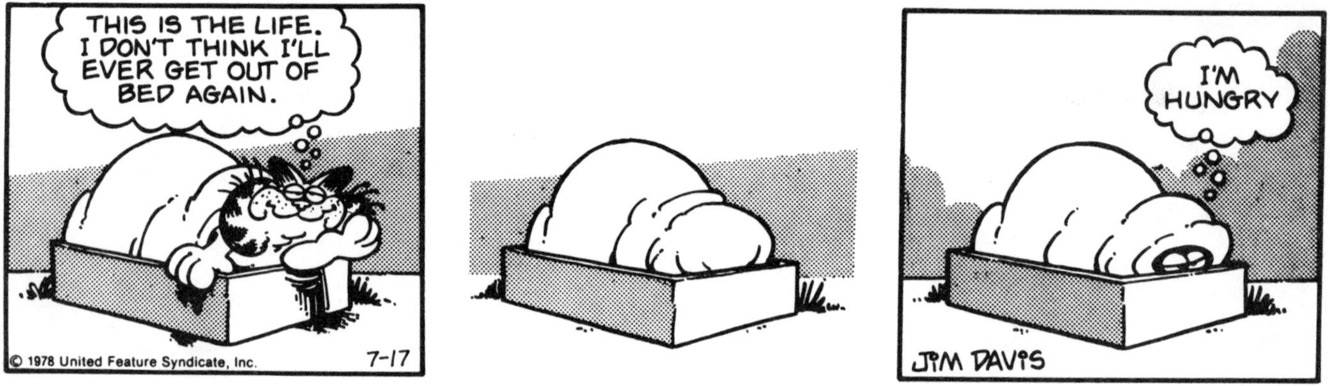
THIS IS THE LIFE. I DON'T THINK I'LL EVER GET OUT OF BED AGAIN.
© 1978 United Feature Syndicate, Inc.
7-17
I'M HUNGRY
JIM DAVIS

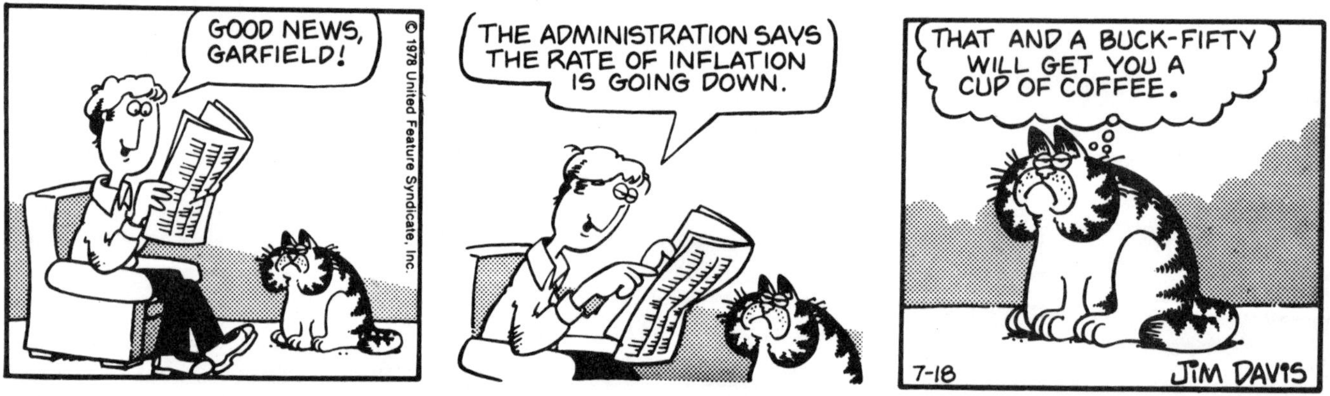
GOOD NEWS, GARFIELD!
© 1978 United Feature Syndicate, Inc.
THE ADMINISTRATION SAYS THE RATE OF INFLATION IS GOING DOWN.
THAT AND A BUCK-FIFTY WILL GET YOU A CUP OF COFFEE.
7-18
JIM DAVIS

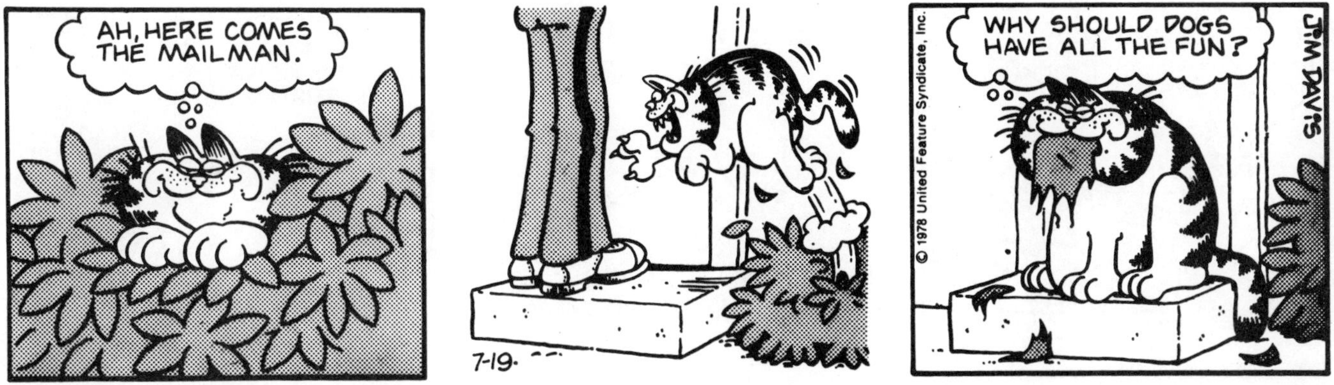
AH, HERE COMES THE MAILMAN.
7-19
© 1978 United Feature Syndicate, Inc.
WHY SHOULD DOGS HAVE ALL THE FUN?
JIM DAVIS

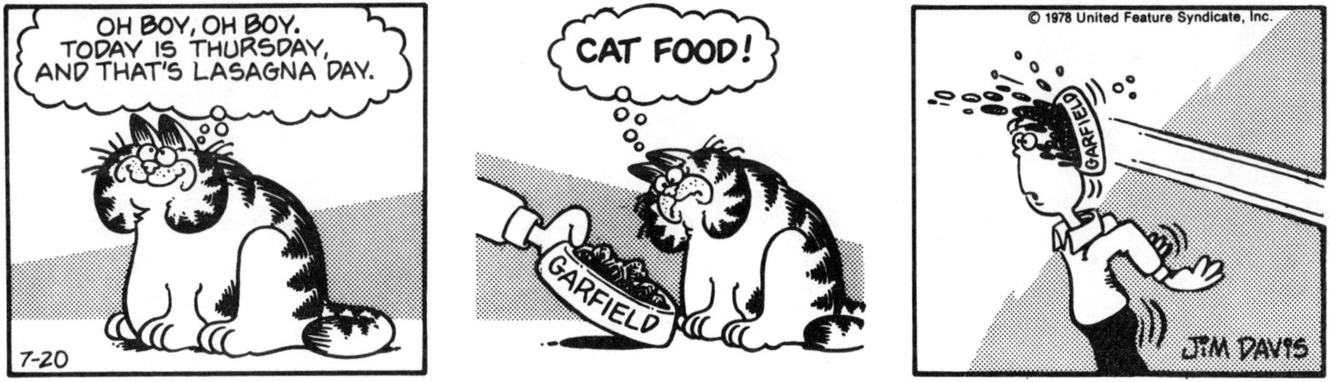
OH BOY, OH BOY. TODAY IS THURSDAY, AND THAT'S LASAGNA DAY.
7-20
CAT FOOD!
GARFIELD
© 1978 United Feature Syndicate, Inc.
GARFIELD
JIM DAVIS

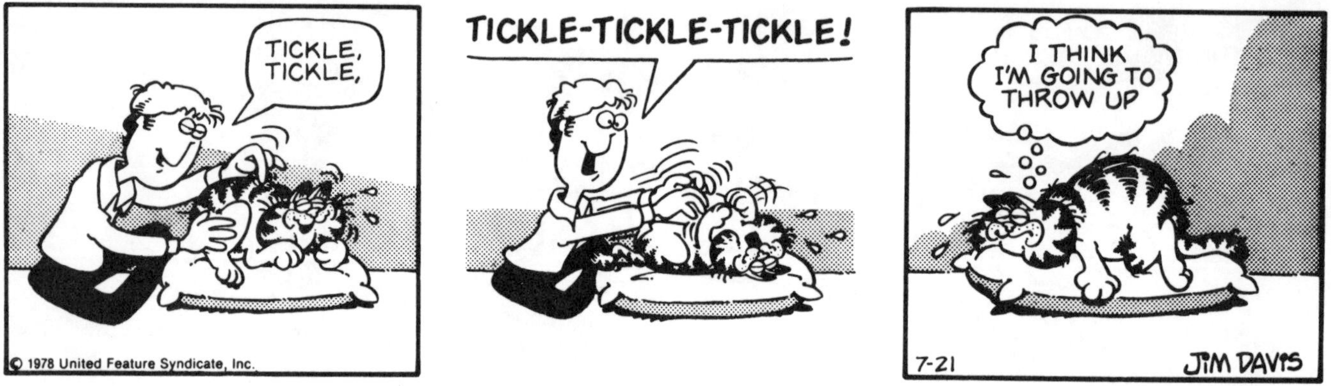
TICKLE, TICKLE,
TICKLE-TICKLE-TICKLE!
I THINK I'M GOING TO THROW UP
© 1978 United Feature Syndicate, Inc.
7-21
JIM DAVIS

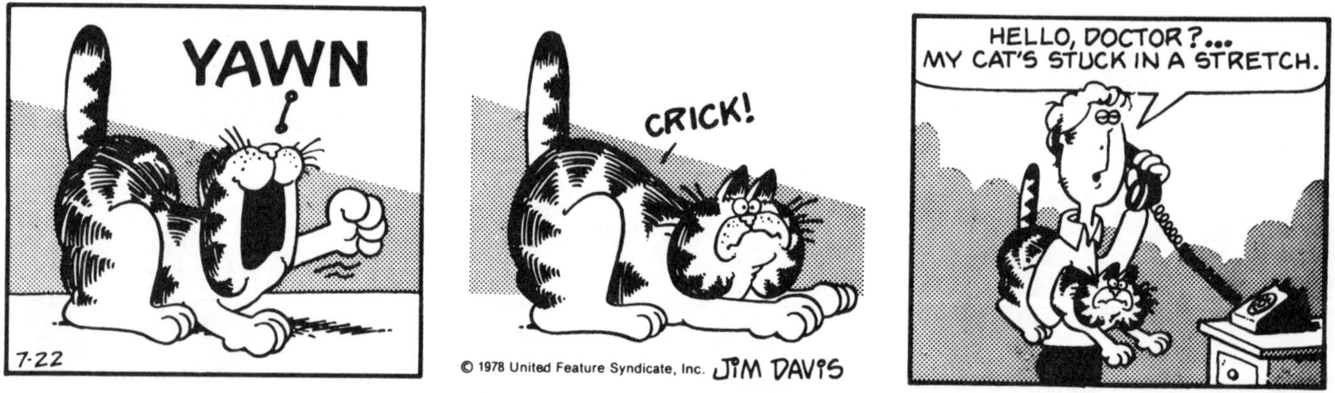
YAWN
CRICK!
HELLO, DOCTOR?... MY CAT'S STUCK IN A STRETCH.
7-22
© 1978 United Feature Syndicate, Inc.
JIM DAVIS

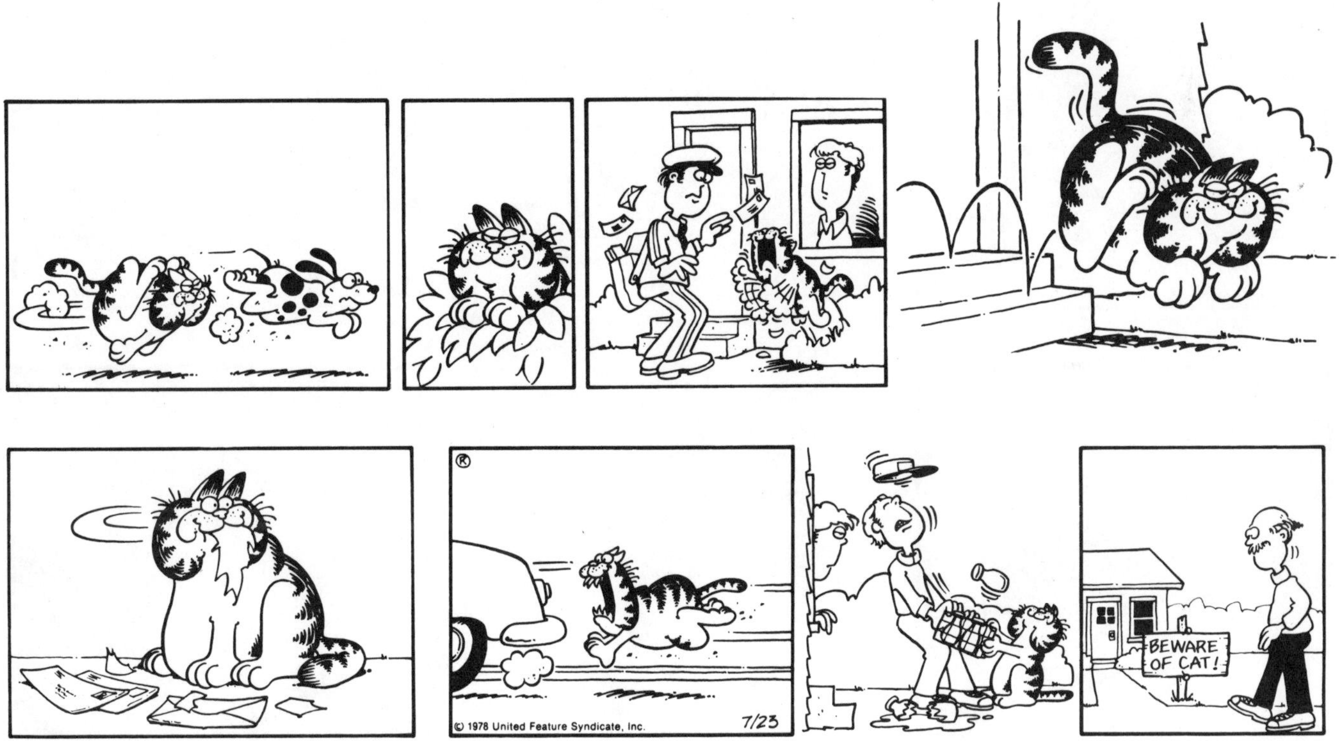
© 1978 United Feature Syndicate, Inc.
7/23
BEWARE OF CAT!

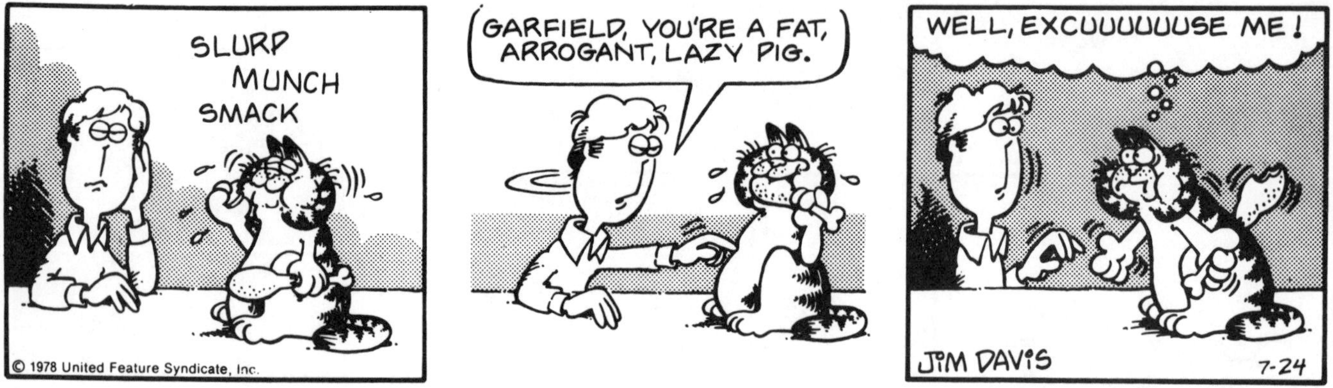
SLURP
MUNCH
SMACK
© 1978 United Feature Syndicate, Inc.
GARFIELD, YOU'RE A FAT, ARROGANT, LAZY PIG.
WELL, EXCUUUUUUSE ME!
JIM DAVIS
7-24

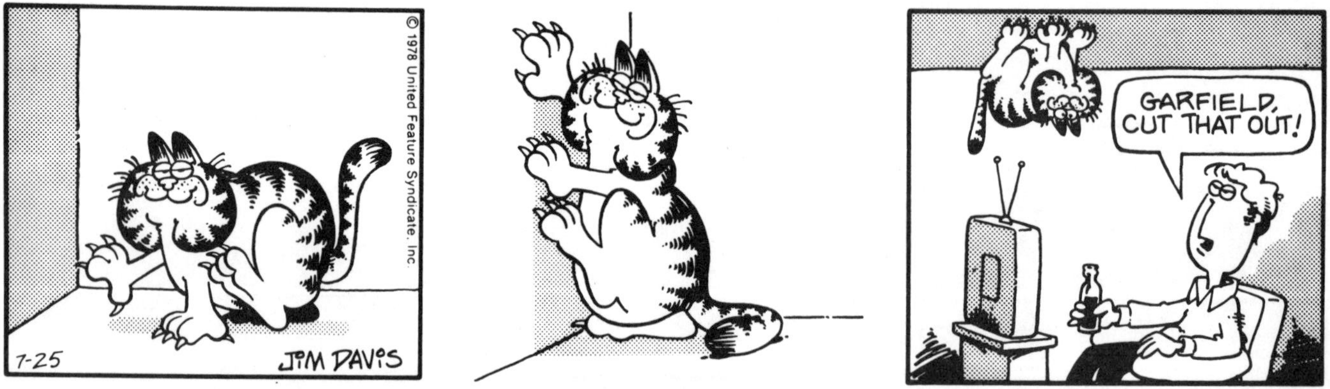
© 1978 United Feature Syndicate, Inc.
7-25
JIM DAVIS
GARFIELD, CUT THAT OUT!

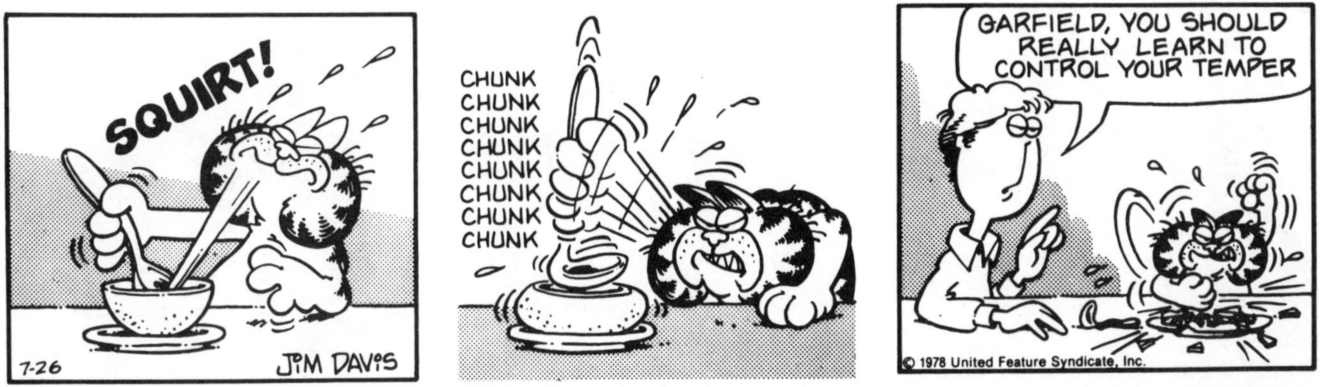
SQUIRT!
7-26
JIM DAVIS
CHUNK
CHUNK
CHUNK
CHUNK
CHUNK
CHUNK
CHUNK
CHUNK
GARFIELD, YOU SHOULD REALLY LEARN TO CONTROL YOUR TEMPER
© 1978 United Feature Syndicate, Inc.

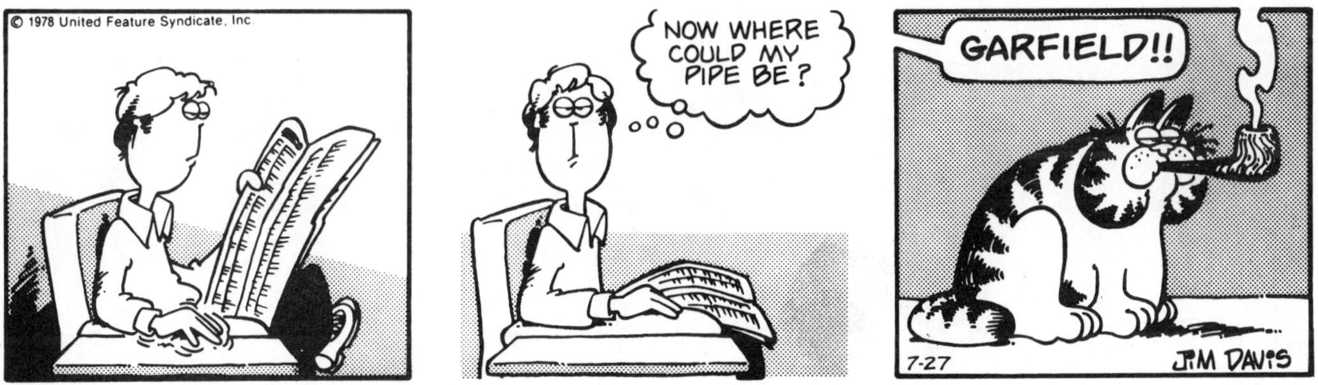
© 1978 United Feature Syndicate, Inc.
NOW WHERE COULD MY PIPE BE?
GARFIELD!!
7-27
JIM DAVIS

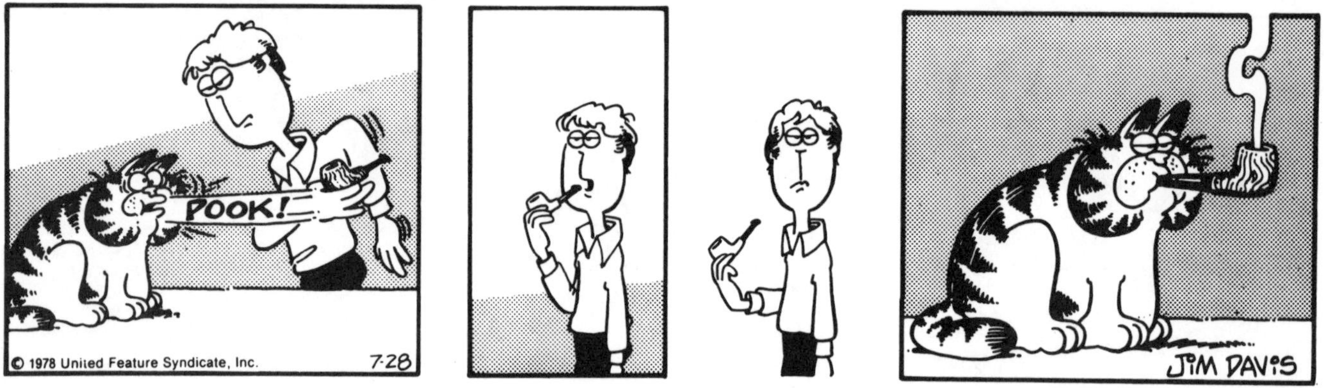
POOK!
© 1978 United Feature Syndicate, Inc.
7-28
JIM DAVIS

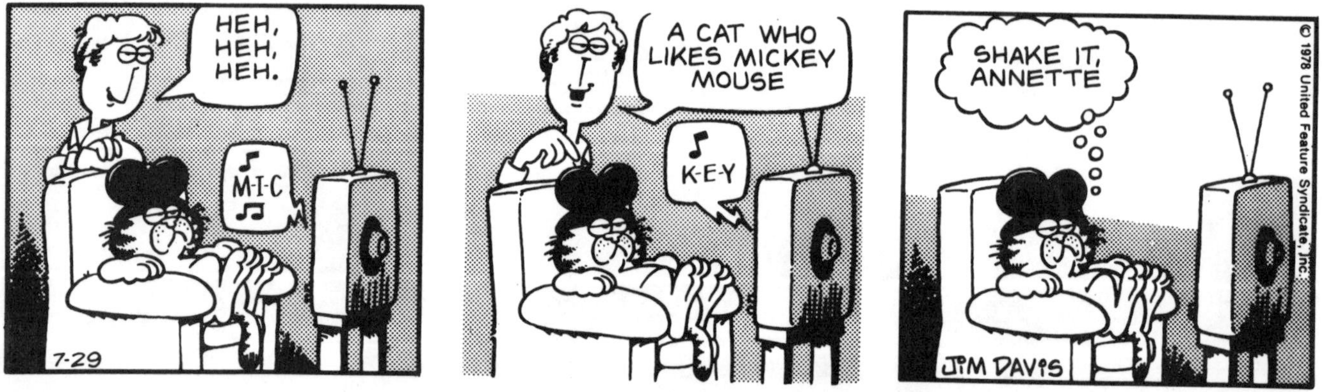
HEH, HEH, HEH.
M-I-C
7-29
A CAT WHO LIKES MICKEY MOUSE
K-E-Y
SHAKE IT, ANNETTE
© 1978 United Feature Syndicate, Inc.
JIM DAVIS

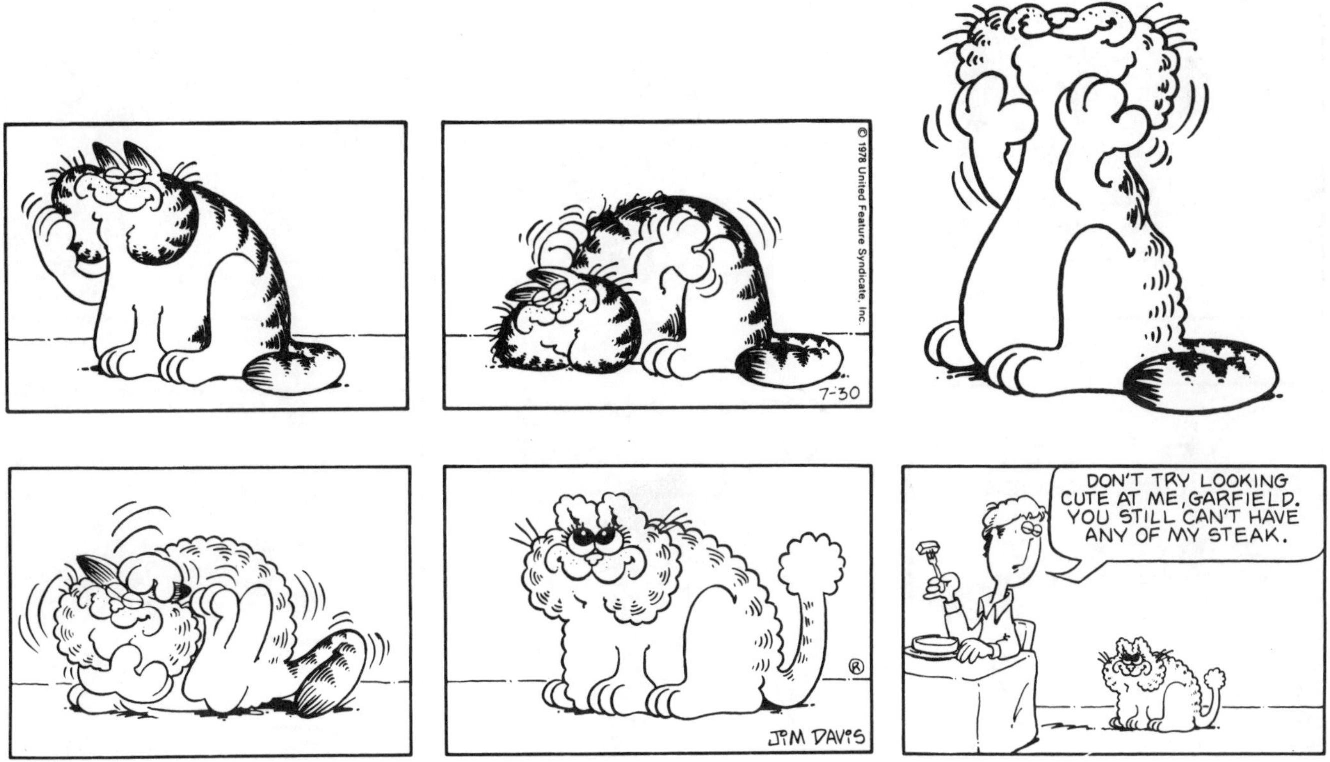
7-30
DON'T TRY LOOKING CUTE AT ME, GARFIELD. YOU STILL CAN'T HAVE ANY OF MY STEAK.
JIM DAVIS

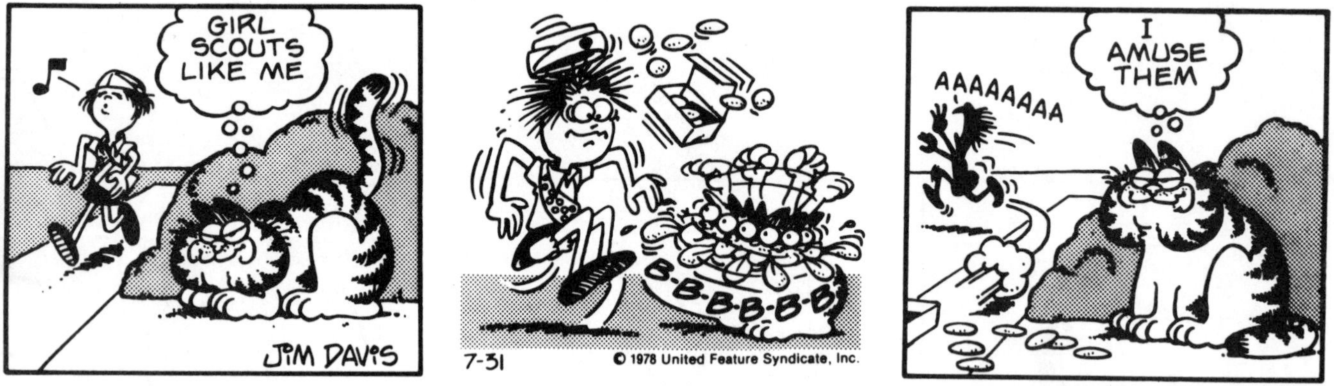
GIRL SCOUTS LIKE ME
JIM DAVIS
B-B-B-B-B-B-B
7-31
© 1978 United Feature Syndicate, Inc.
AAAAAAAA
I AMUSE THEM

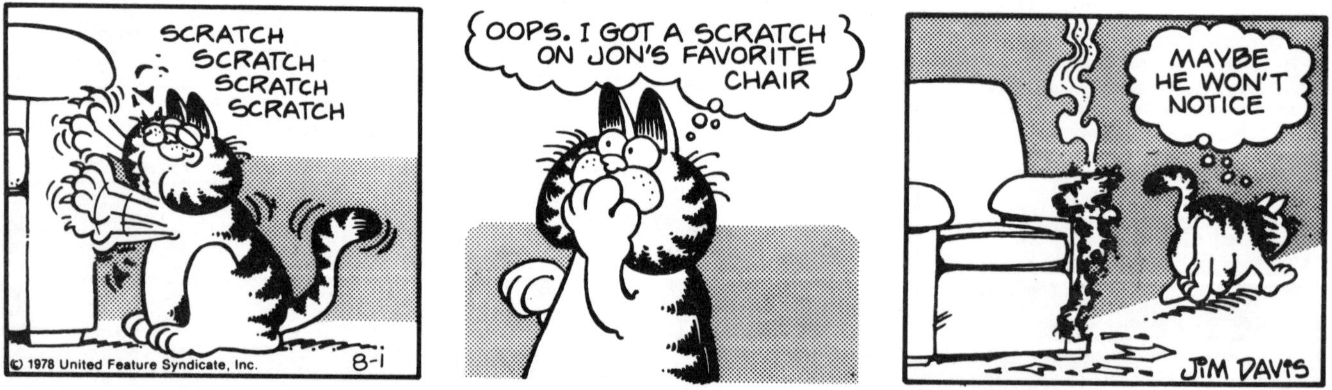
SCRATCH SCRATCH SCRATCH SCRATCH
© 1978 United Feature Syndicate, Inc.
8-1
OOPS. I GOT A SCRATCH ON JON'S FAVORITE CHAIR
MAYBE HE WON'T NOTICE
JIM DAVIS

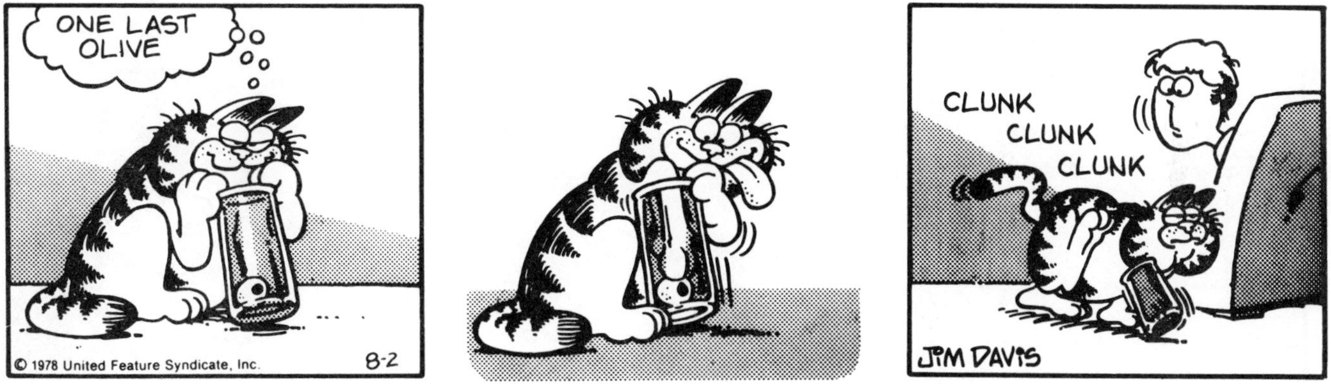
ONE LAST OLIVE
© 1978 United Feature Syndicate, Inc.
8-2
CLUNK
CLUNK
CLUNK
JIM DAVIS

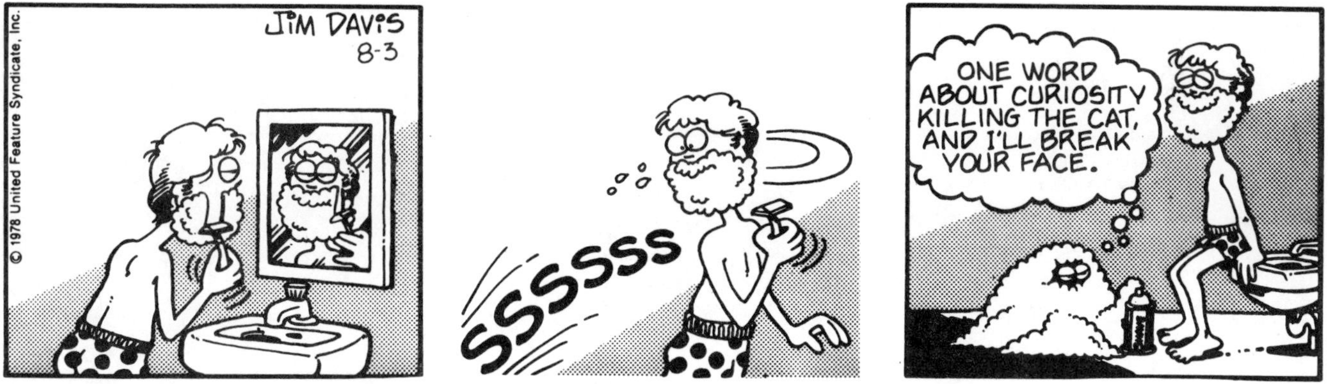
JIM DAVIS
8-3
© 1978 United Feature Syndicate, Inc.
SSSSSS
ONE WORD ABOUT CURIOSITY KILLING THE CAT, AND I'LL BREAK YOUR FACE.

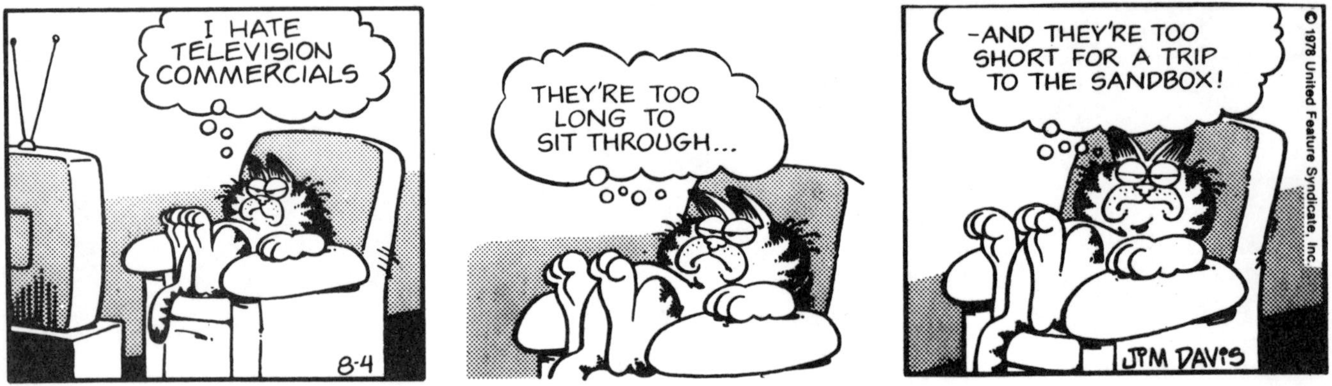
I HATE TELEVISION COMMERCIALS
8-4
THEY'RE TOO LONG TO SIT THROUGH...
-AND THEY'RE TOO SHORT FOR A TRIP TO THE SANDBOX!
© 1978 United Feature Syndicate, Inc.
JIM DAVIS

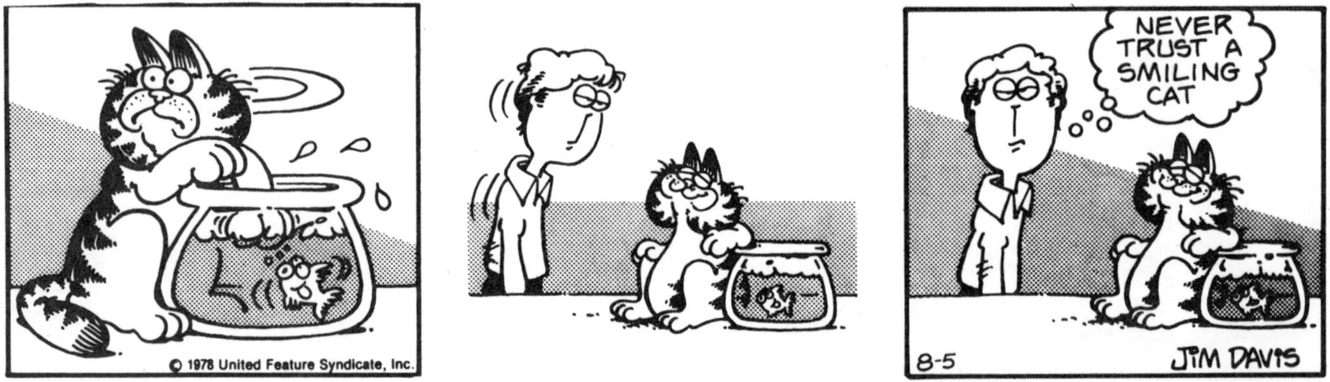
© 1978 United Feature Syndicate, Inc.
NEVER TRUST A SMILING CAT
8-5
JIM DAVIS

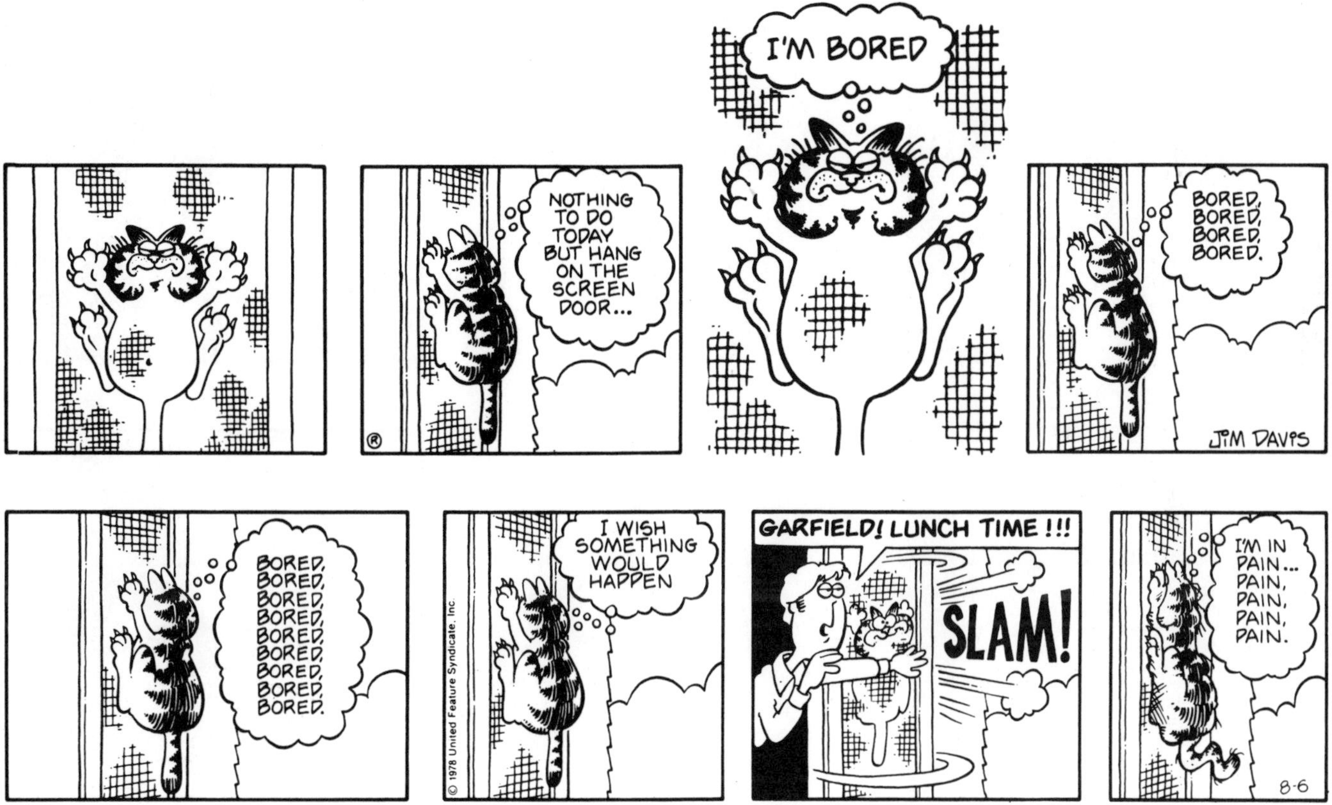

NOTHING TO DO TODAY BUT HANG ON THE SCREEN DOOR...
I'M BORED
BORED, BORED, BORED, BORED.
JIM DAVIS
BORED, BORED, BORED, BORED, BORED, BORED, BORED, BORED, BORED.
I WISH SOMETHING WOULD HAPPEN
© 1978 United Feature Syndicate, Inc.
GARFIELD! LUNCH TIME !!!
SLAM!
I'M IN PAIN... PAIN, PAIN, PAIN, PAIN.
8-6

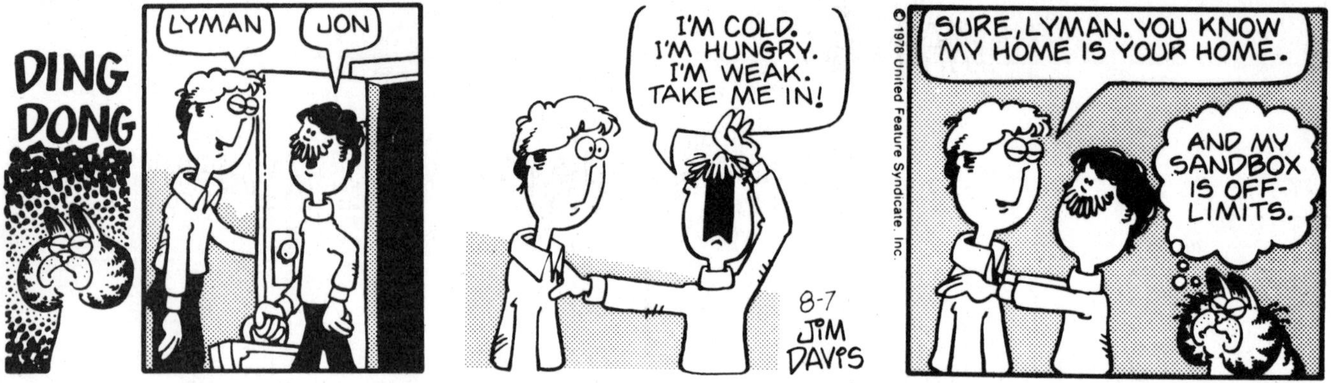
DING DONG
LYMAN
JON
I'M COLD. I'M HUNGRY. I'M WEAK. TAKE ME IN!
8-7
JIM DAVIS
© 1978 United Feature Syndicate, Inc.
SURE, LYMAN. YOU KNOW MY HOME IS YOUR HOME.
AND MY SANDBOX IS OFF-LIMITS.

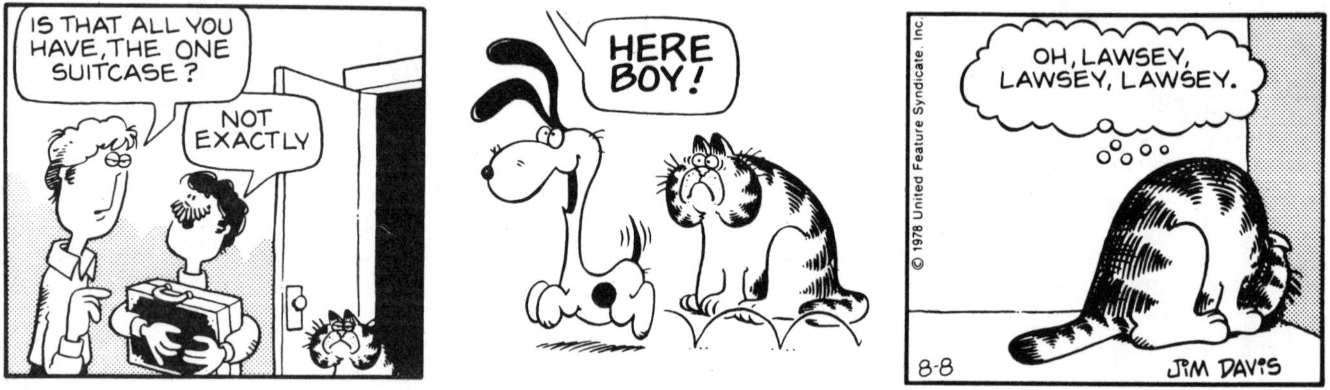
IS THAT ALL YOU HAVE, THE ONE SUITCASE?
NOT EXACTLY
HERE BOY!
© 1978 United Feature Syndicate, Inc.
OH, LAWSEY, LAWSEY, LAWSEY.
8-8
JIM DAVIS

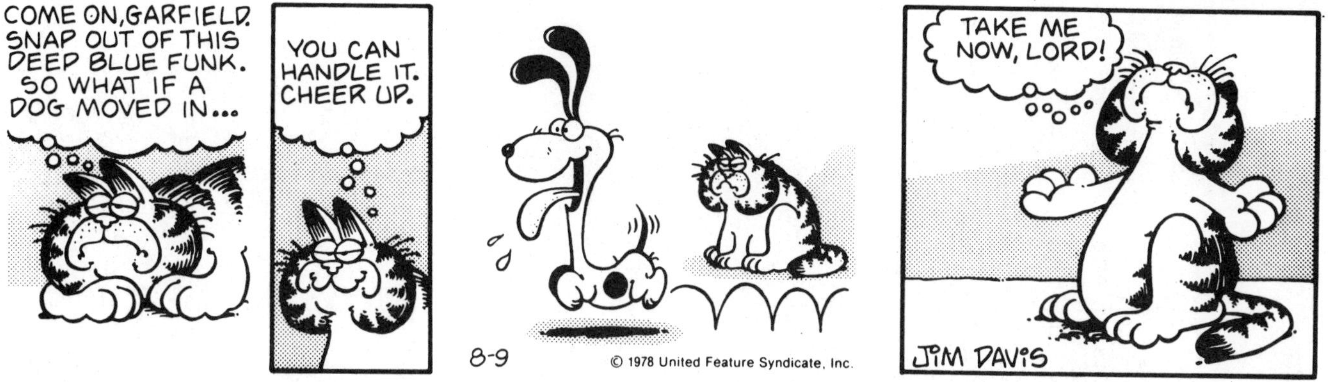
COME ON, GARFIELD. SNAP OUT OF THIS DEEP BLUE FUNK. SO WHAT IF A DOG MOVED IN...
YOU CAN HANDLE IT. CHEER UP.
8-9
© 1978 United Feature Syndicate, Inc.
TAKE ME NOW, LORD!
JIM DAVIS

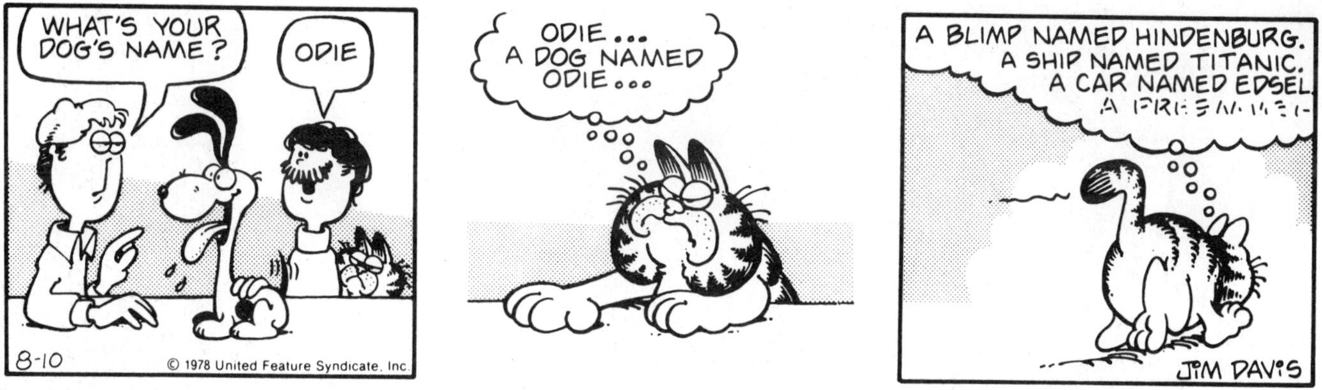
WHAT'S YOUR DOG'S NAME?
ODIE
8-10
© 1978 United Feature Syndicate, Inc.
ODIE... A DOG NAMED ODIE...
A BLIMP NAMED HINDENBURG.
A SHIP NAMED TITANIC.
A CAR NAMED EDSEL.
JIM DAVIS

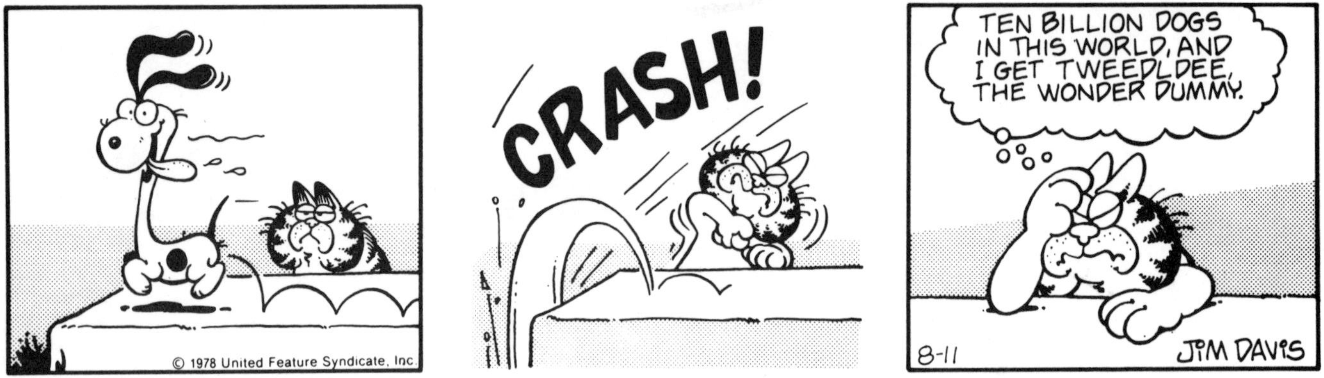
© 1978 United Feature Syndicate, Inc.
CRASH!
TEN BILLION DOGS IN THIS WORLD, AND I GET TWEEDLDEE, THE WONDER DUMMY.
8-11
JIM DAVIS

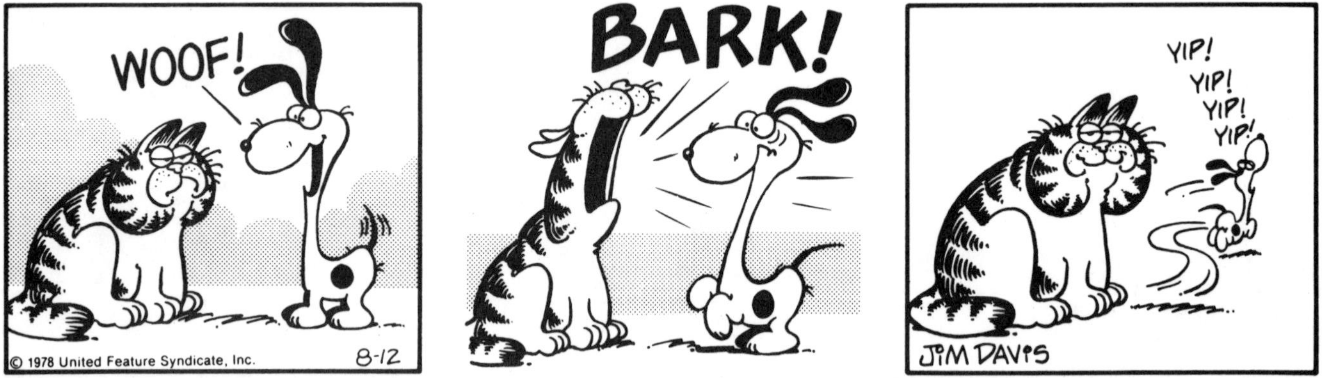
WOOF!
© 1978 United Feature Syndicate, Inc.
8-12
BARK!
YIP!
YIP!
YIP!
YIP!
JIM DAVIS

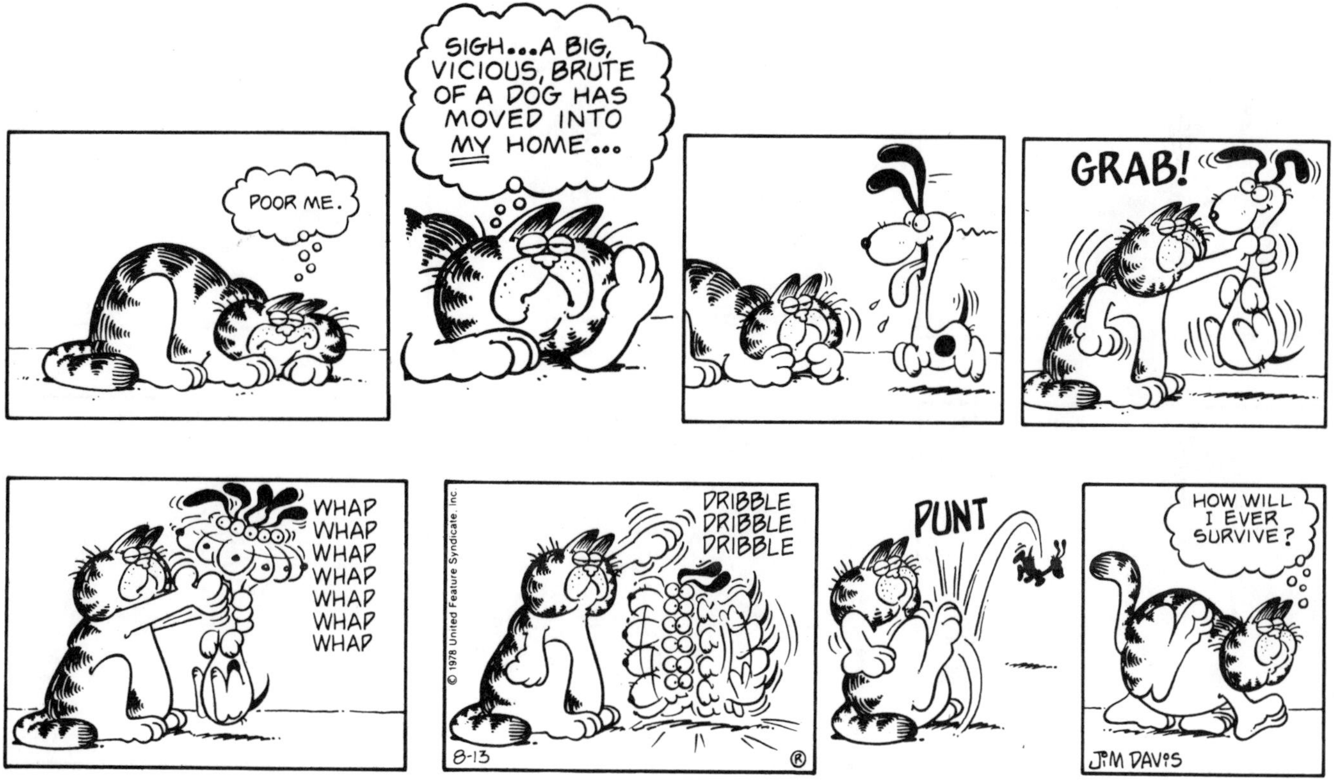
POOR ME.
SIGH...A BIG, VICIOUS, BRUTE OF A DOG HAS MOVED INTO MY HOME...
GRAB!
WHAP WHAP WHAP WHAP WHAP WHAP WHAP
© 1978 United Feature Syndicate, Inc.
DRIBBLE DRIBBLE DRIBBLE
8-13
PUNT
HOW WILL I EVER SURVIVE?
JIM DAVIS

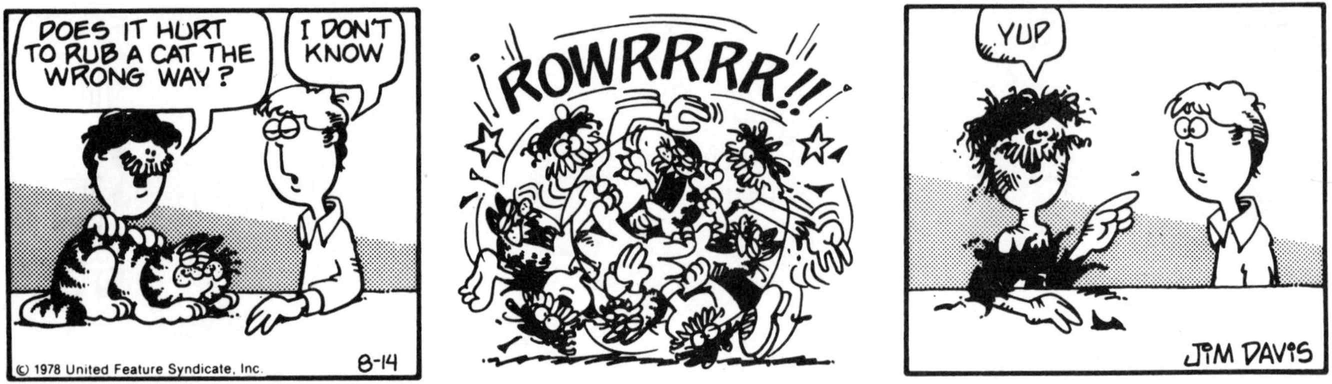
DOES IT HURT TO RUB A CAT THE WRONG WAY?
I DON'T KNOW
© 1978 United Feature Syndicate, Inc.
8-14
ROWRRRRR!!!
YUP
JIM DAVIS

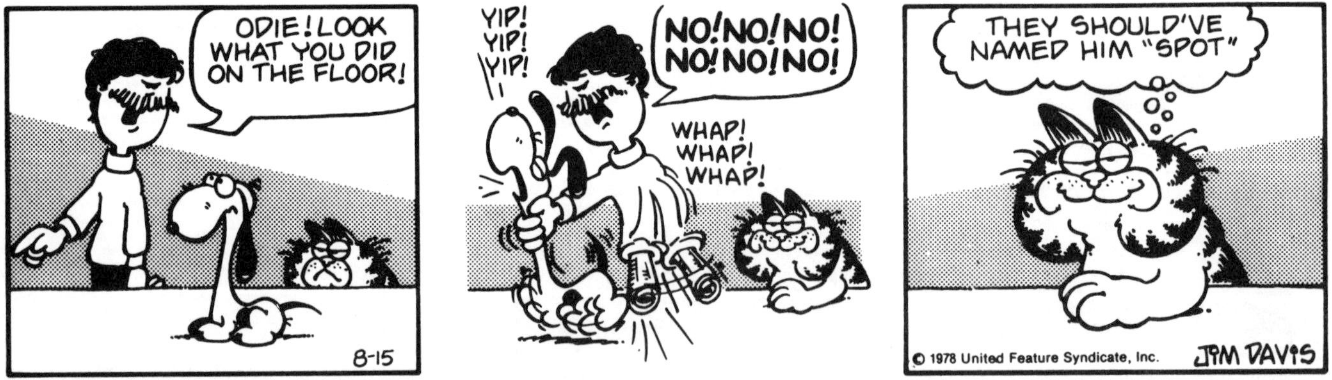
ODIE! LOOK WHAT YOU DID ON THE FLOOR!
8-15
YIP! YIP! YIP!
NO! NO! NO! NO! NO! NO!
WHAP! WHAP! WHAP!
THEY SHOULD'VE NAMED HIM "SPOT"
© 1978 United Feature Syndicate, Inc.
JIM DAVIS

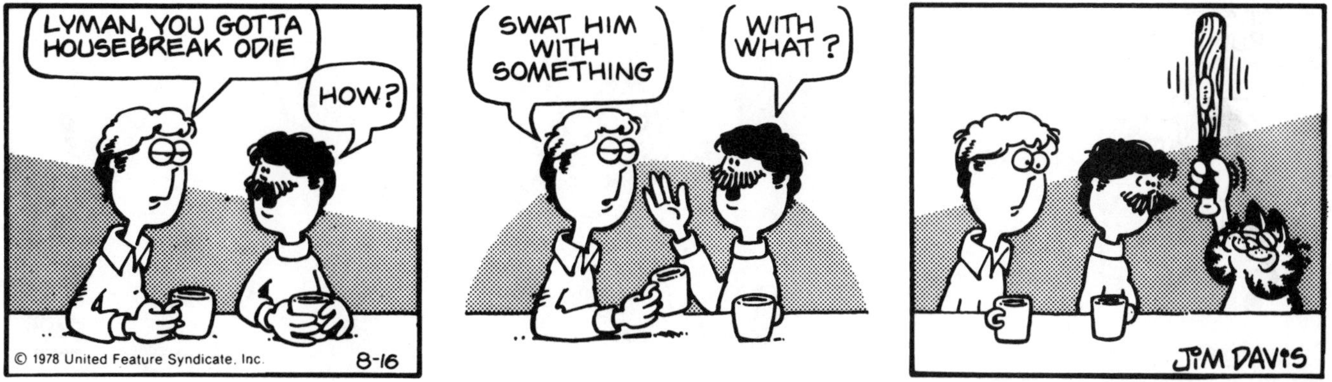
LYMAN, YOU GOTTA HOUSEBREAK ODIE
HOW?
SWAT HIM WITH SOMETHING
WITH WHAT ?
© 1978 United Feature Syndicate, Inc.
8-16
JIM DAVIS

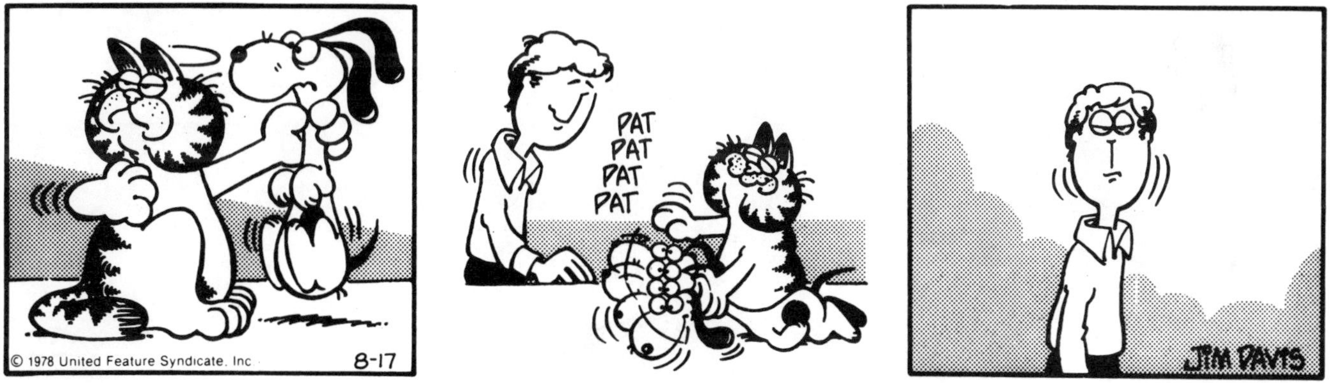
PAT
PAT
PAT
PAT
© 1978 United Feature Syndicate, Inc.
8-17
JIM DAVIS

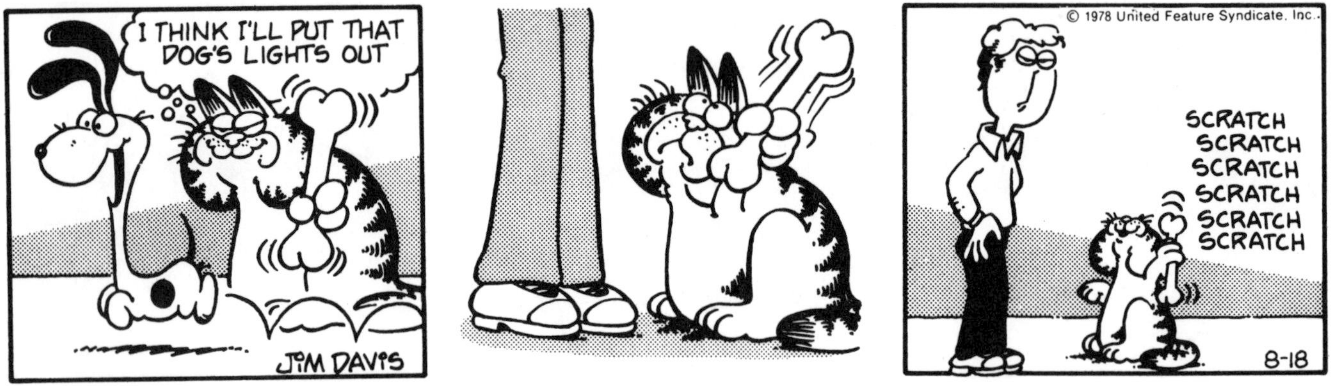
I THINK I'LL PUT THAT DOG'S LIGHTS OUT
JIM DAVIS
© 1978 United Feature Syndicate, Inc.
SCRATCH SCRATCH SCRATCH SCRATCH SCRATCH SCRATCH
8-18

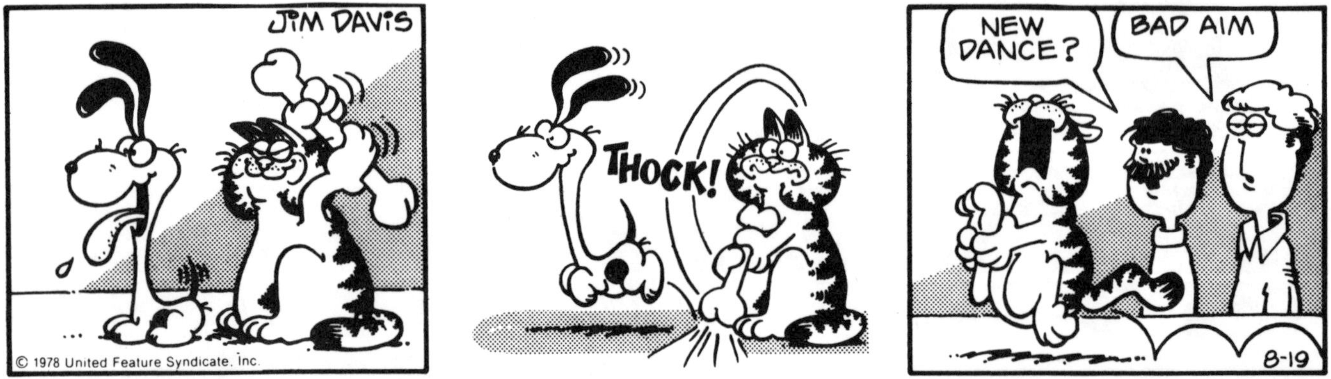
JIM DAVIS
© 1978 United Feature Syndicate, Inc.
THOCK!
NEW DANCE?
BAD AIM
8-19

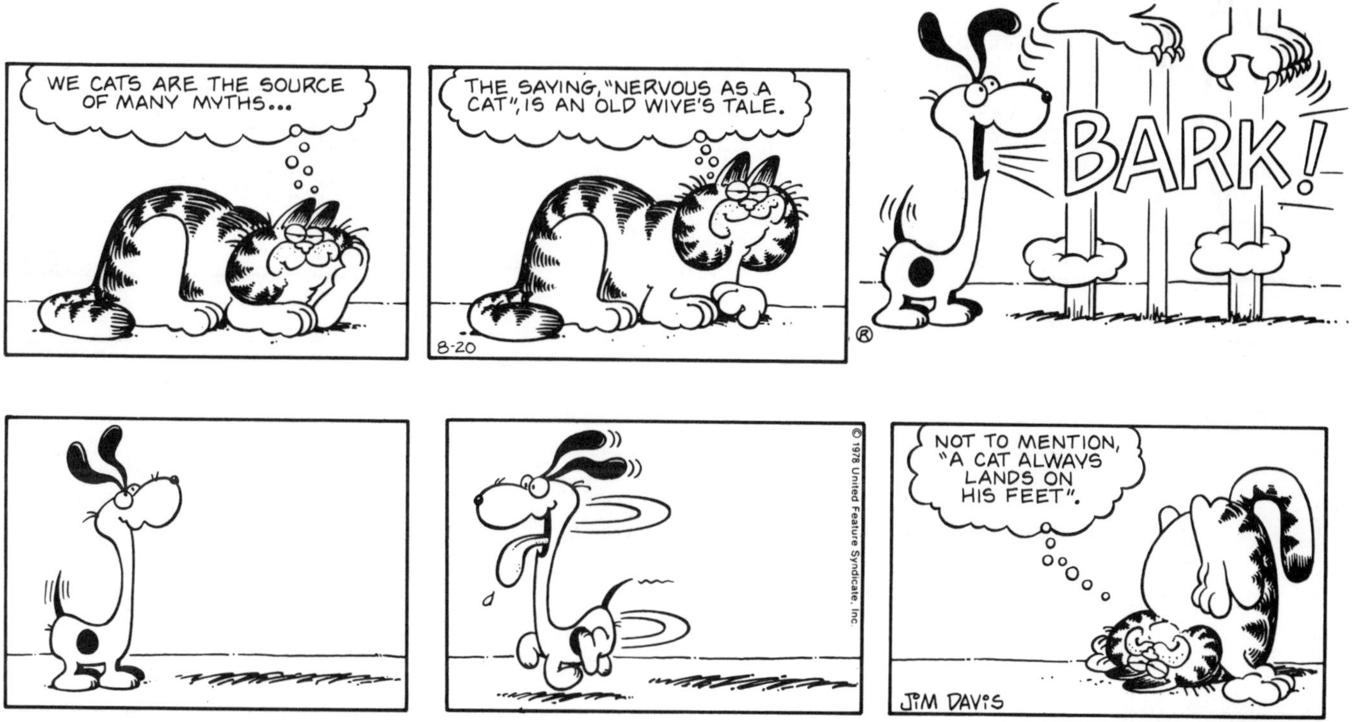
WE CATS ARE THE SOURCE OF MANY MYTHS...
THE SAYING, "NERVOUS AS A CAT", IS AN OLD WIVE'S TALE.
8-20
BARK!
© 1978 United Feature Syndicate, Inc.
NOT TO MENTION, "A CAT ALWAYS LANDS ON HIS FEET".
JIM DAVIS

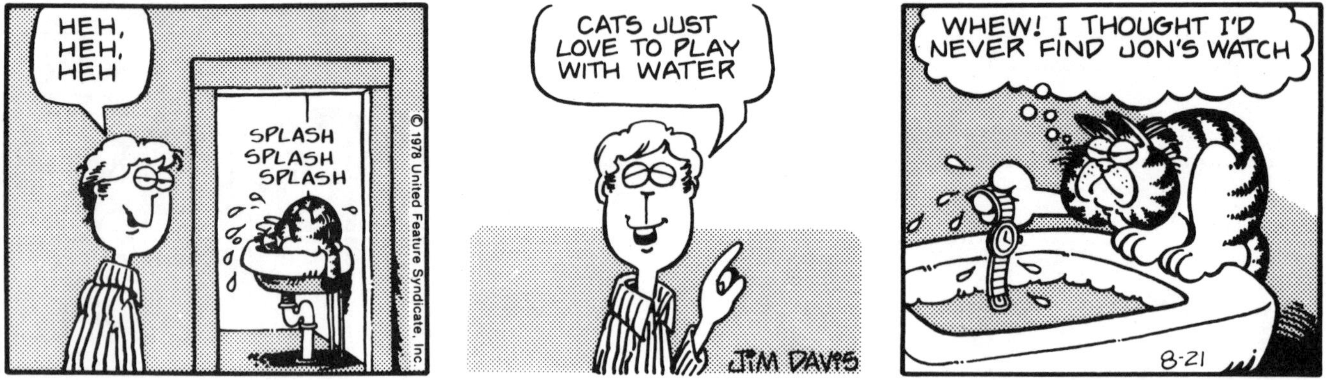
HEH, HEH, HEH
SPLASH SPLASH SPLASH
© 1978 United Feature Syndicate, Inc.
CATS JUST LOVE TO PLAY WITH WATER
JIM DAVIS
WHEW! I THOUGHT I'D NEVER FIND JON'S WATCH
8-21

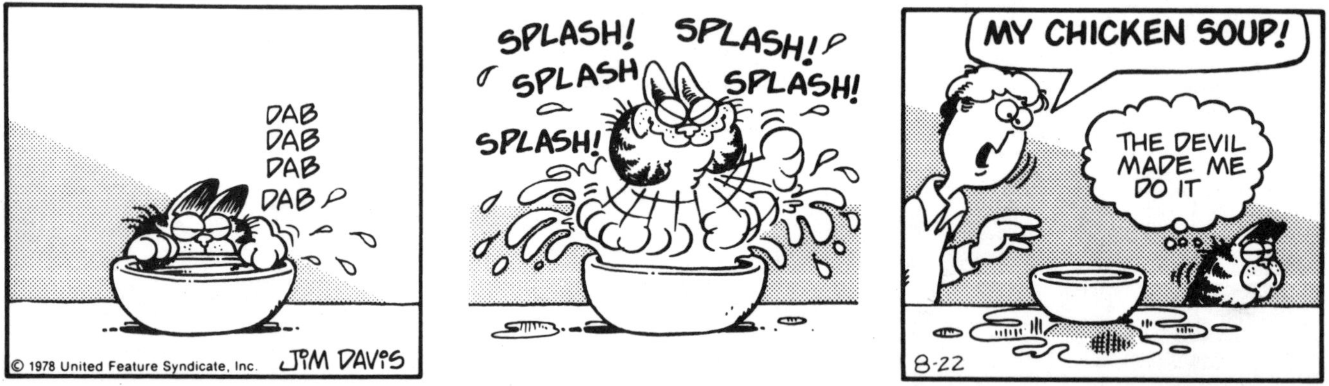
DAB DAB DAB DAB
© 1978 United Feature Syndicate, Inc.
JIM DAVIS
SPLASH! SPLASH! SPLASH SPLASH! SPLASH!
MY CHICKEN SOUP!
THE DEVIL MADE ME DO IT
8-22

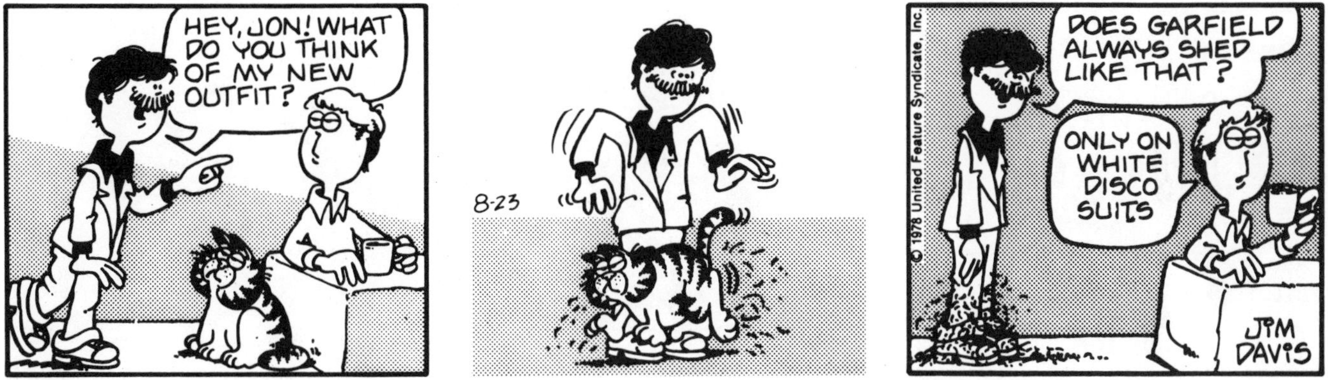
HEY, JON! WHAT DO YOU THINK OF MY NEW OUTFIT?
8-23
DOES GARFIELD ALWAYS SHED LIKE THAT?
ONLY ON WHITE DISCO SUITS
© 1978 United Feature Syndicate, Inc.
JIM DAVIS

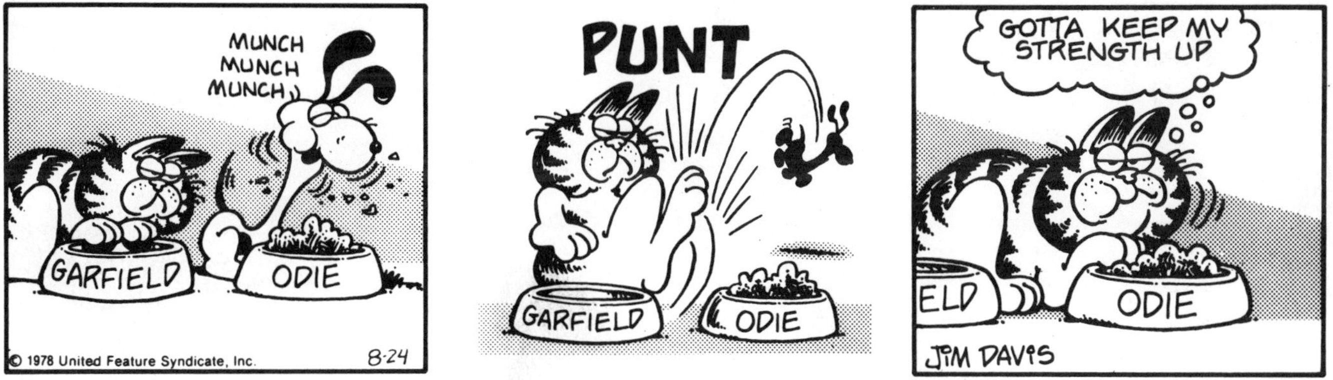
MUNCH MUNCH MUNCH
GARFIELD
ODIE
© 1978 United Feature Syndicate, Inc.
8-24
PUNT
GARFIELD
ODIE
GOTTA KEEP MY STRENGTH UP
ELD
ODIE
JIM DAVIS

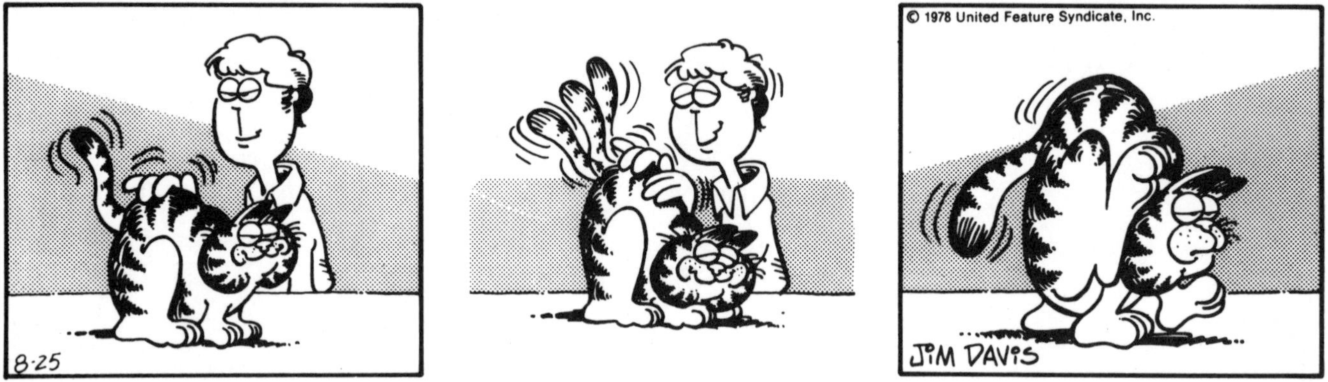
© 1978 United Feature Syndicate, Inc.
8-25
JIM DAVIS

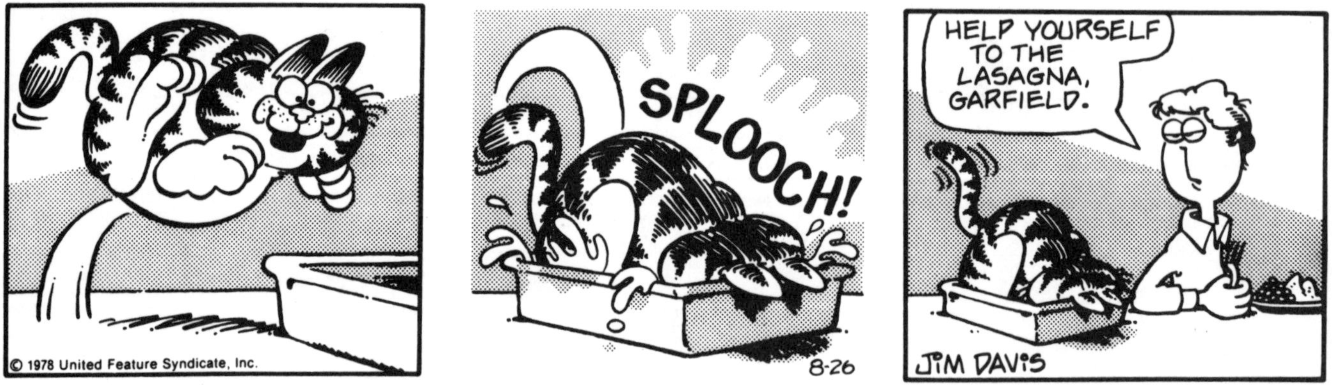
© 1978 United Feature Syndicate, Inc.
SPLOOCH!
8-26
HELP YOURSELF TO THE LASAGNA, GARFIELD.
JIM DAVIS

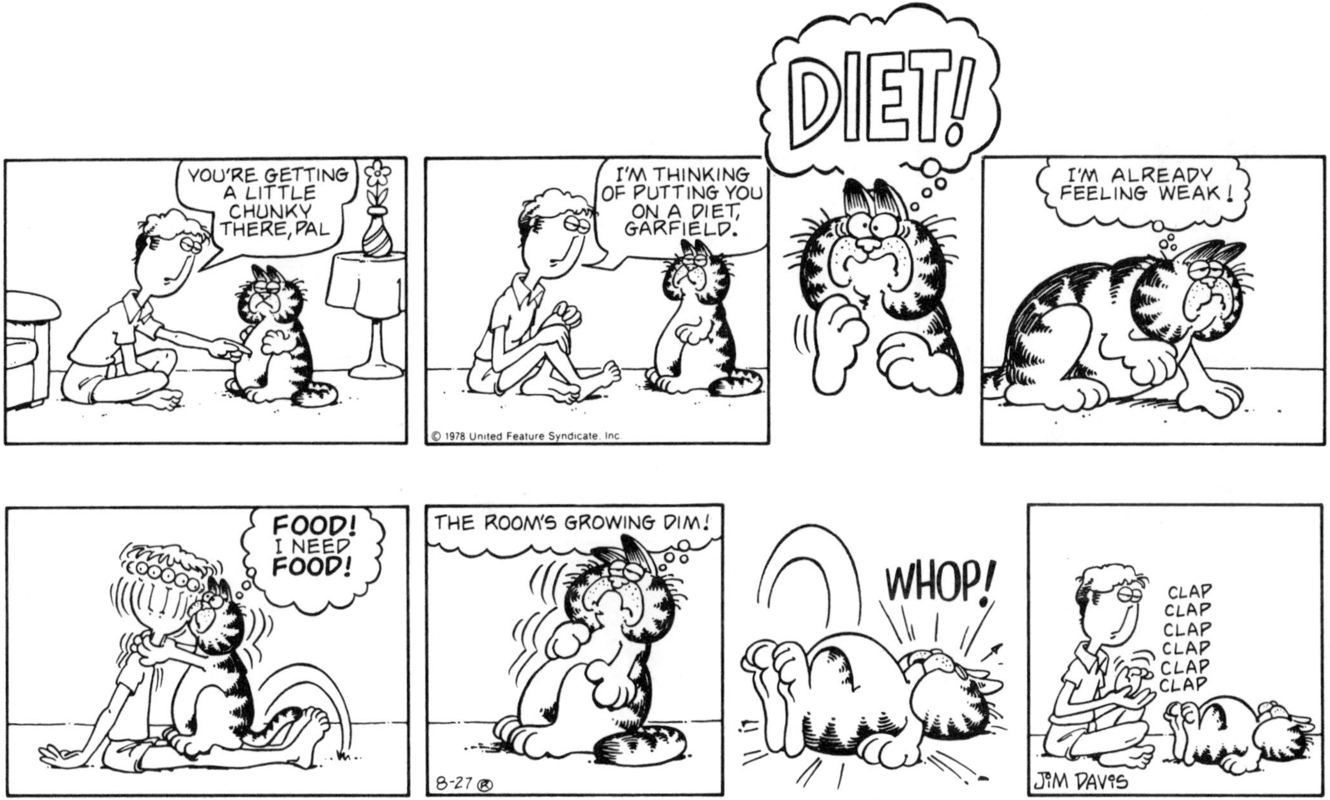
YOU'RE GETTING A LITTLE CHUNKY THERE, PAL
I'M THINKING OF PUTTING YOU ON A DIET, GARFIELD.
© 1978 United Feature Syndicate, Inc.
DIET!
I'M ALREADY FEELING WEAK!
FOOD! I NEED FOOD!
THE ROOM'S GROWING DIM!
8-27 ®
WHOP!
CLAP
CLAP
CLAP
CLAP
CLAP
CLAP
JIM DAVIS

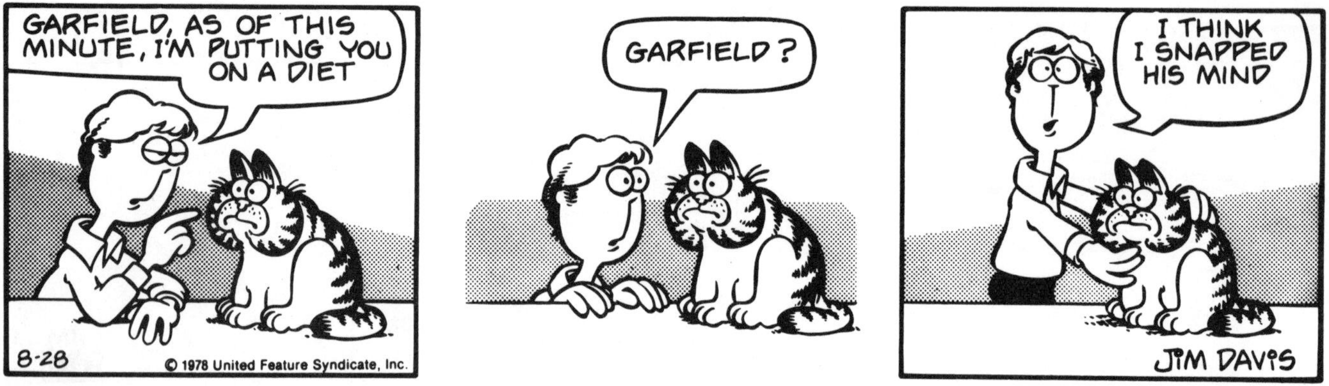
GARFIELD, AS OF THIS MINUTE, I'M PUTTING YOU ON A DIET
8-28
© 1978 United Feature Syndicate, Inc.
GARFIELD?
I THINK I SNAPPED HIS MIND
JIM DAVIS

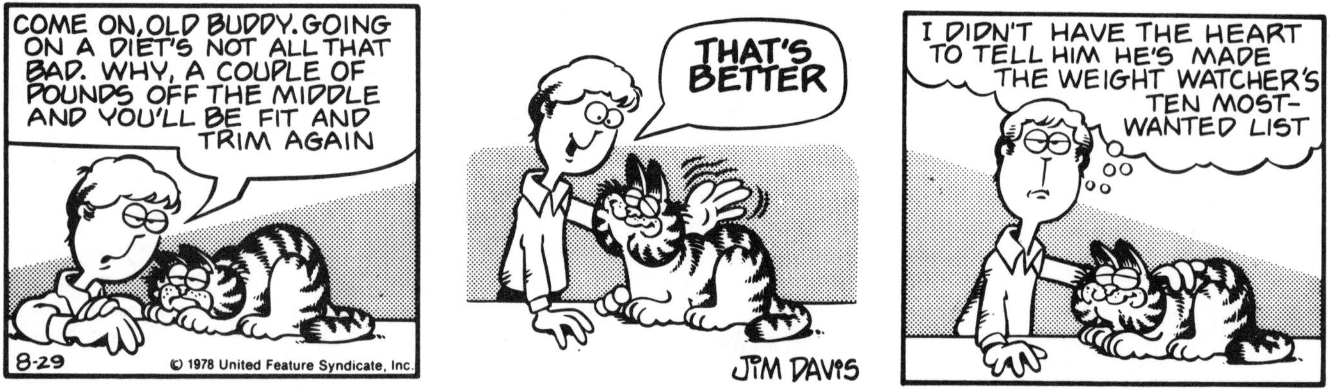
COME ON, OLD BUDDY. GOING ON A DIET'S NOT ALL THAT BAD. WHY, A COUPLE OF POUNDS OFF THE MIDDLE AND YOU'LL BE FIT AND TRIM AGAIN
8-29
© 1978 United Feature Syndicate, Inc.
THAT'S BETTER
JIM DAVIS
I DIDN'T HAVE THE HEART TO TELL HIM HE'S MADE THE WEIGHT WATCHER'S TEN MOST-WANTED LIST

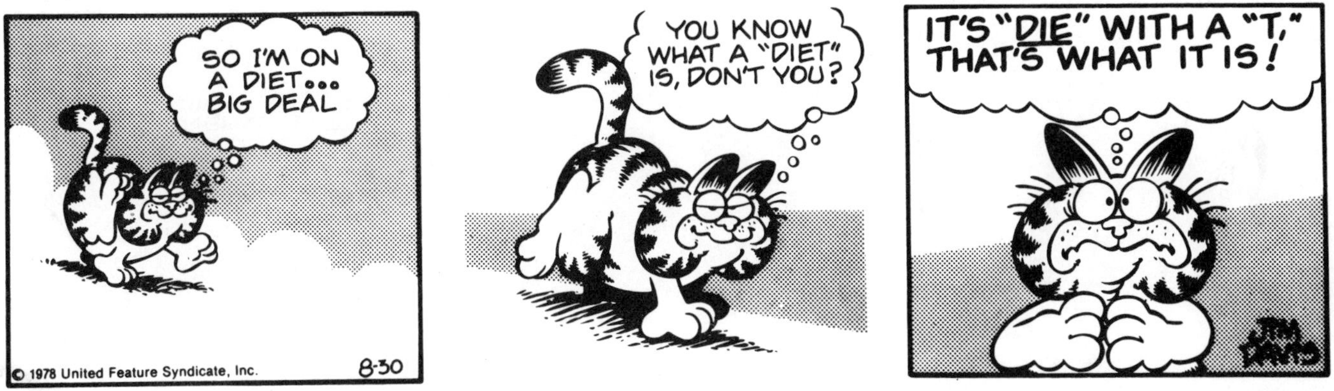
SO I'M ON A DIET... BIG DEAL
© 1978 United Feature Syndicate, Inc.
8-30
YOU KNOW WHAT A "DIET" IS, DON'T YOU?
IT'S "DIE" WITH A "T," THAT'S WHAT IT IS!
JIM DAVIS

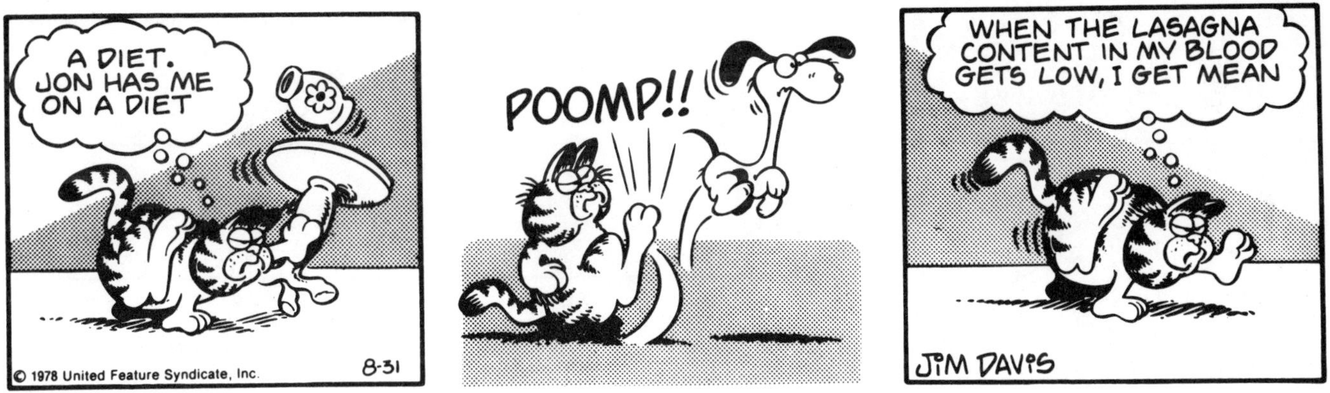
A DIET. JON HAS ME ON A DIET
© 1978 United Feature Syndicate, Inc.
8-31
POOMP!!
WHEN THE LASAGNA CONTENT IN MY BLOOD GETS LOW, I GET MEAN
JIM DAVIS

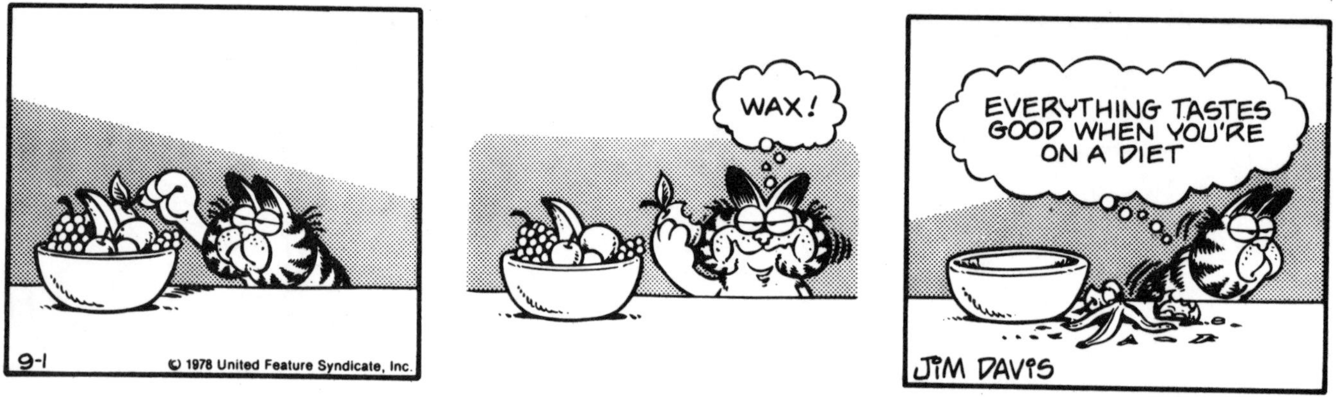

9-1
© 1978 United Feature Syndicate, Inc.
WAX!
EVERYTHING TASTES GOOD WHEN YOU'RE ON A DIET
JIM DAVIS

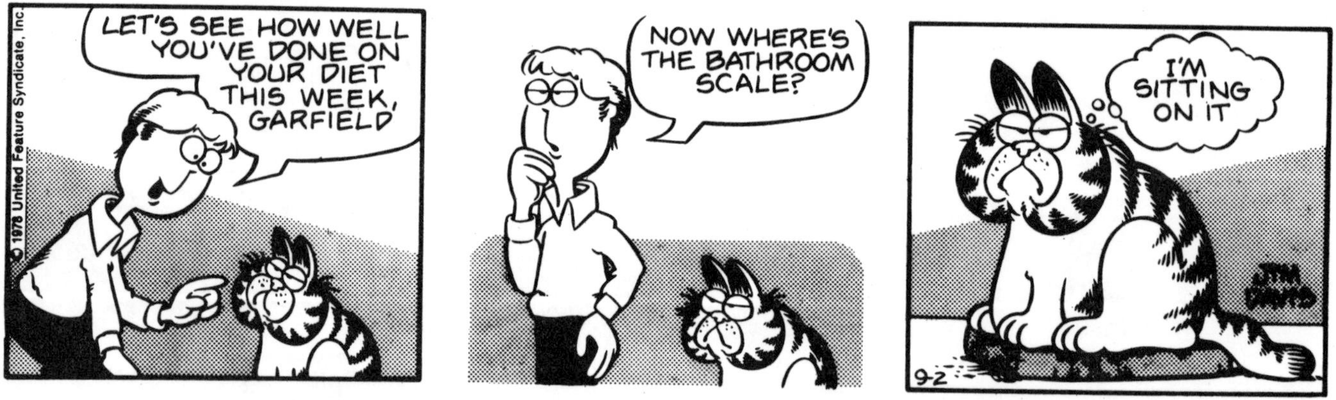

© 1978 United Feature Syndicate, Inc.
LET'S SEE HOW WELL YOU'VE DONE ON YOUR DIET THIS WEEK, GARFIELD
NOW WHERE'S THE BATHROOM SCALE?
I'M SITTING ON IT
JIM DAVIS
9-2

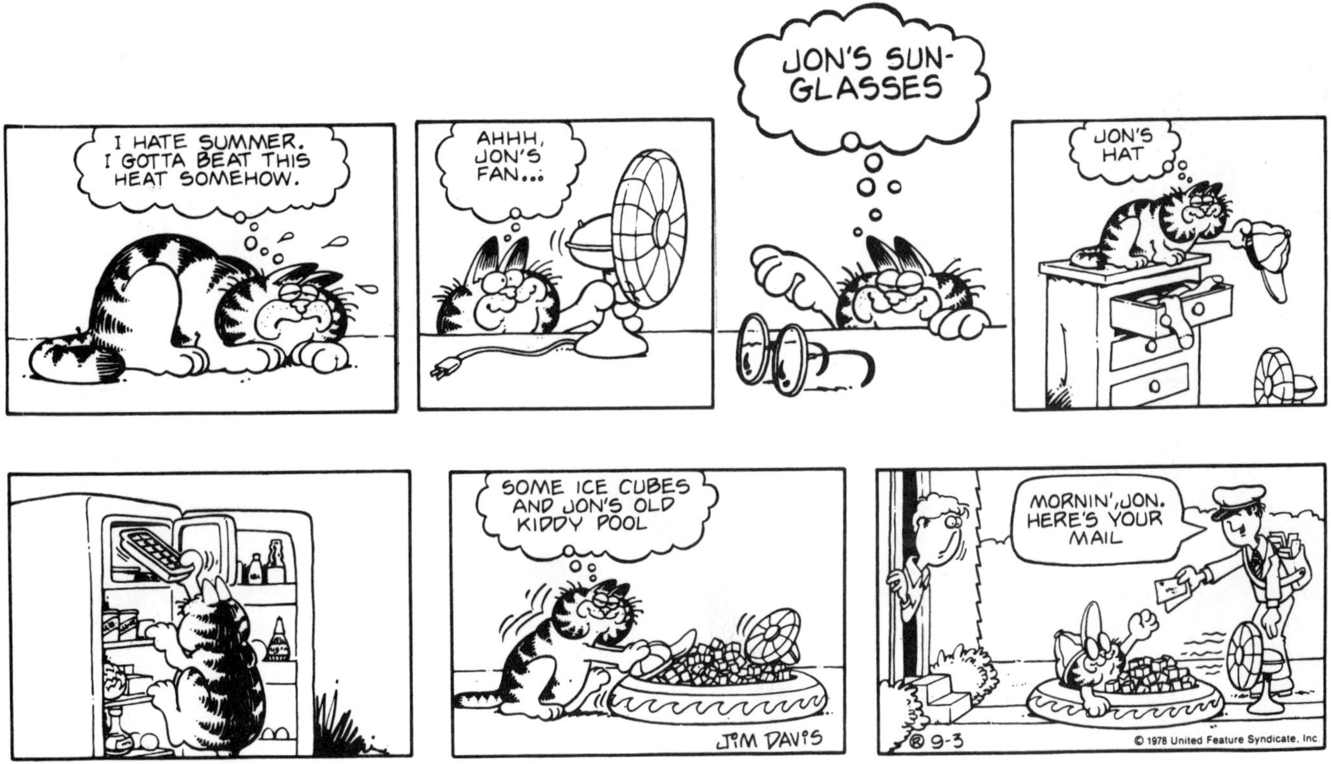
I HATE SUMMER. I GOTTA BEAT THIS HEAT SOMEHOW.
AHHH, JON'S FAN...
JON'S SUN-GLASSES
JON'S HAT
SOME ICE CUBES AND JON'S OLD KIDDY POOL
MORNIN', JON. HERE'S YOUR MAIL
JIM DAVIS
® 9-3
© 1978 United Feature Syndicate, Inc.

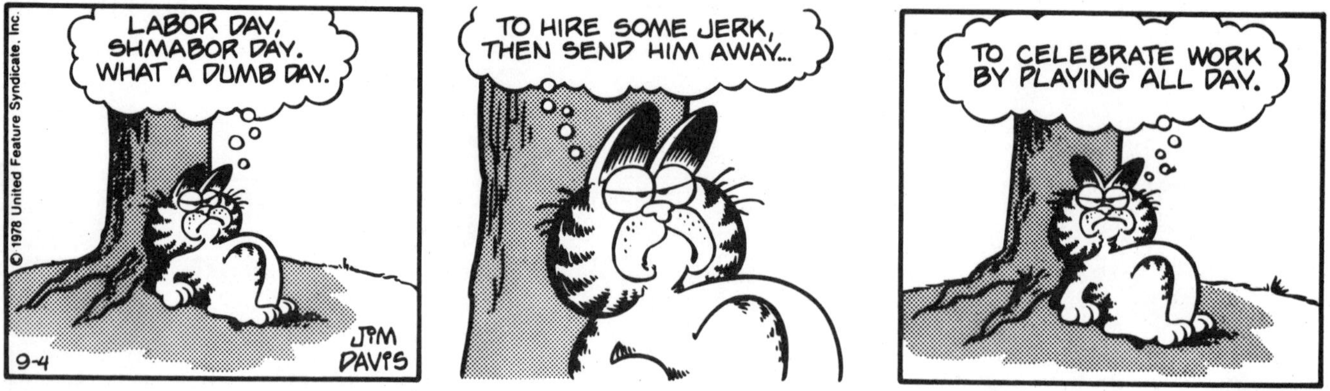
© 1978 United Feature Syndicate, Inc.
LABOR DAY, SHMABOR DAY. WHAT A DUMB DAY.
9-4
JIM DAVIS
TO HIRE SOME JERK, THEN SEND HIM AWAY...
TO CELEBRATE WORK BY PLAYING ALL DAY.

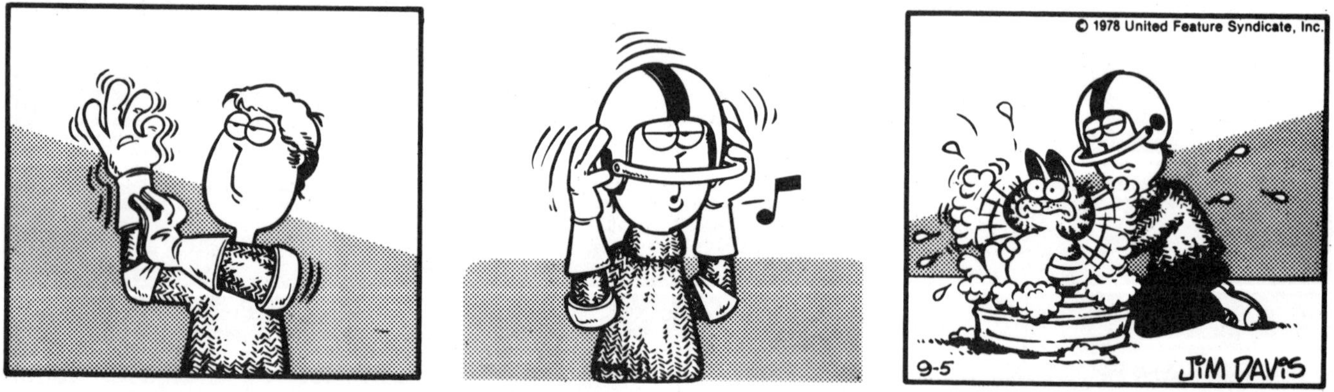
© 1978 United Feature Syndicate, Inc.
9-5
JIM DAVIS

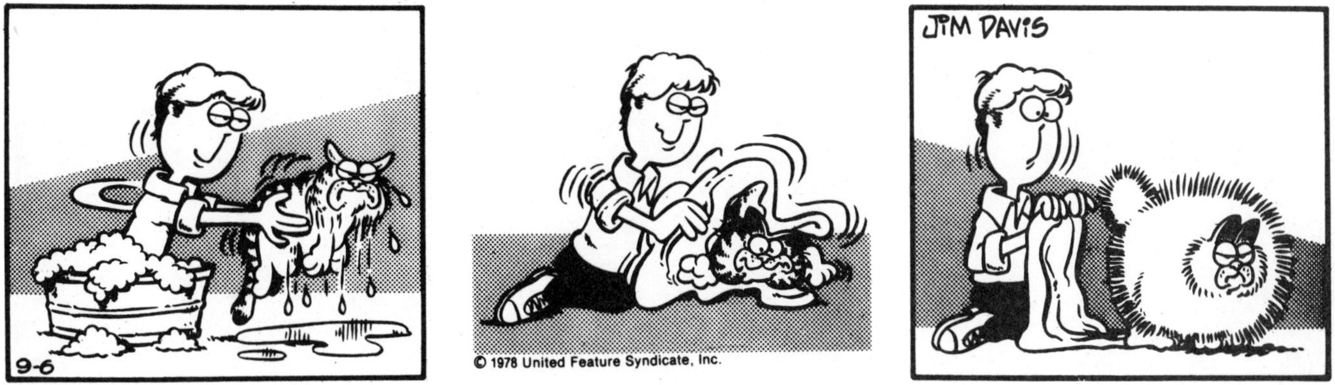
9-6
© 1978 United Feature Syndicate, Inc.
JIM DAVIS

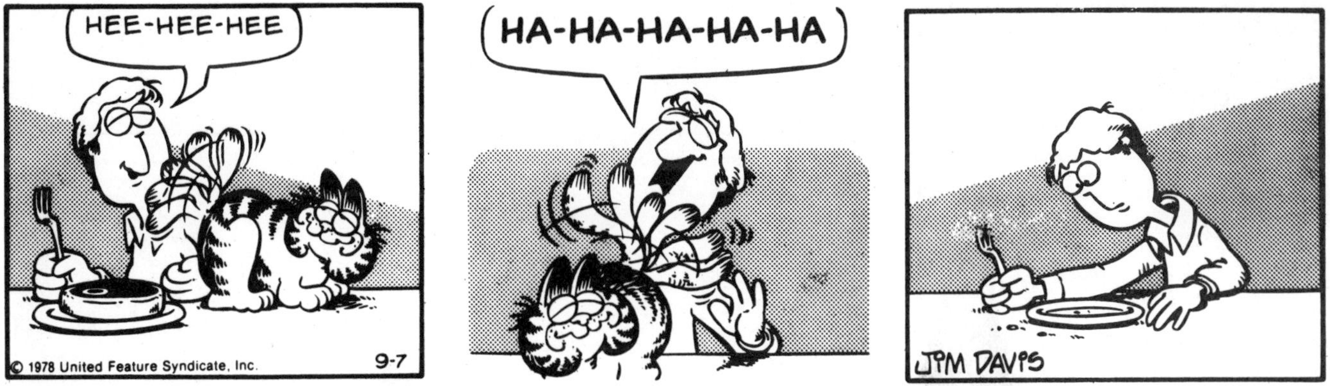
HEE-HEE-HEE
© 1978 United Feature Syndicate, Inc.
9-7
HA-HA-HA-HA-HA
JIM DAVIS

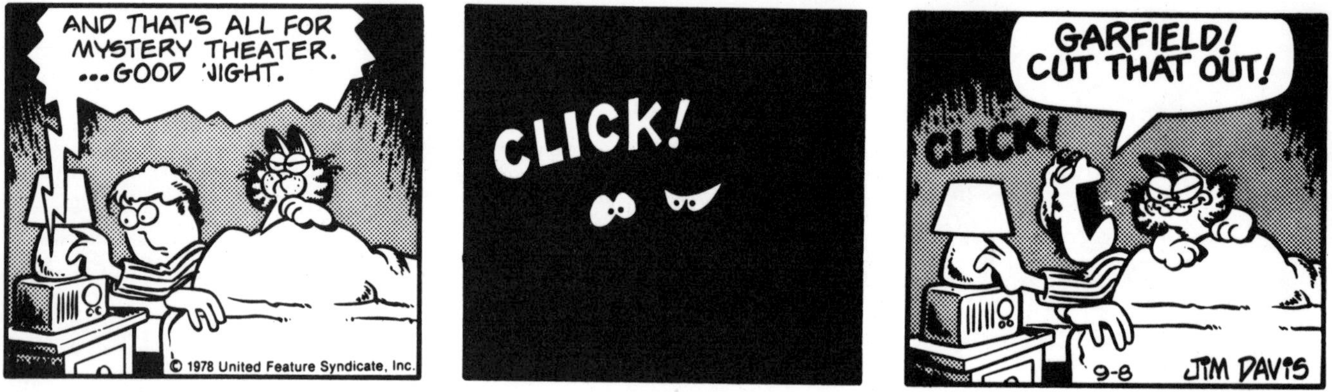
AND THAT'S ALL FOR MYSTERY THEATER. ...GOOD 'NIGHT.
© 1978 United Feature Syndicate, Inc.
CLICK!
CLICK!
GARFIELD! CUT THAT OUT!
9-8
JIM DAVIS

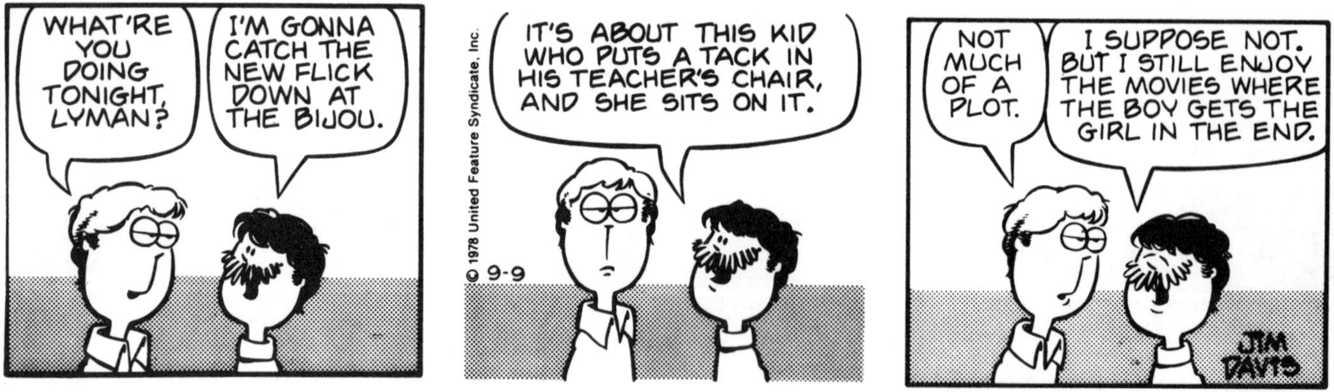
WHAT'RE YOU DOING TONIGHT, LYMAN?
I'M GONNA CATCH THE NEW FLICK DOWN AT THE BIJOU.
© 1978 United Feature Syndicate, Inc.
9-9
IT'S ABOUT THIS KID WHO PUTS A TACK IN HIS TEACHER'S CHAIR, AND SHE SITS ON IT.
NOT MUCH OF A PLOT.
I SUPPOSE NOT. BUT I STILL ENJOY THE MOVIES WHERE THE BOY GETS THE GIRL IN THE END.
JIM DAVIS

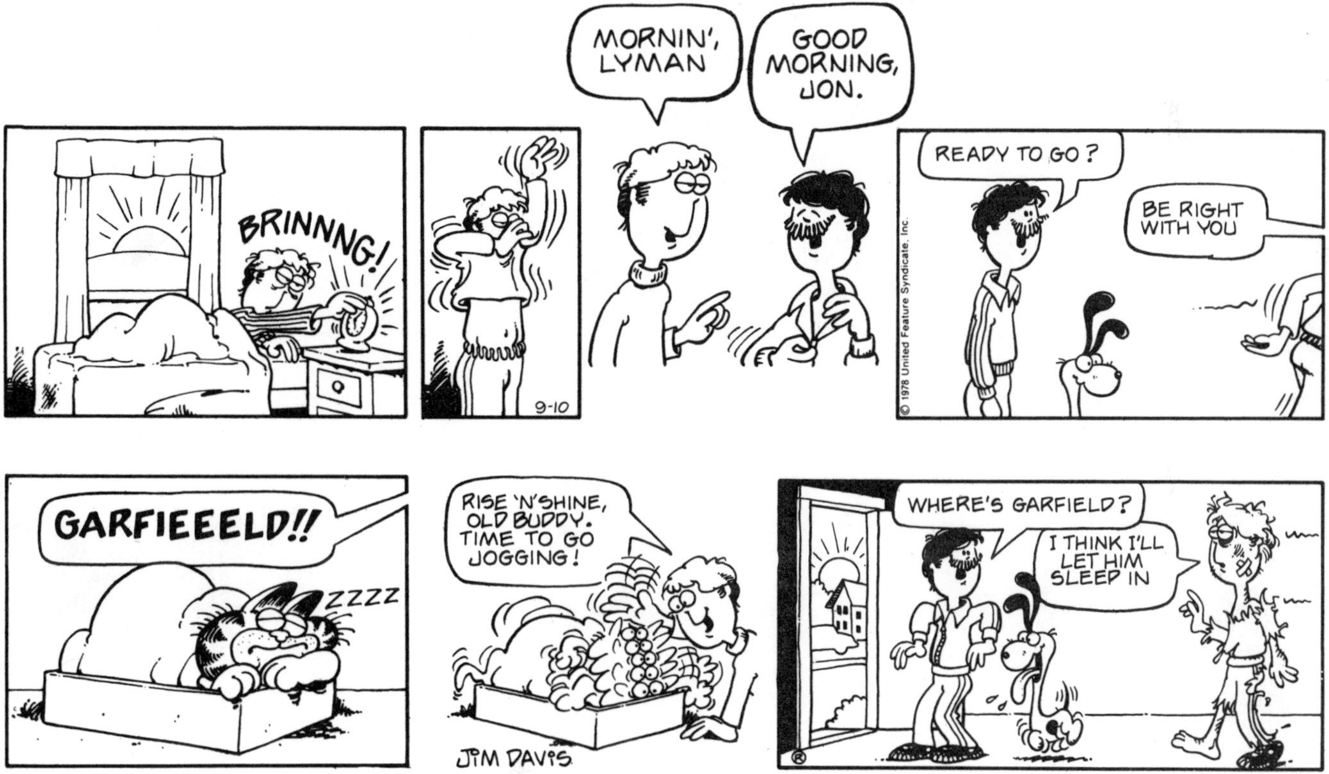
BRINNNG!
9-10
MORNIN', LYMAN
GOOD MORNING, JON.
© 1978 United Feature Syndicate, Inc.
READY TO GO?
BE RIGHT WITH YOU
GARFIEEELD!!
ZZZZ
RISE 'N' SHINE, OLD BUDDY. TIME TO GO JOGGING!
JIM DAVIS
WHERE'S GARFIELD?
I THINK I'LL LET HIM SLEEP IN

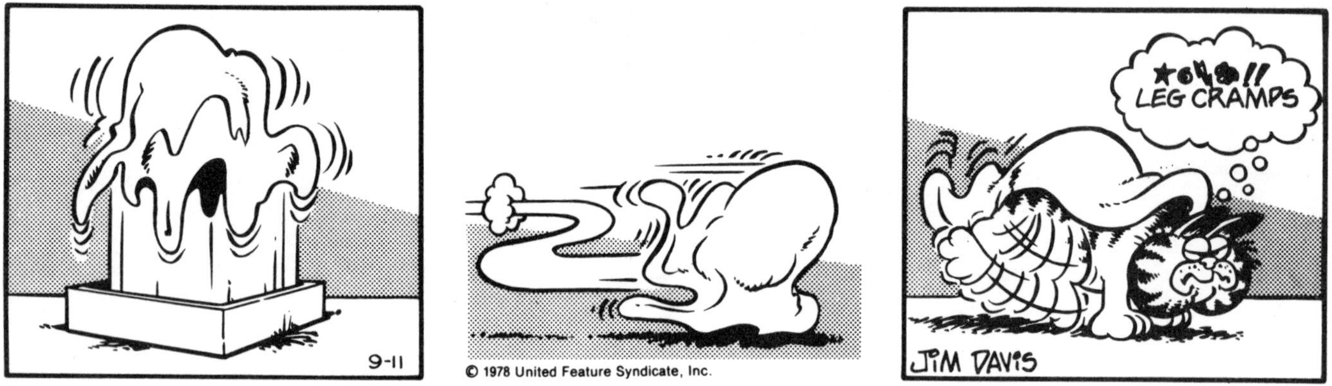
9-11
© 1978 United Feature Syndicate, Inc.
LEG CRAMPS
JIM DAVIS

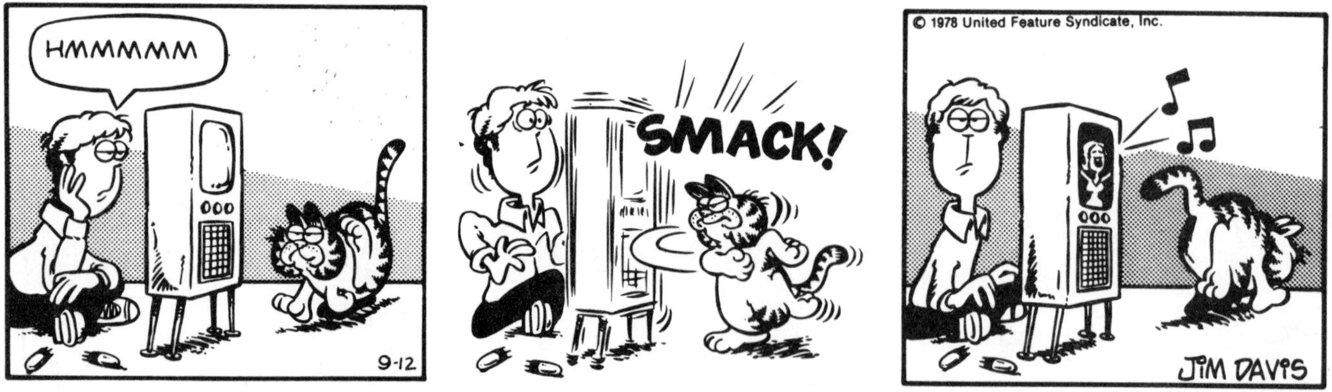
HMMMMM
9-12
SMACK!
© 1978 United Feature Syndicate, Inc.
JIM DAVIS

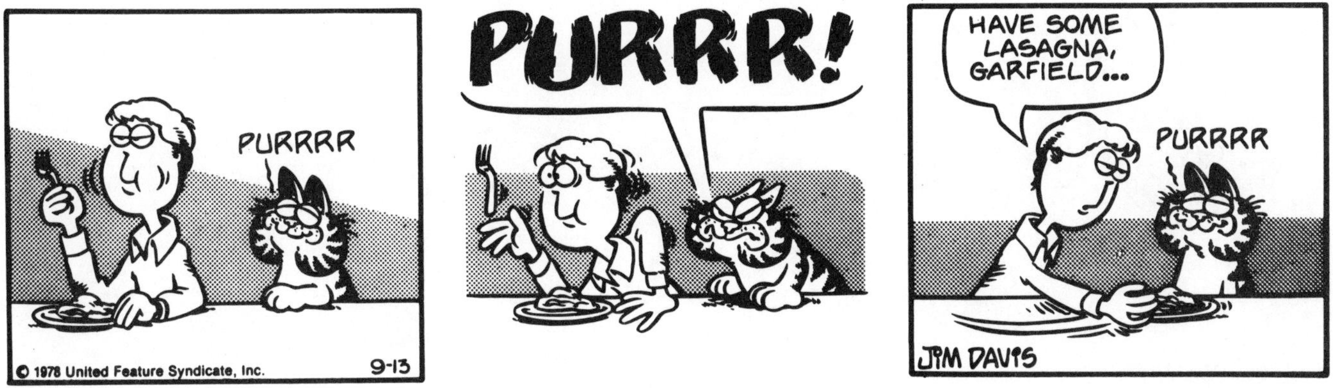
PURRRR
PURRR!
HAVE SOME LASAGNA, GARFIELD...
PURRRR
JIM DAVIS
9-13

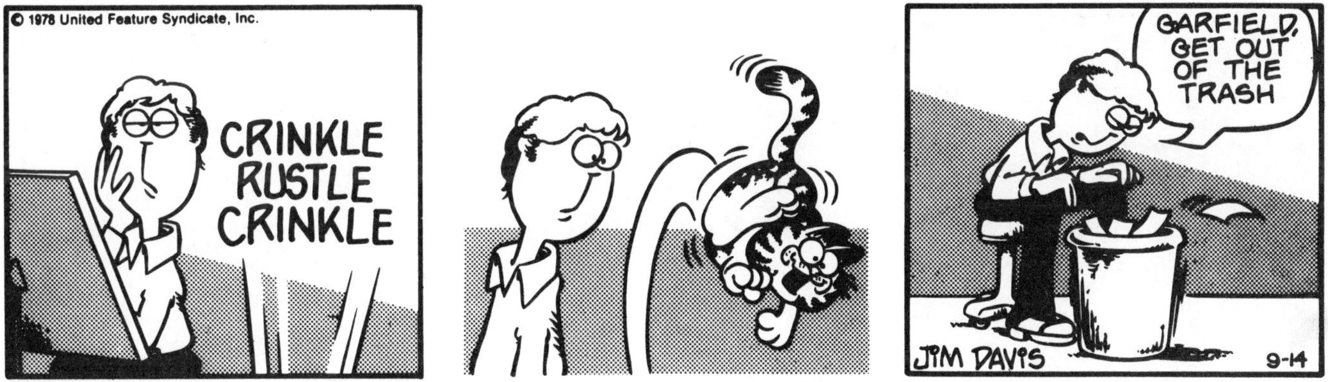
CRINKLE RUSTLE CRINKLE
GARFIELD, GET OUT OF THE TRASH
JIM DAVIS
9-14

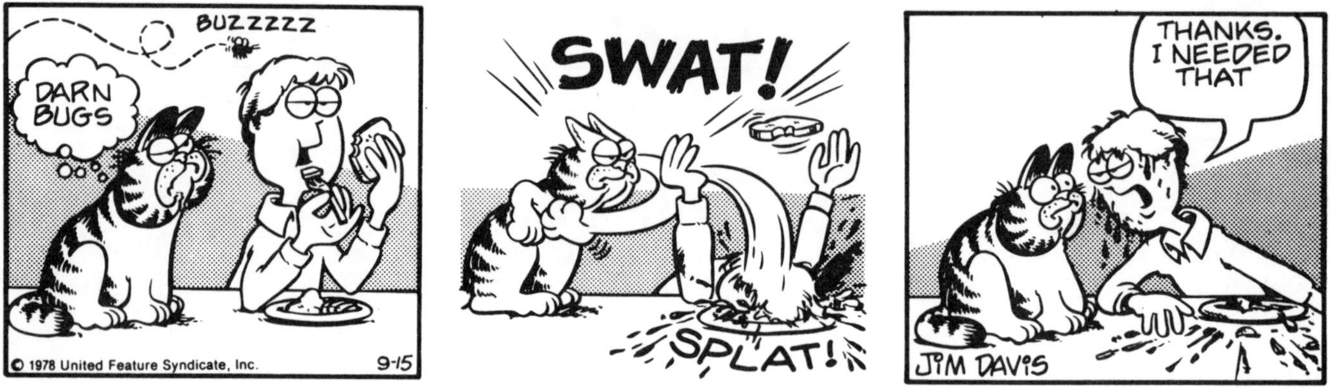
BUZZZZZ
DARN BUGS
SWAT!
SPLAT!
THANKS. I NEEDED THAT
JIM DAVIS
© 1978 United Feature Syndicate, Inc.
9-15

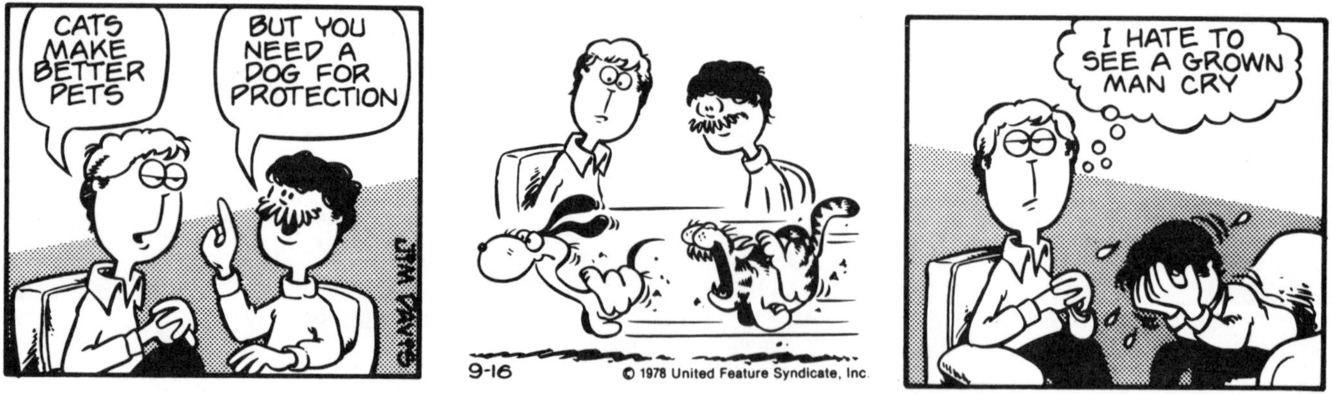
CATS MAKE BETTER PETS
BUT YOU NEED A DOG FOR PROTECTION
JIM DAVIS
I HATE TO SEE A GROWN MAN CRY
9-16
© 1978 United Feature Syndicate, Inc.

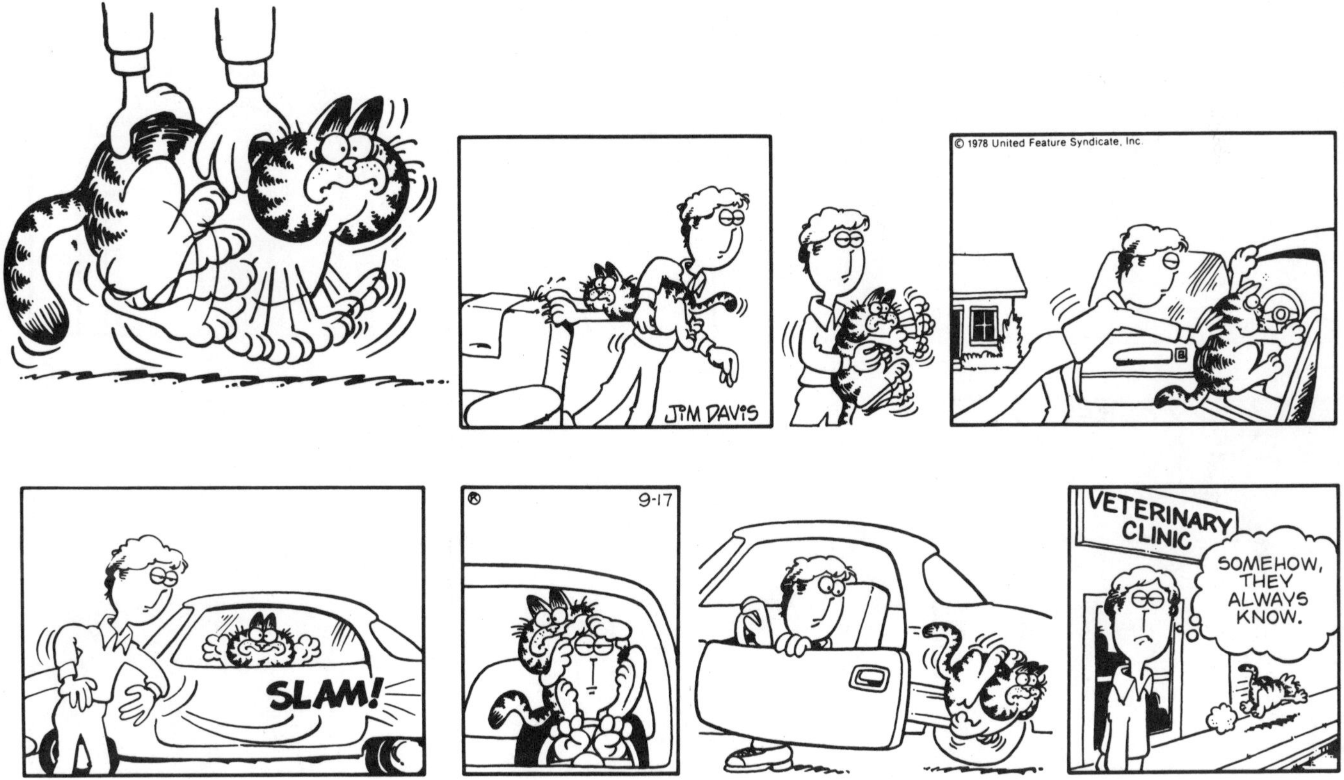
© 1978 United Feature Syndicate, Inc.
JIM DAVIS
SLAM!
9-17
VETERINARY CLINIC
SOMEHOW, THEY ALWAYS KNOW.

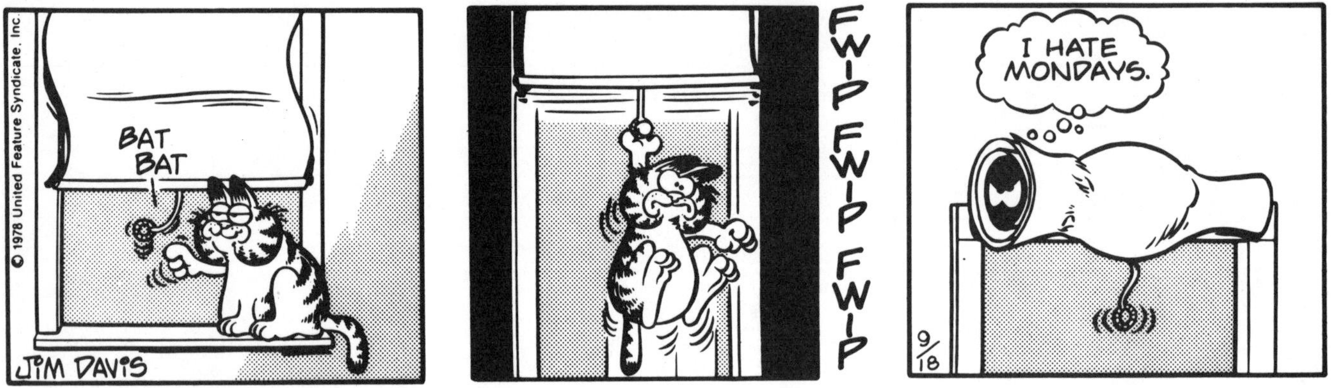
© 1978 United Feature Syndicate, Inc.
JIM DAVIS
BAT
BAT
FWIP FWIP FWIP FWIP
I HATE MONDAYS.
9/18

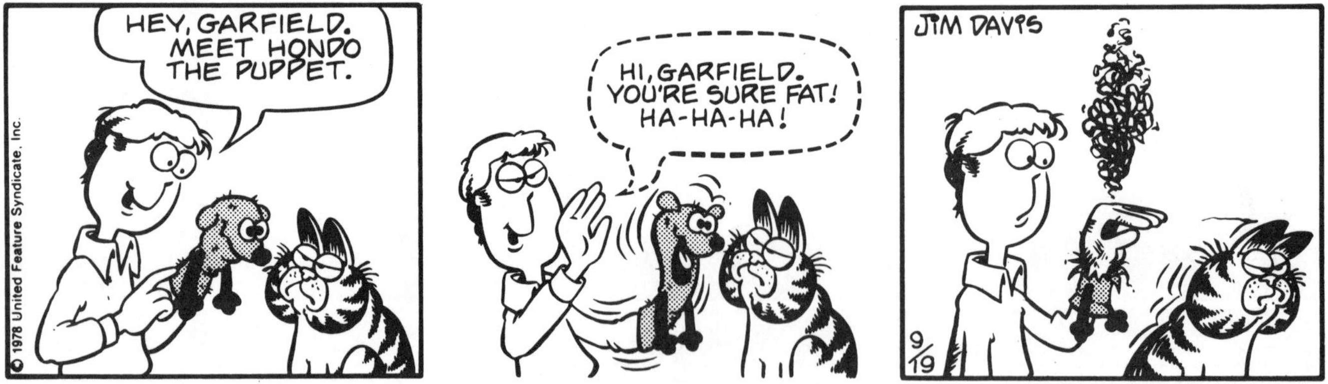
© 1978 United Feature Syndicate, Inc.
HEY, GARFIELD. MEET HONDO THE PUPPET.
HI, GARFIELD. YOU'RE SURE FAT! HA-HA-HA!
JIM DAVIS
9/19

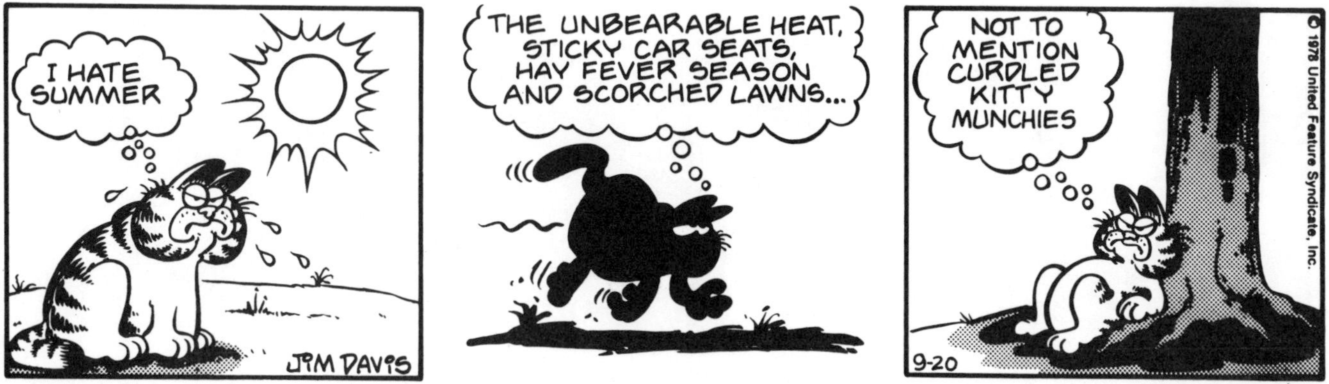
I HATE SUMMER
JIM DAVIS
THE UNBEARABLE HEAT, STICKY CAR SEATS, HAY FEVER SEASON AND SCORCHED LAWNS...
NOT TO MENTION CURDLED KITTY MUNCHIES
© 1978 United Feature Syndicate, Inc.
9-20

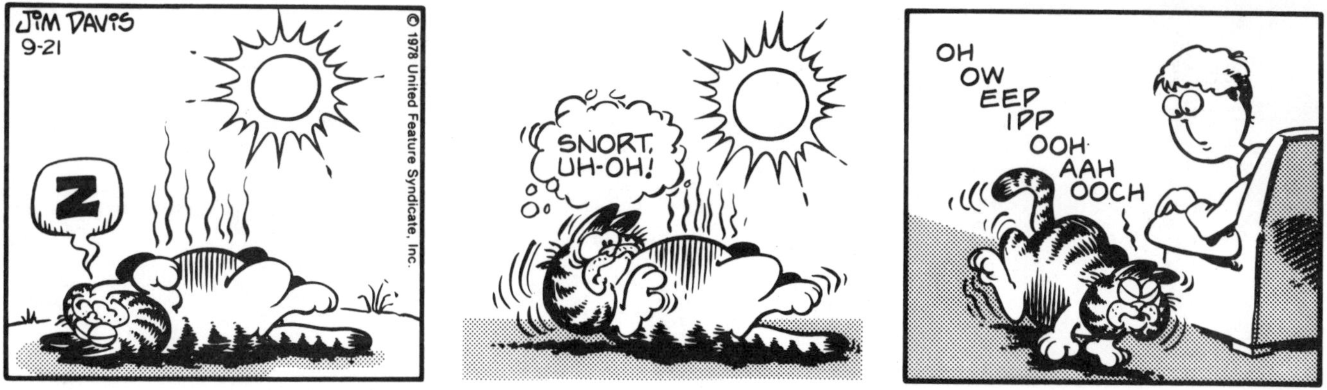
JIM DAVIS
9-21
© 1978 United Feature Syndicate, Inc.
Z
SNORT, UH-OH!
OH
OW
EEP
IPP
OOH
AAH
OOCH

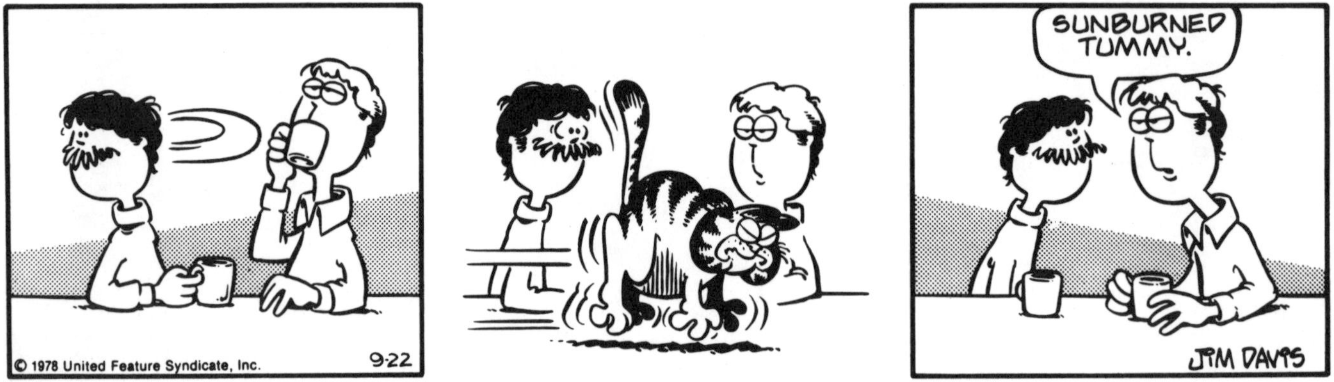
© 1978 United Feature Syndicate, Inc.
9-22
SUNBURNED TUMMY.
JIM DAVIS

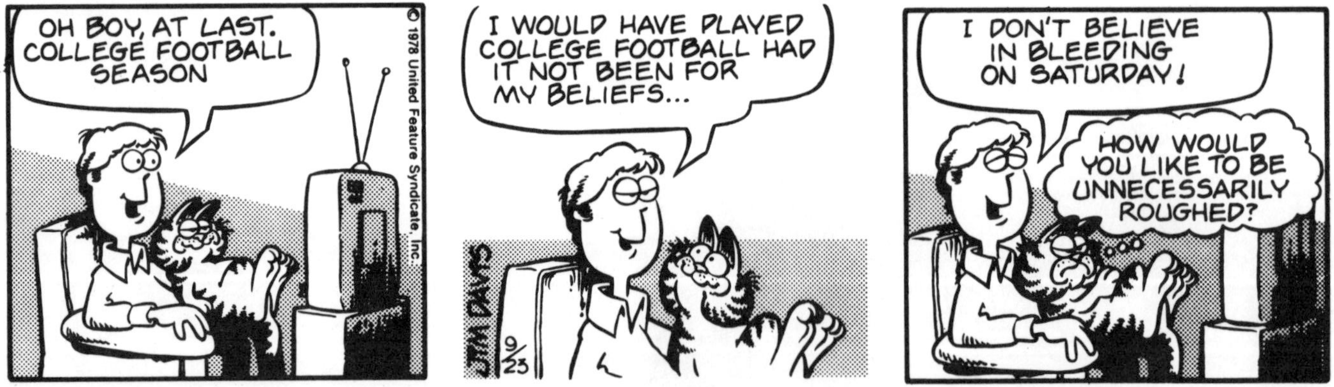
OH BOY, AT LAST. COLLEGE FOOTBALL SEASON
© 1978 United Feature Syndicate, Inc.
I WOULD HAVE PLAYED COLLEGE FOOTBALL HAD IT NOT BEEN FOR MY BELIEFS...
JIM DAVIS
9/23
I DON'T BELIEVE IN BLEEDING ON SATURDAY!
HOW WOULD YOU LIKE TO BE UNNECESSARILY ROUGHED?

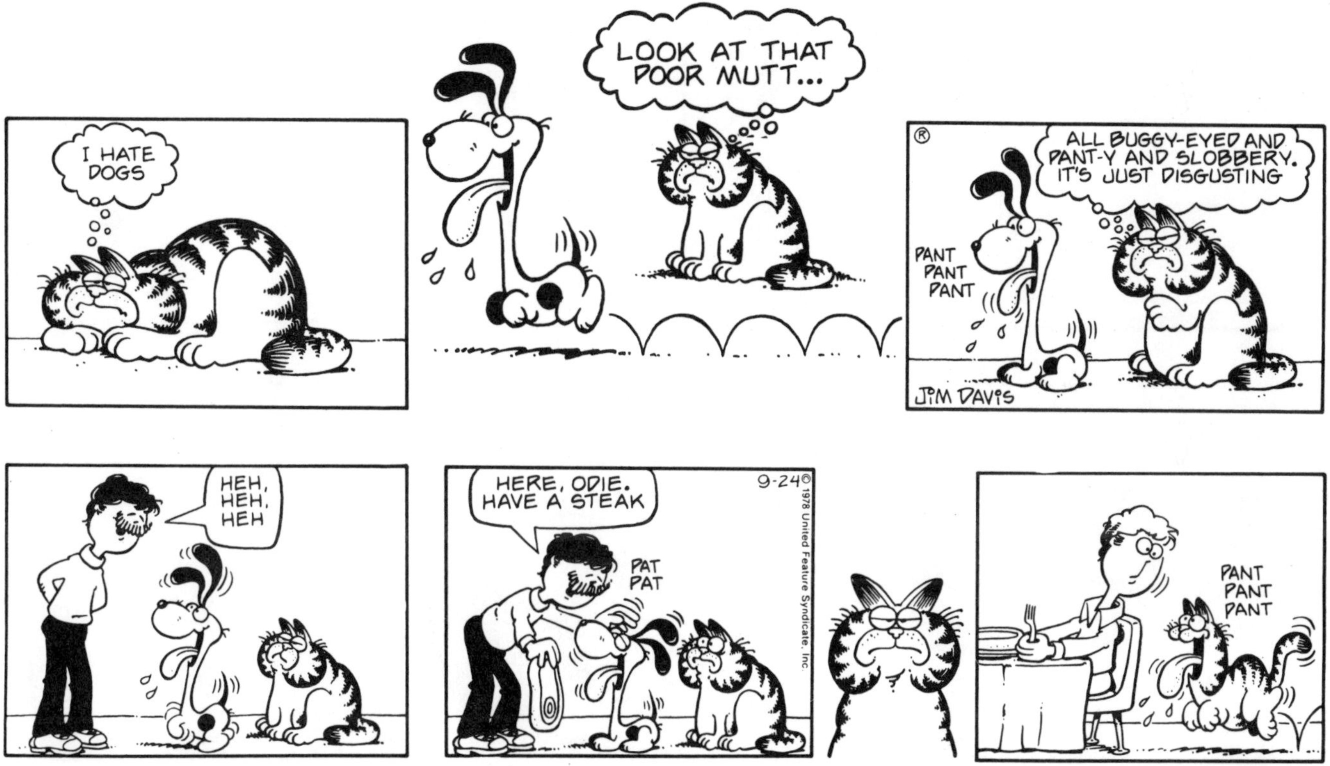

I HATE DOGS
LOOK AT THAT POOR MUTT...
ALL BUGGY-EYED AND PANT-Y AND SLOBBERY. IT'S JUST DISGUSTING
PANT PANT PANT
JIM DAVIS
HEH, HEH, HEH
HERE, ODIE. HAVE A STEAK
PAT PAT
9-24 © 1978 United Feature Syndicate, Inc.
PANT PANT PANT

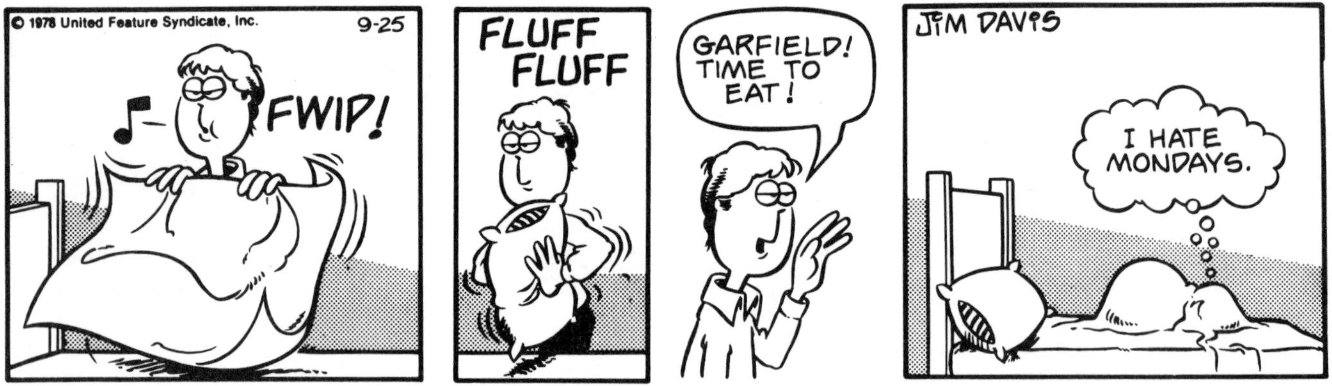
© 1978 United Feature Syndicate, Inc.
9-25
FWIP!
FLUFF FLUFF
GARFIELD! TIME TO EAT!
JIM DAVIS
I HATE MONDAYS.

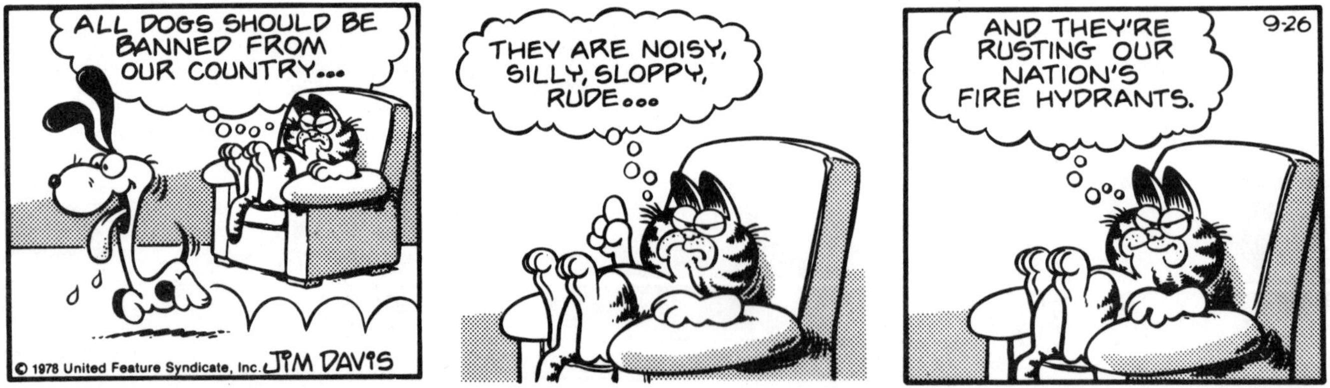
ALL DOGS SHOULD BE BANNED FROM OUR COUNTRY...
© 1978 United Feature Syndicate, Inc. JIM DAVIS
THEY ARE NOISY, SILLY, SLOPPY, RUDE...
9-26
AND THEY'RE RUSTING OUR NATION'S FIRE HYDRANTS.

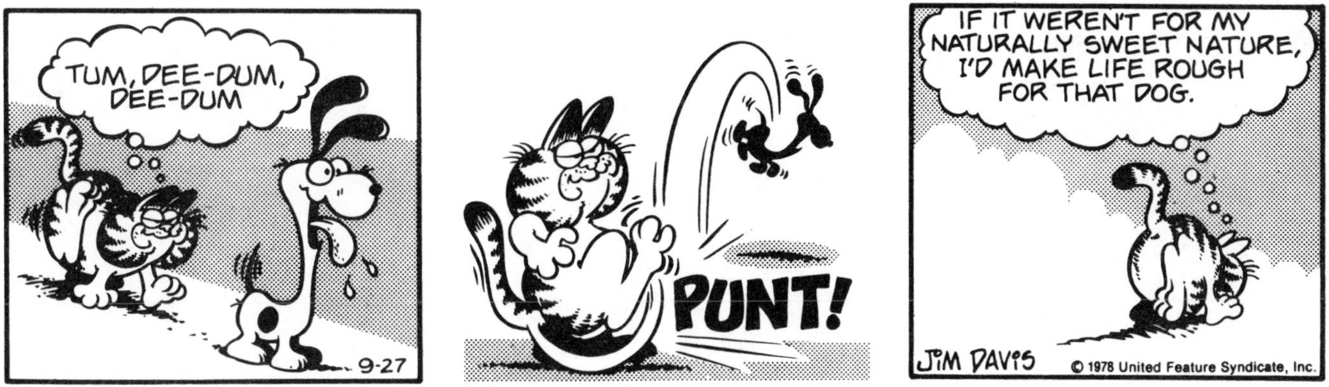
TUM, DEE-DUM, DEE-DUM
9-27
PUNT!
IF IT WEREN'T FOR MY NATURALLY SWEET NATURE, I'D MAKE LIFE ROUGH FOR THAT DOG.
JIM DAVIS
© 1978 United Feature Syndicate, Inc.

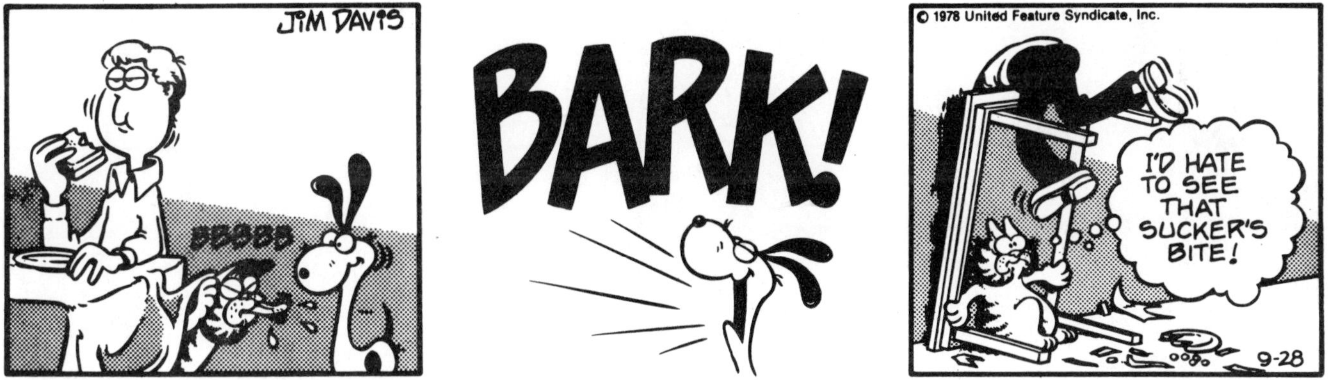
JIM DAVIS
BBBBB
BARK!
© 1978 United Feature Syndicate, Inc.
I'D HATE TO SEE THAT SUCKER'S BITE!
9-28

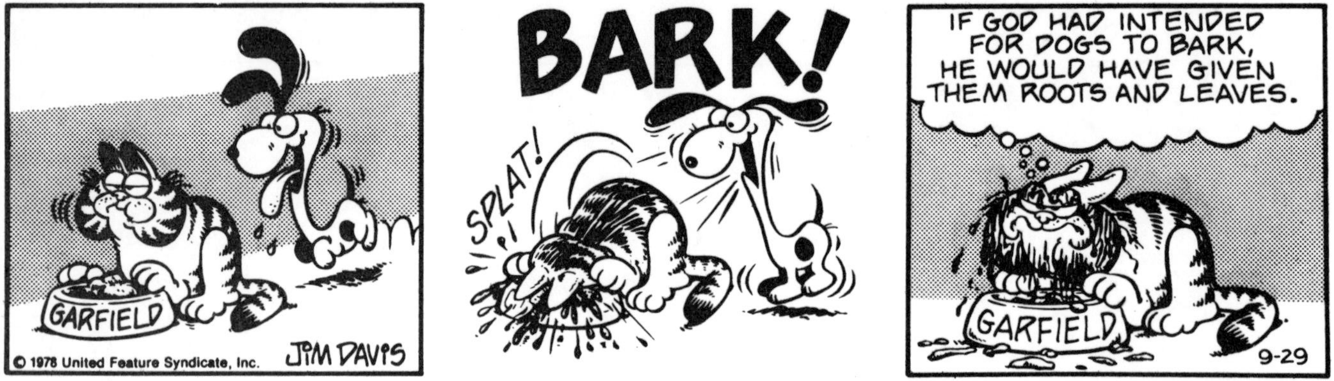
GARFIELD
© 1978 United Feature Syndicate, Inc.
JIM DAVIS
BARK!
SPLAT!
IF GOD HAD INTENDED FOR DOGS TO BARK, HE WOULD HAVE GIVEN THEM ROOTS AND LEAVES.
GARFIELD
9-29

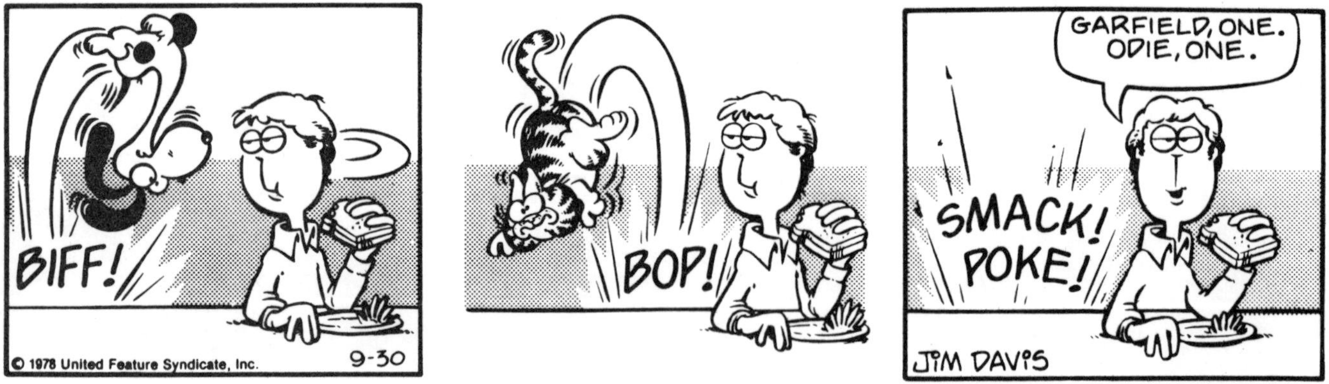
BIFF!
© 1978 United Feature Syndicate, Inc.
9-30
BOP!
GARFIELD, ONE. ODIE, ONE.
SMACK! POKE!
JIM DAVIS

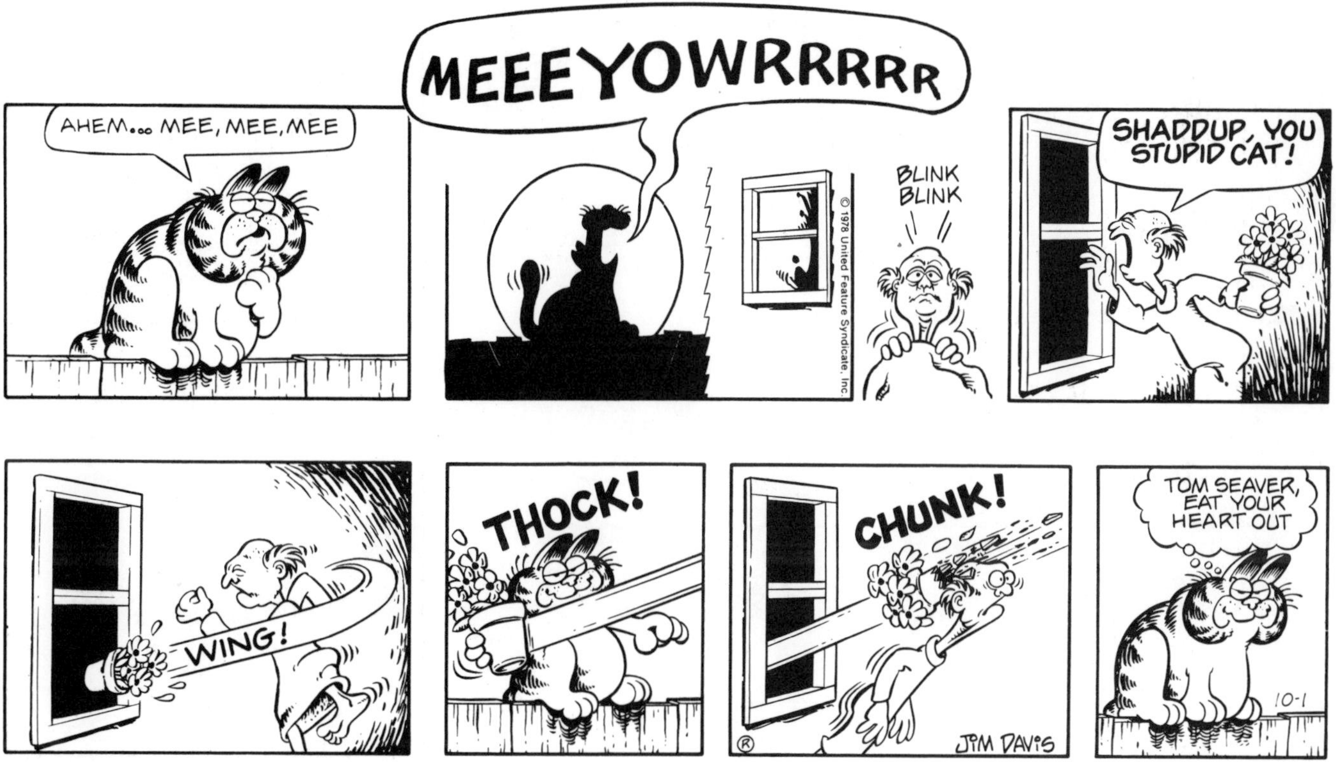
AHEM... MEE, MEE, MEE
MEEEYOWRRRRR
© 1978 United Feature Syndicate, Inc.
BLINK BLINK
SHADDUP, YOU STUPID CAT!
WING!
THOCK!
CHUNK!
JIM DAVIS
TOM SEAVER, EAT YOUR HEART OUT
10-1

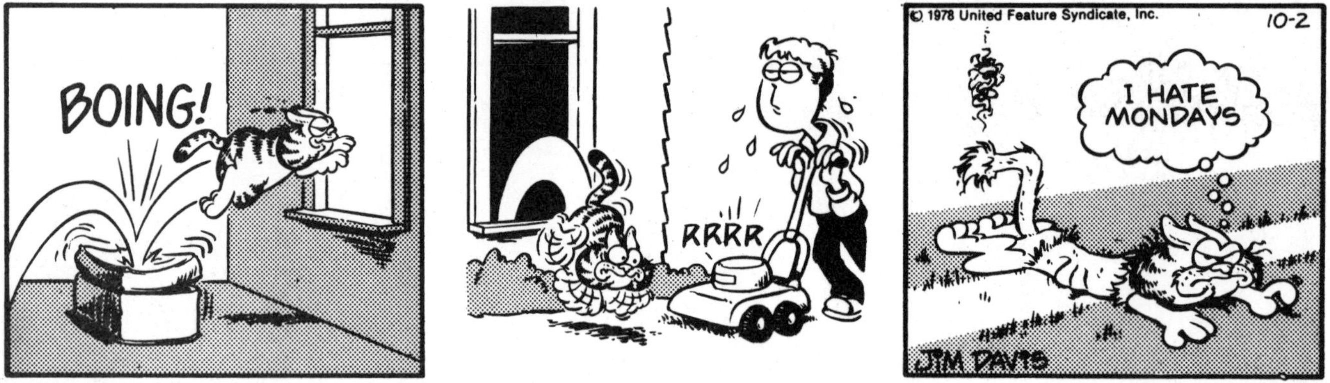
BOING!
RRRR
© 1978 United Feature Syndicate, Inc.
10-2
I HATE MONDAYS
JIM DAVIS

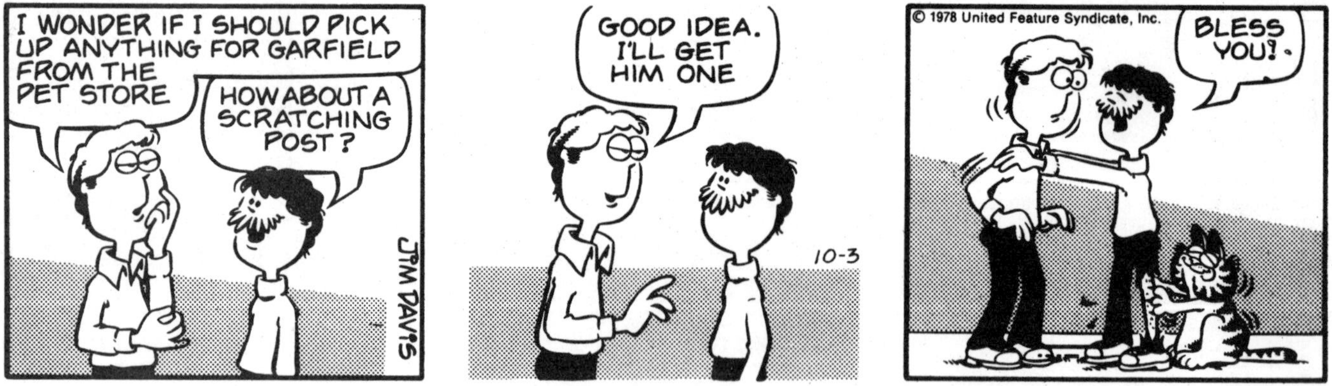
I WONDER IF I SHOULD PICK UP ANYTHING FOR GARFIELD FROM THE PET STORE
HOW ABOUT A SCRATCHING POST?
JIM DAVIS
GOOD IDEA. I'LL GET HIM ONE
10-3
© 1978 United Feature Syndicate, Inc.
BLESS YOU!

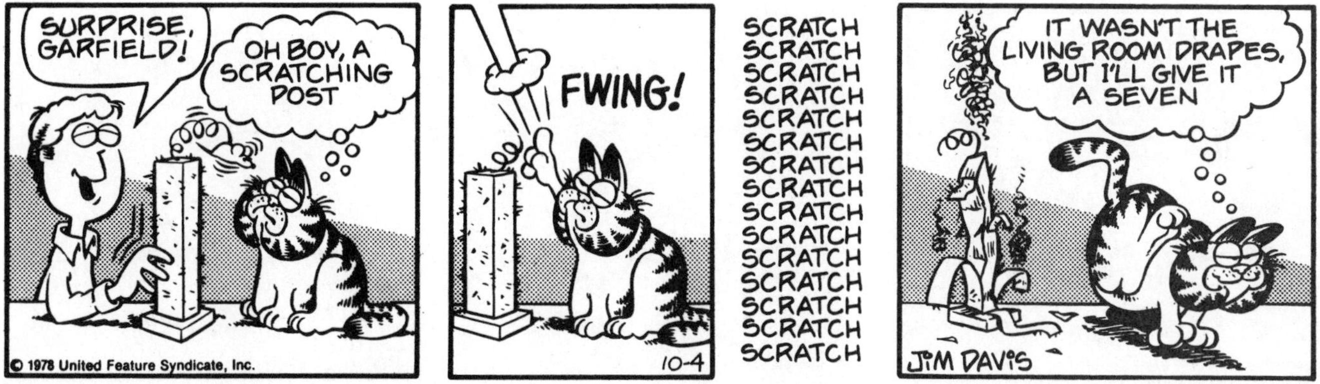
SURPRISE, GARFIELD!
OH BOY, A SCRATCHING POST
© 1978 United Feature Syndicate, Inc.
FWING!
10-4
SCRATCH SCRATCH SCRATCH SCRATCH SCRATCH SCRATCH SCRATCH SCRATCH SCRATCH SCRATCH SCRATCH SCRATCH SCRATCH SCRATCH SCRATCH
IT WASN'T THE LIVING ROOM DRAPES, BUT I'LL GIVE IT A SEVEN
JIM DAVIS

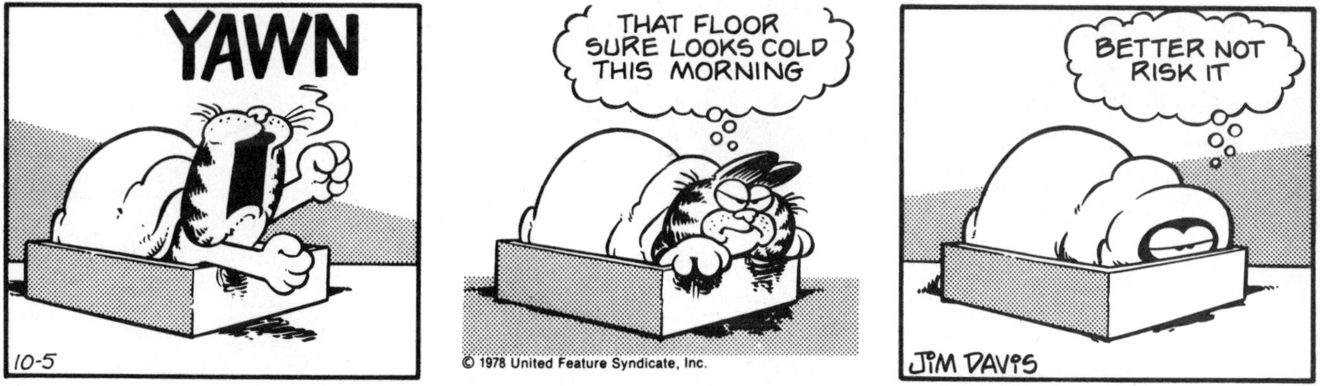
YAWN
10-5
THAT FLOOR SURE LOOKS COLD THIS MORNING
© 1978 United Feature Syndicate, Inc.
BETTER NOT RISK IT
JIM DAVIS

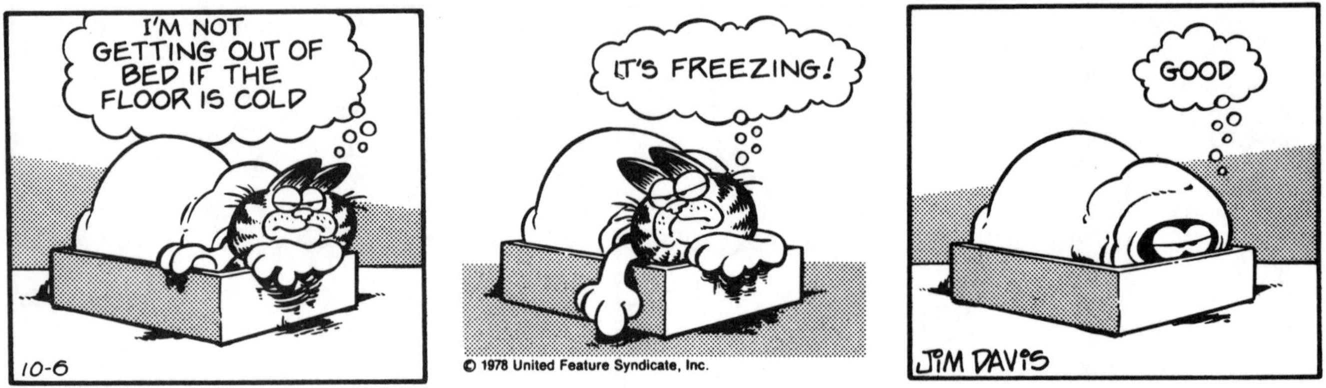
I'M NOT GETTING OUT OF BED IF THE FLOOR IS COLD
IT'S FREEZING!
GOOD
10-6
© 1978 United Feature Syndicate, Inc.
JIM DAVIS

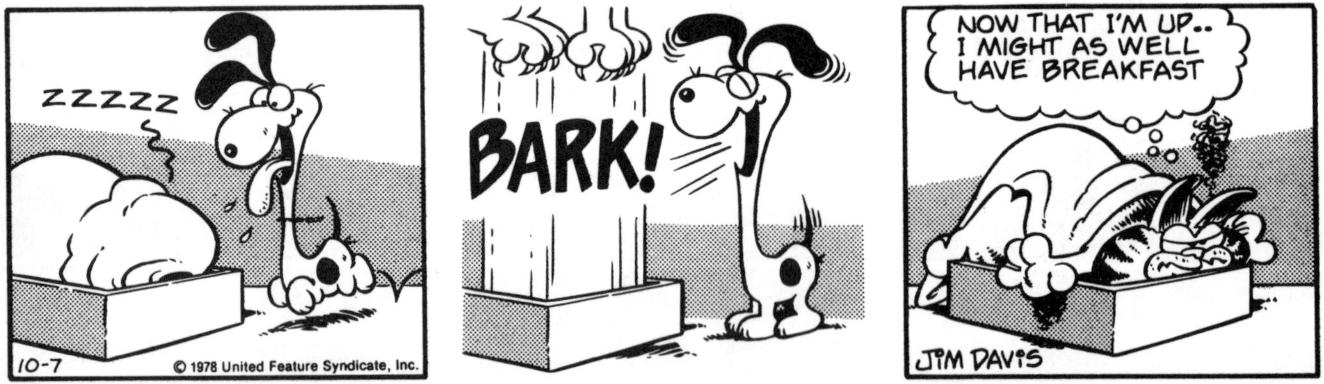
ZZZZZ
BARK!
NOW THAT I'M UP.. I MIGHT AS WELL HAVE BREAKFAST
10-7
© 1978 United Feature Syndicate, Inc.
JIM DAVIS

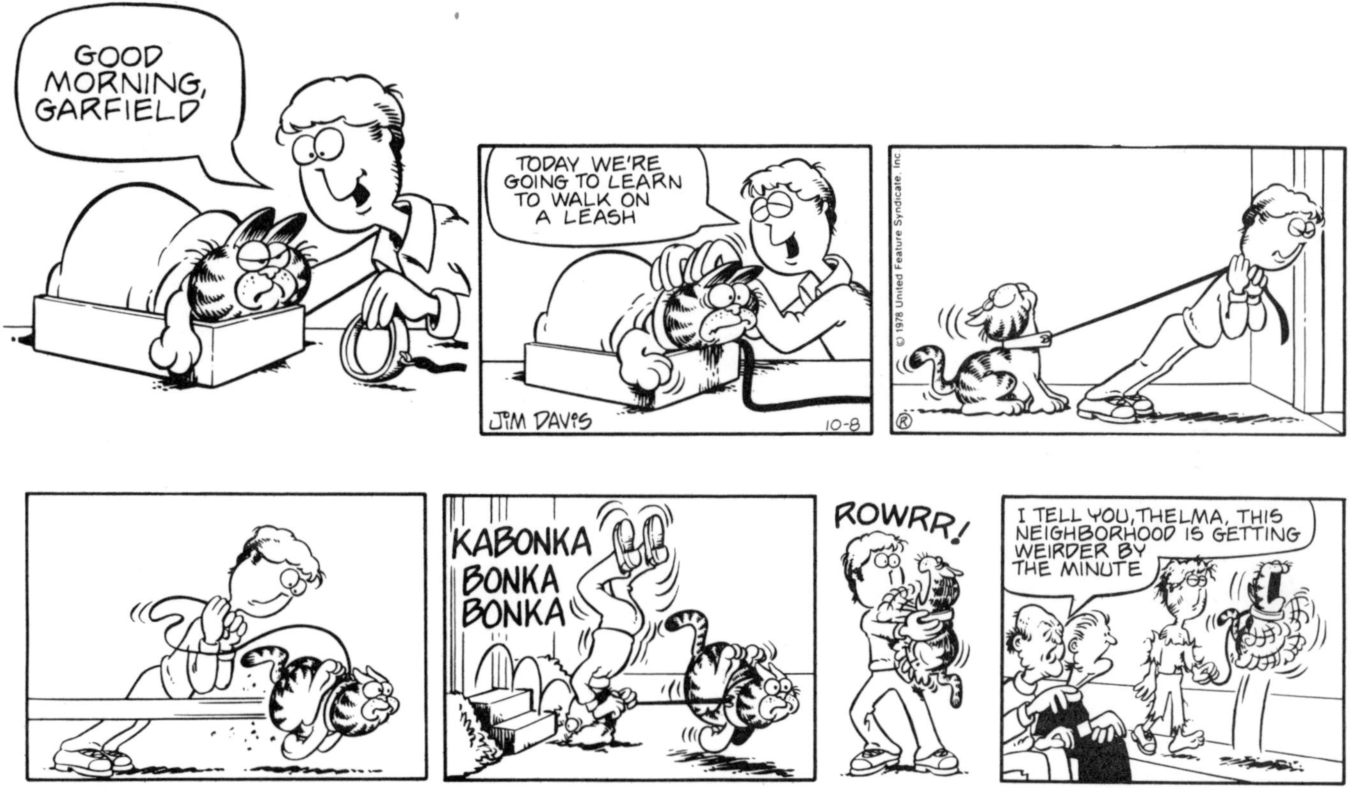
GOOD MORNING, GARFIELD
TODAY WE'RE GOING TO LEARN TO WALK ON A LEASH
JIM DAVIS
10-8
© 1978 United Feature Syndicate, Inc.
KABONKA BONKA BONKA
ROWRR!
I TELL YOU, THELMA, THIS NEIGHBORHOOD IS GETTING WEIRDER BY THE MINUTE

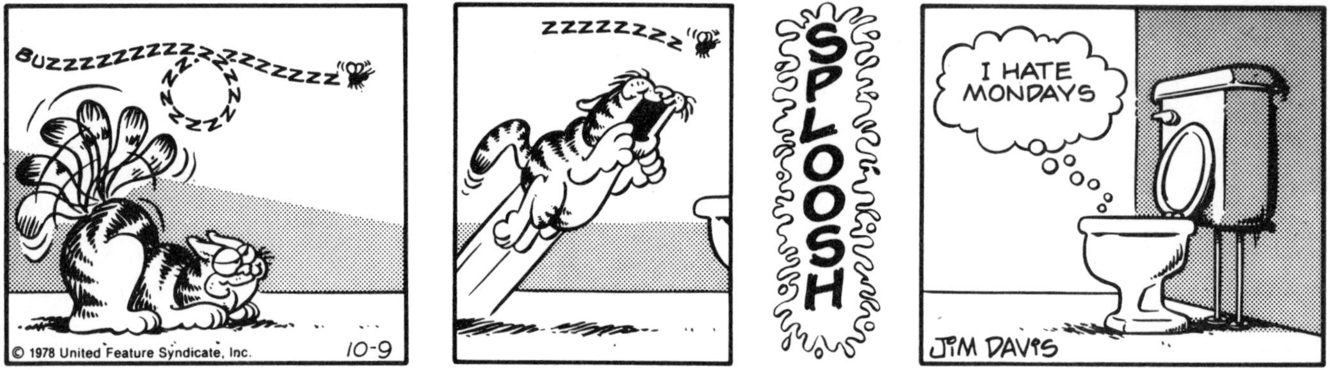
BUZZZZZZZZZZZZZZZZZZZZZZZZ
ZZZZZZZZZ
SPLOOSH
I HATE MONDAYS
JIM DAVIS

10-9

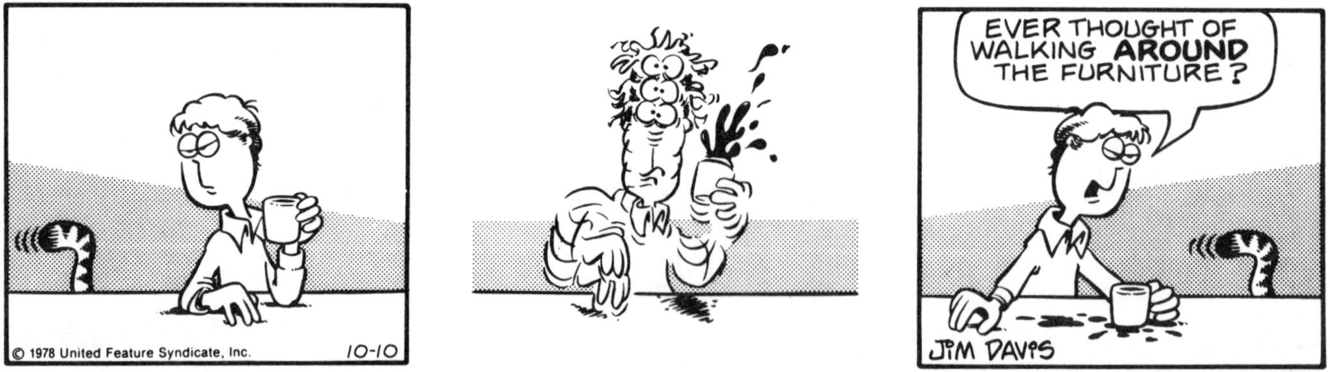
EVER THOUGHT OF WALKING **AROUND** THE FURNITURE?
JIM DAVIS

10-10

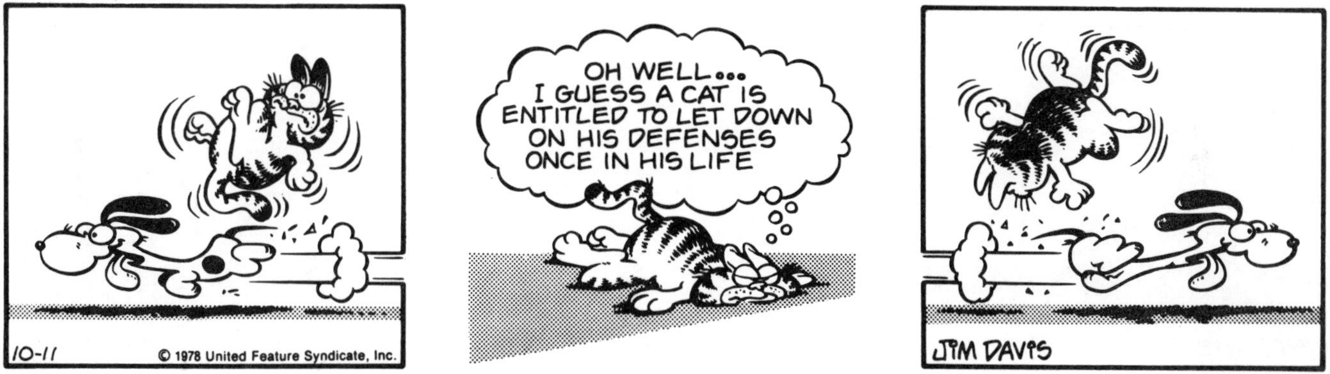
OH WELL...
I GUESS A CAT IS ENTITLED TO LET DOWN ON HIS DEFENSES ONCE IN HIS LIFE
10-11
© 1978 United Feature Syndicate, Inc.
JIM DAVIS

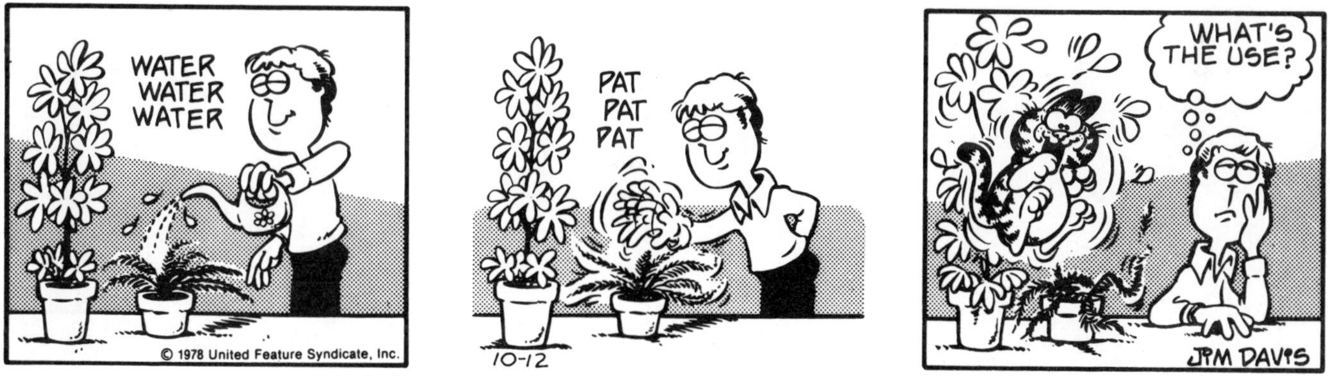
WATER WATER WATER
PAT PAT PAT
WHAT'S THE USE?
© 1978 United Feature Syndicate, Inc.
10-12
JIM DAVIS

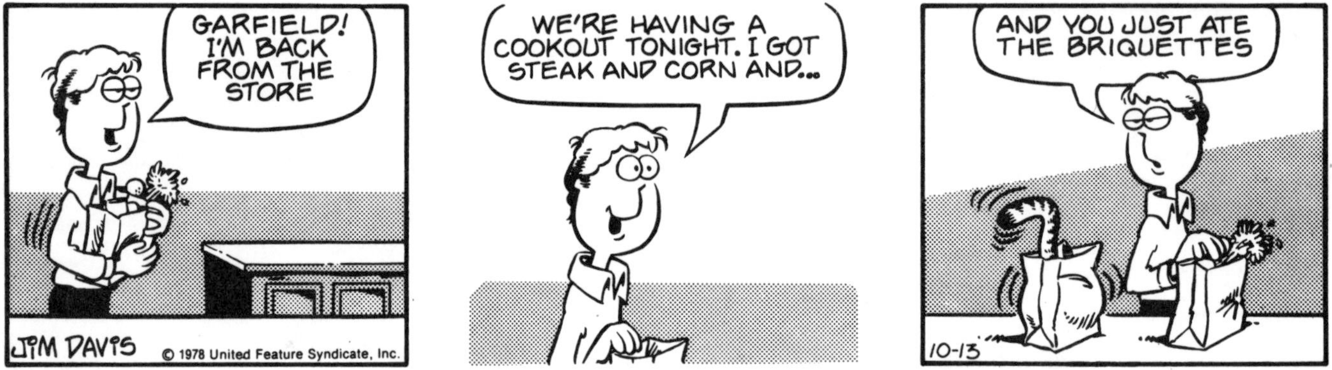
GARFIELD! I'M BACK FROM THE STORE
JIM DAVIS
© 1978 United Feature Syndicate, Inc.
WE'RE HAVING A COOKOUT TONIGHT. I GOT STEAK AND CORN AND...
AND YOU JUST ATE THE BRIQUETTES
10-13

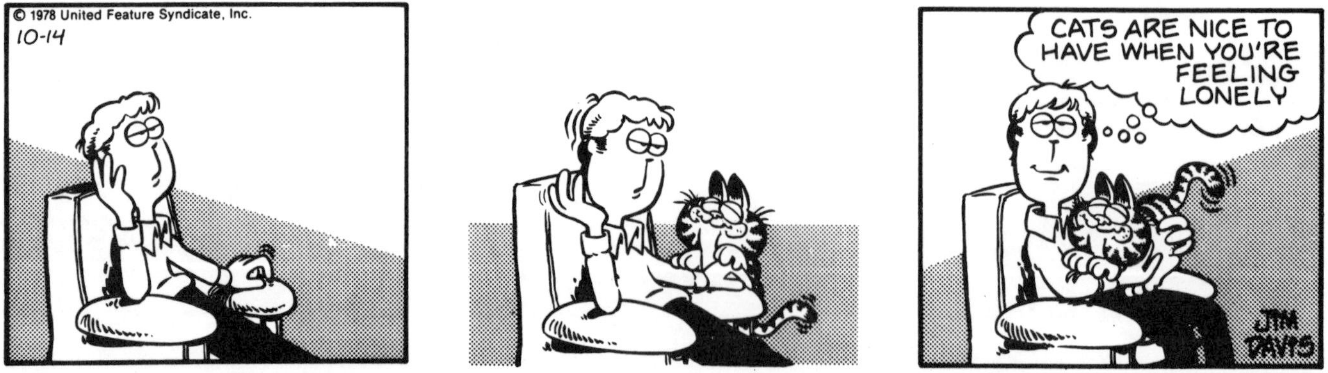
© 1978 United Feature Syndicate, Inc.
10-14
CATS ARE NICE TO HAVE WHEN YOU'RE FEELING LONELY
JIM DAVIS

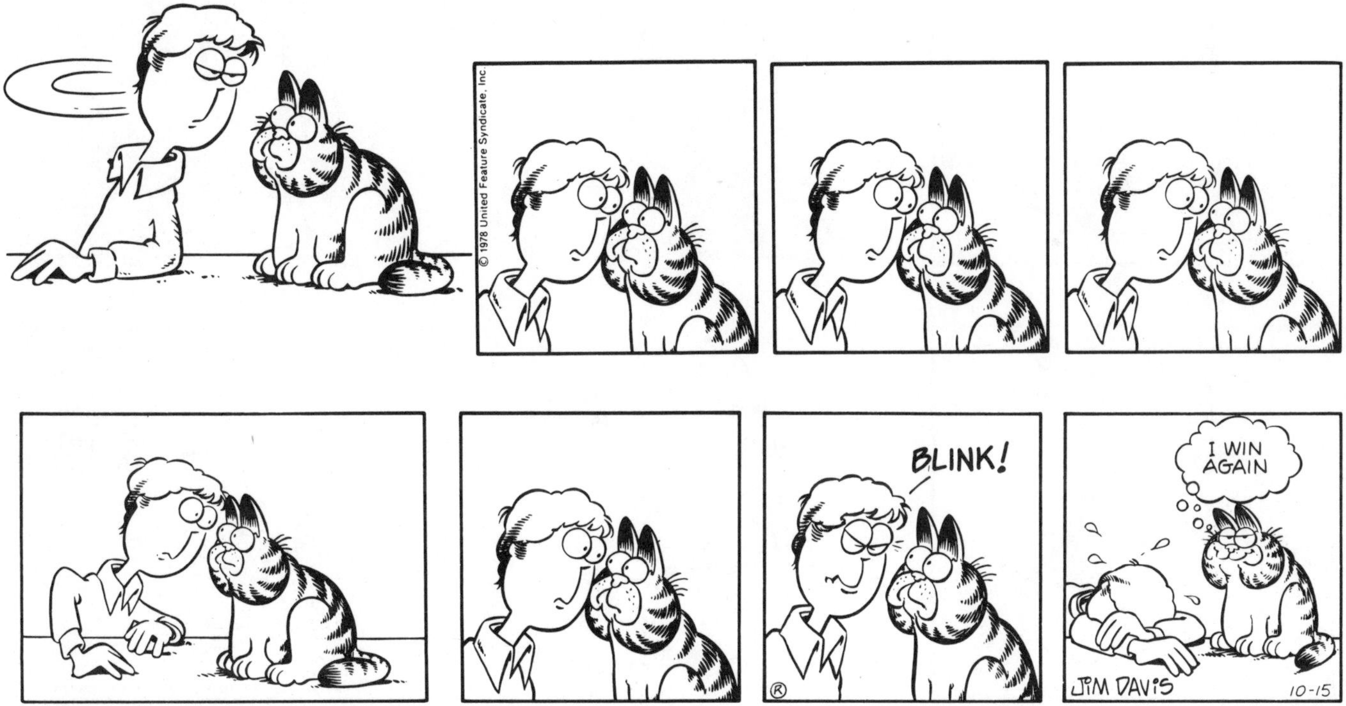

© 1978 United Feature Syndicate, Inc.
BLINK!
I WIN AGAIN
JIM DAVIS
10-15

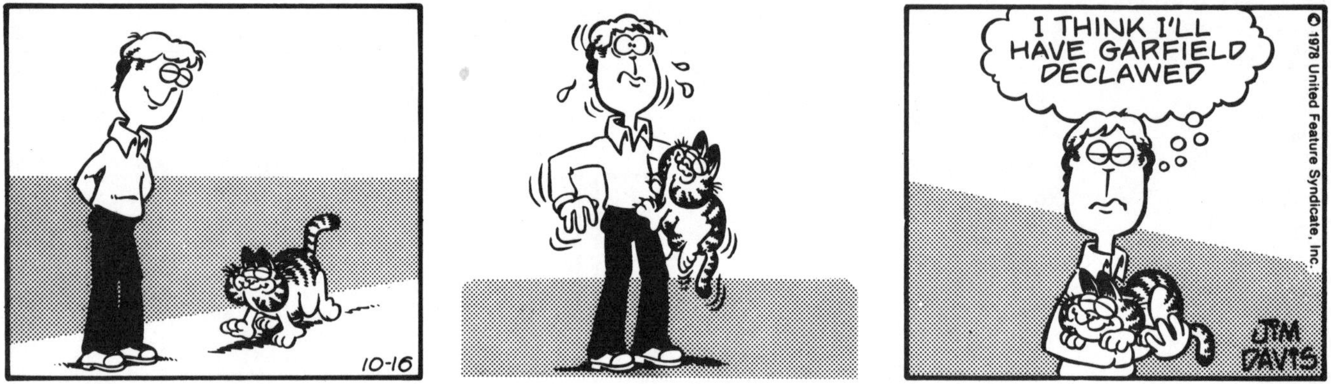
10-16
I THINK I'LL HAVE GARFIELD DECLAWED
JIM DAVIS
© 1978 United Feature Syndicate, Inc.

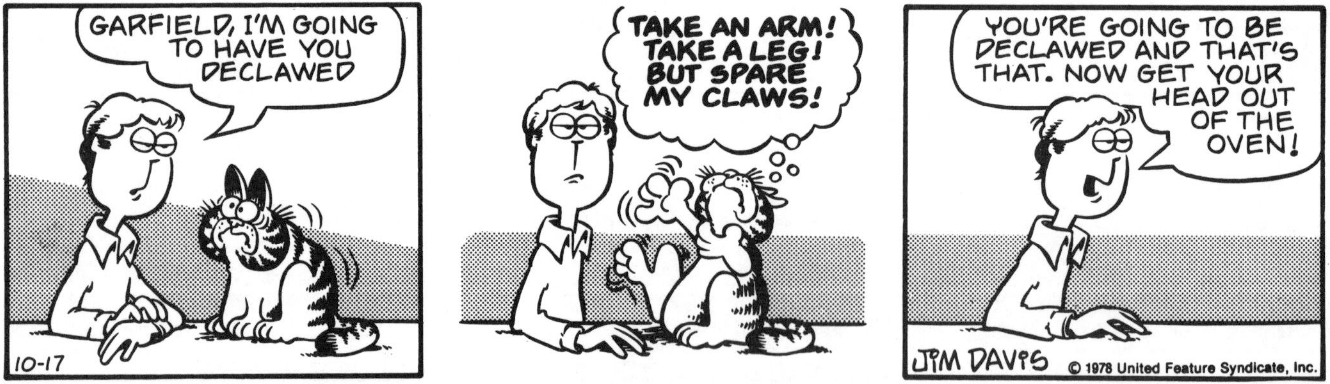
GARFIELD, I'M GOING TO HAVE YOU DECLAWED
10-17
TAKE AN ARM! TAKE A LEG! BUT SPARE MY CLAWS!
YOU'RE GOING TO BE DECLAWED AND THAT'S THAT. NOW GET YOUR HEAD OUT OF THE OVEN!
JIM DAVIS
© 1978 United Feature Syndicate, Inc.

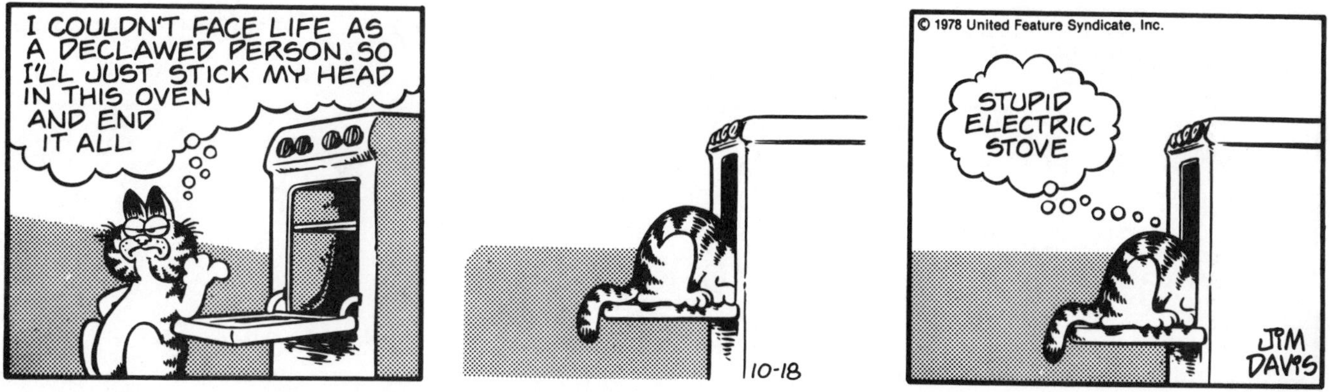
I COULDN'T FACE LIFE AS A DECLAWED PERSON. SO I'LL JUST STICK MY HEAD IN THIS OVEN AND END IT ALL
10-18
© 1978 United Feature Syndicate, Inc.
STUPID ELECTRIC STOVE
JIM DAVIS

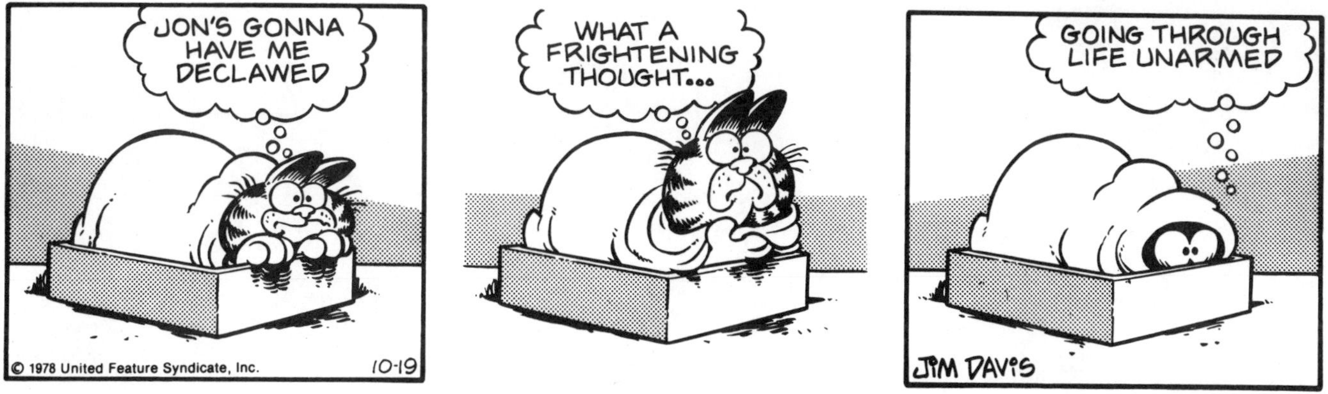
JON'S GONNA HAVE ME DECLAWED
© 1978 United Feature Syndicate, Inc.
10-19
WHAT A FRIGHTENING THOUGHT...
GOING THROUGH LIFE UNARMED
JIM DAVIS

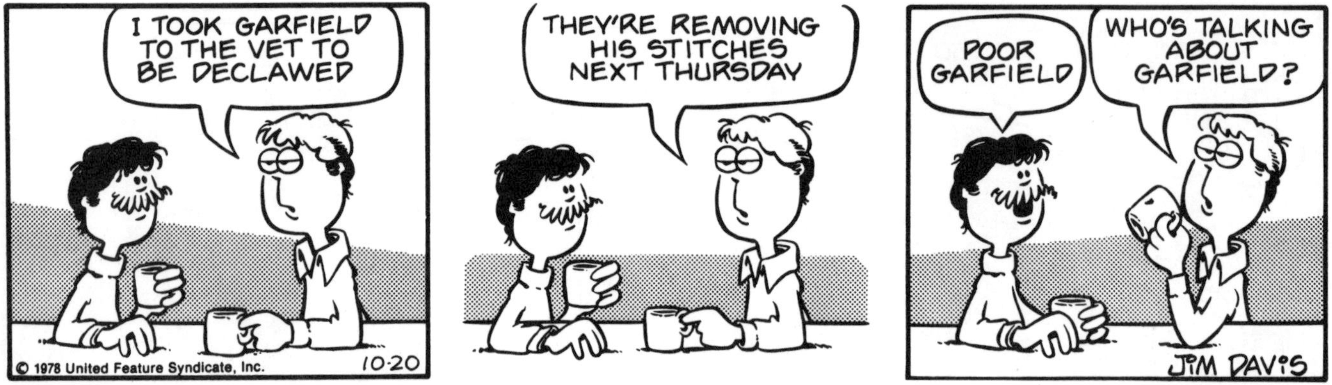
I TOOK GARFIELD TO THE VET TO BE DECLAWED
THEY'RE REMOVING HIS STITCHES NEXT THURSDAY
POOR GARFIELD
WHO'S TALKING ABOUT GARFIELD?
© 1978 United Feature Syndicate, Inc.
10-20
JIM DAVIS

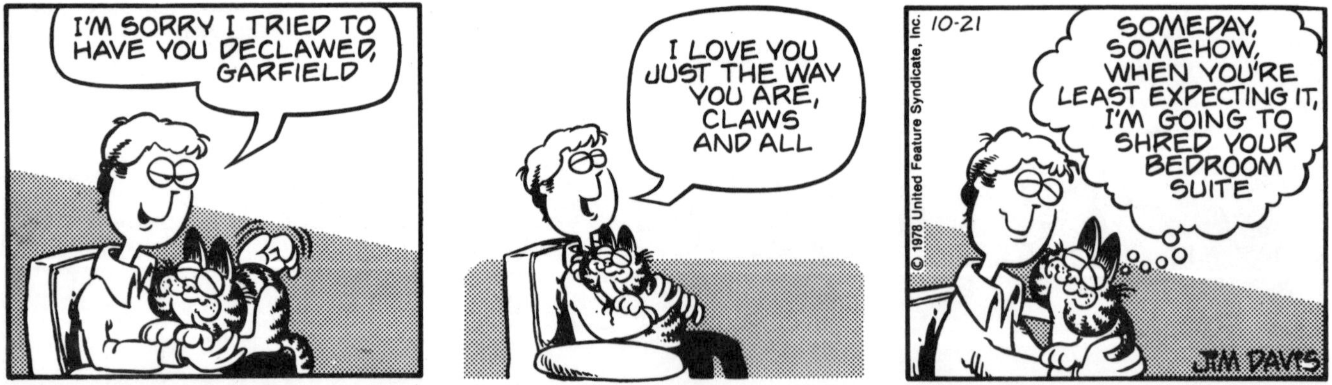
I'M SORRY I TRIED TO HAVE YOU DECLAWED, GARFIELD
I LOVE YOU JUST THE WAY YOU ARE, CLAWS AND ALL
SOMEDAY, SOMEHOW, WHEN YOU'RE LEAST EXPECTING IT, I'M GOING TO SHRED YOUR BEDROOM SUITE
© 1978 United Feature Syndicate, Inc.
10-21
JIM DAVIS

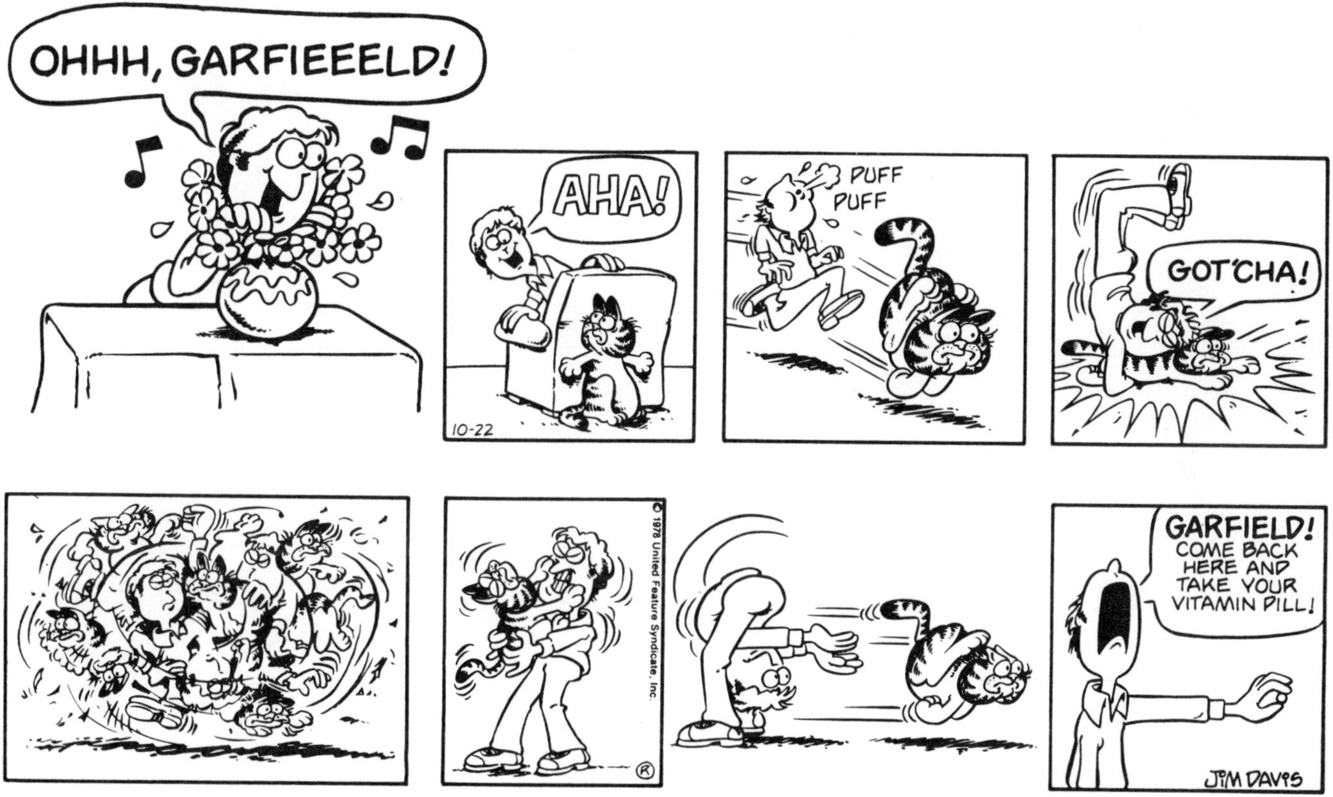
OHHH, GARFIEEELD!
AHA!
10-22
PUFF
PUFF
GOT'CHA!
© 1978 United Feature Syndicate, Inc.
GARFIELD! COME BACK HERE AND TAKE YOUR VITAMIN PILL!
JIM DAVIS

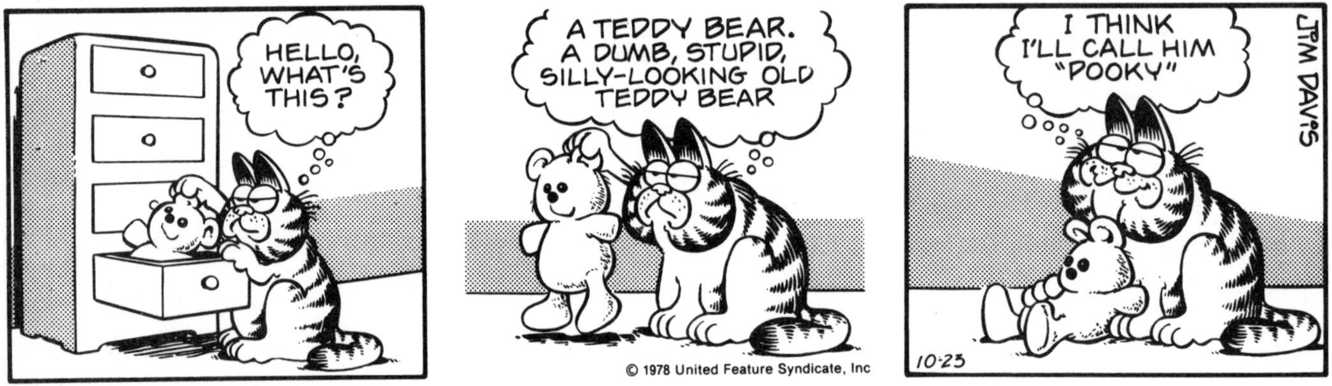
HELLO, WHAT'S THIS?
A TEDDY BEAR. A DUMB, STUPID, SILLY-LOOKING OLD TEDDY BEAR
I THINK I'LL CALL HIM "POOKY"
JIM DAVIS
10-23
© 1978 United Feature Syndicate, Inc

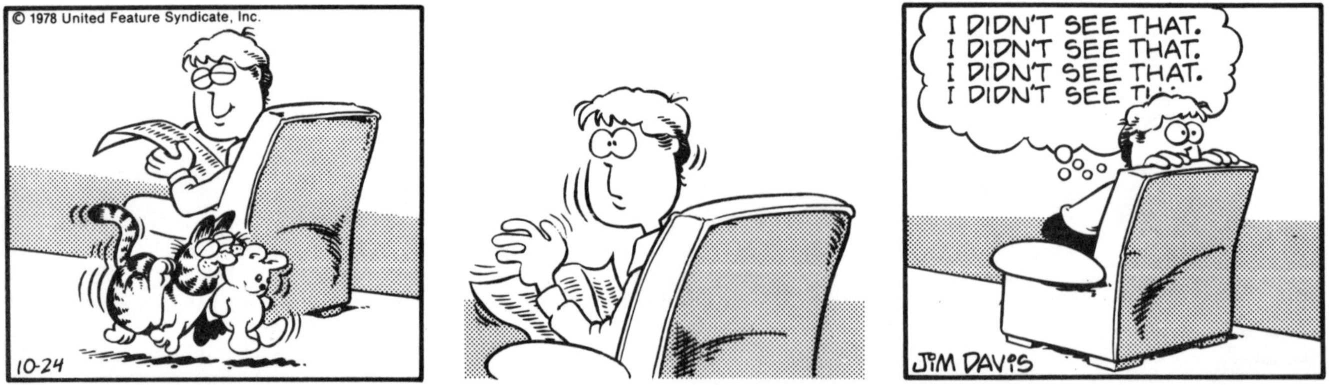
© 1978 United Feature Syndicate, Inc.
10-24
I DIDN'T SEE THAT.
I DIDN'T SEE THAT.
I DIDN'T SEE THAT.
I DIDN'T SEE
JIM DAVIS

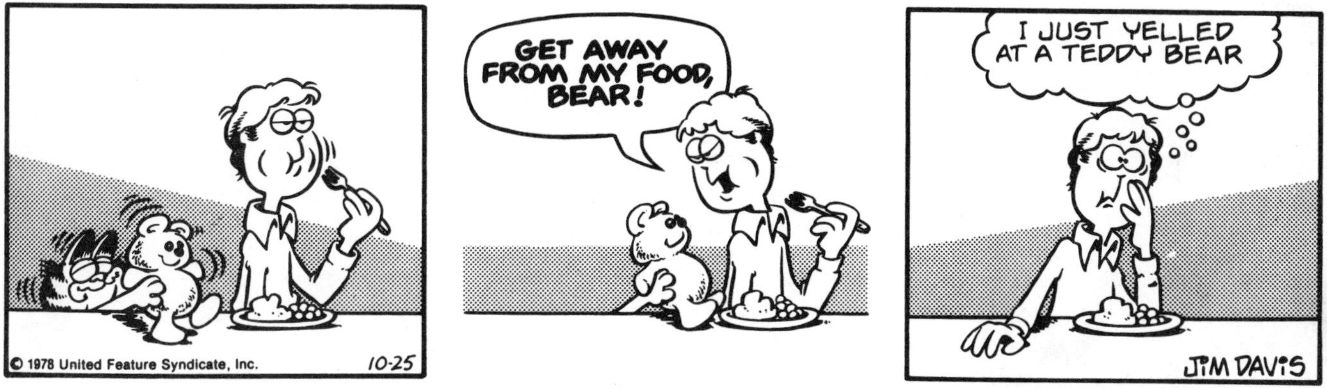
© 1978 United Feature Syndicate, Inc.
10-25
GET AWAY FROM MY FOOD, BEAR!
I JUST YELLED AT A TEDDY BEAR
JIM DAVIS

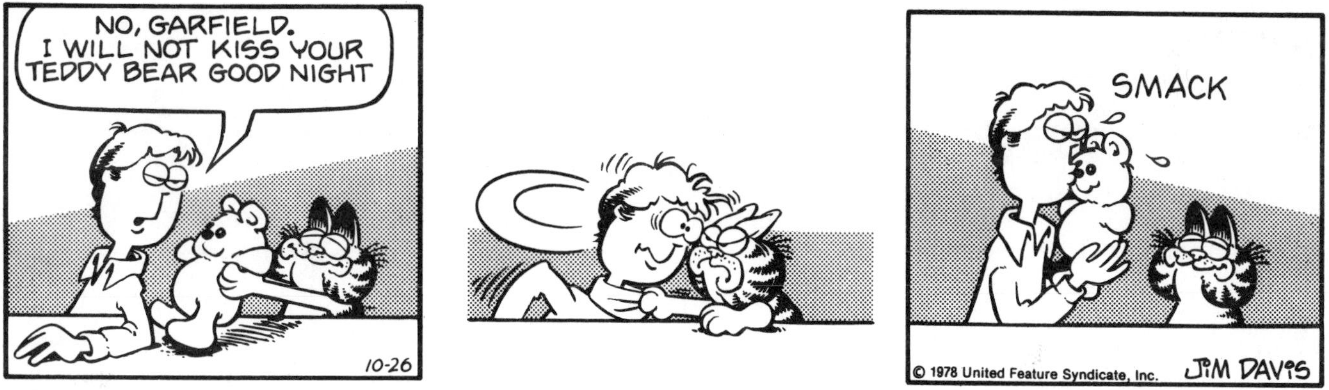
NO, GARFIELD. I WILL NOT KISS YOUR TEDDY BEAR GOOD NIGHT
10-26
SMACK
© 1978 United Feature Syndicate, Inc.
JIM DAVIS

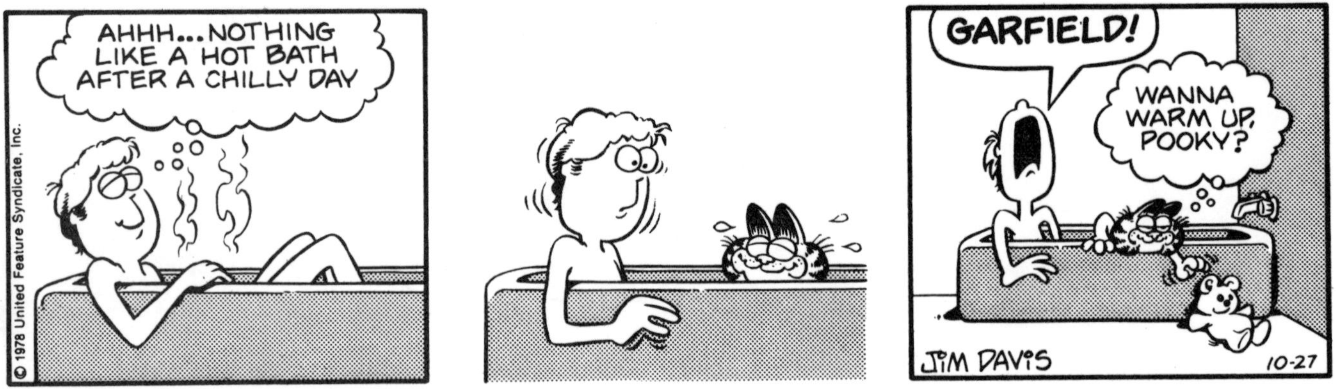
© 1978 United Feature Syndicate, Inc.
AHHH...NOTHING LIKE A HOT BATH AFTER A CHILLY DAY
GARFIELD!
WANNA WARM UP, POOKY?
JiM DAViS
10-27

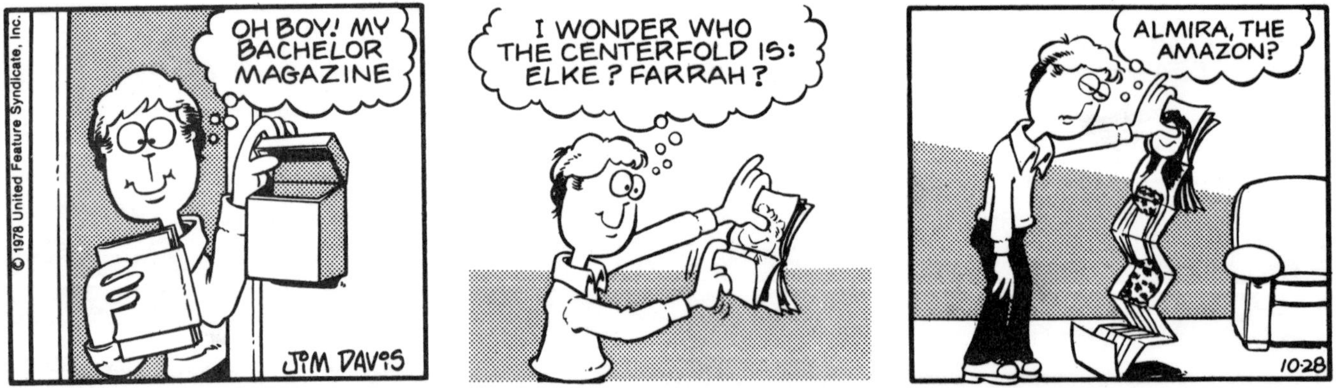
© 1978 United Feature Syndicate, Inc.
OH BOY! MY BACHELOR MAGAZINE
JiM DAViS
I WONDER WHO THE CENTERFOLD IS: ELKE? FARRAH?
ALMIRA, THE AMAZON?
10-28

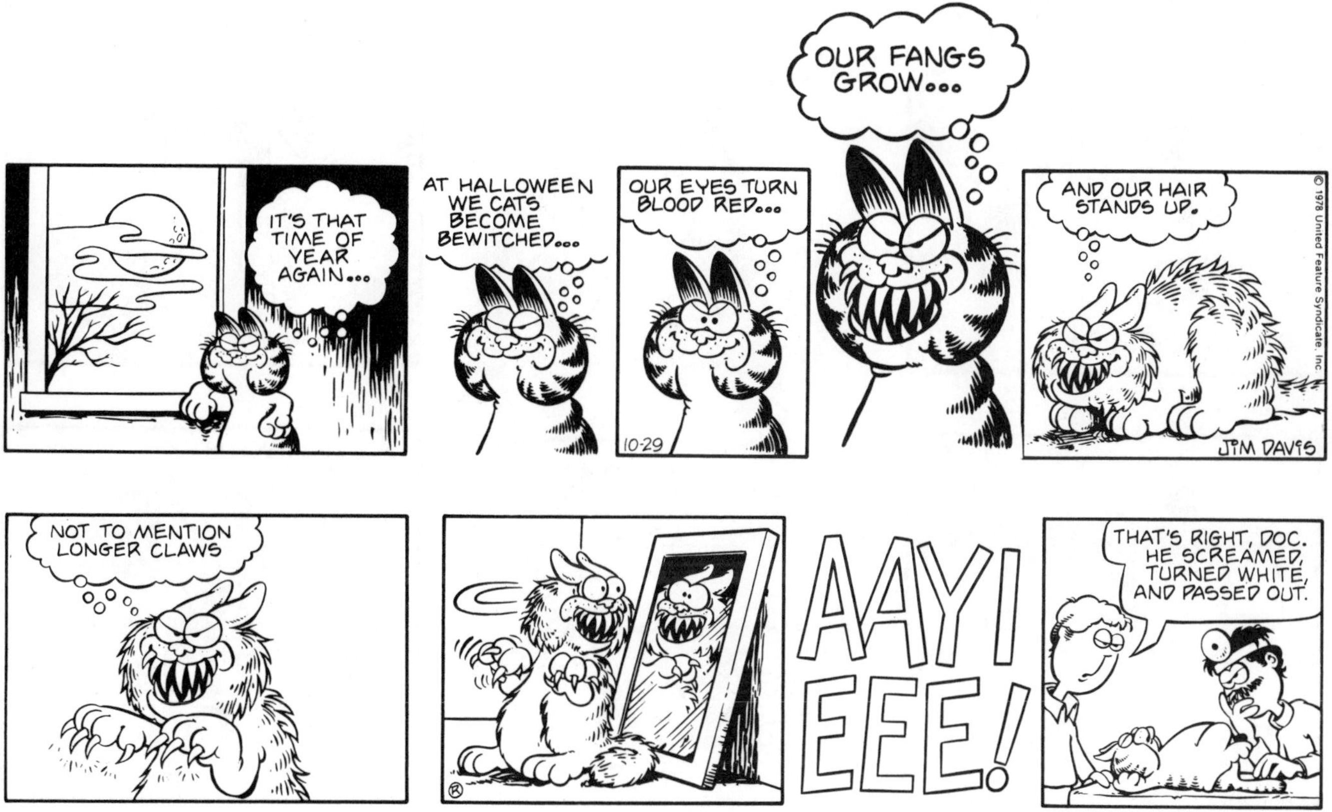
IT'S THAT TIME OF YEAR AGAIN...
AT HALLOWEEN WE CATS BECOME BEWITCHED...
OUR EYES TURN BLOOD RED...
10-29
OUR FANGS GROW...
AND OUR HAIR STANDS UP.
© 1978 United Feature Syndicate, Inc.
JIM DAVIS
NOT TO MENTION LONGER CLAWS
AAYIEEE!
THAT'S RIGHT, DOC. HE SCREAMED, TURNED WHITE, AND PASSED OUT.

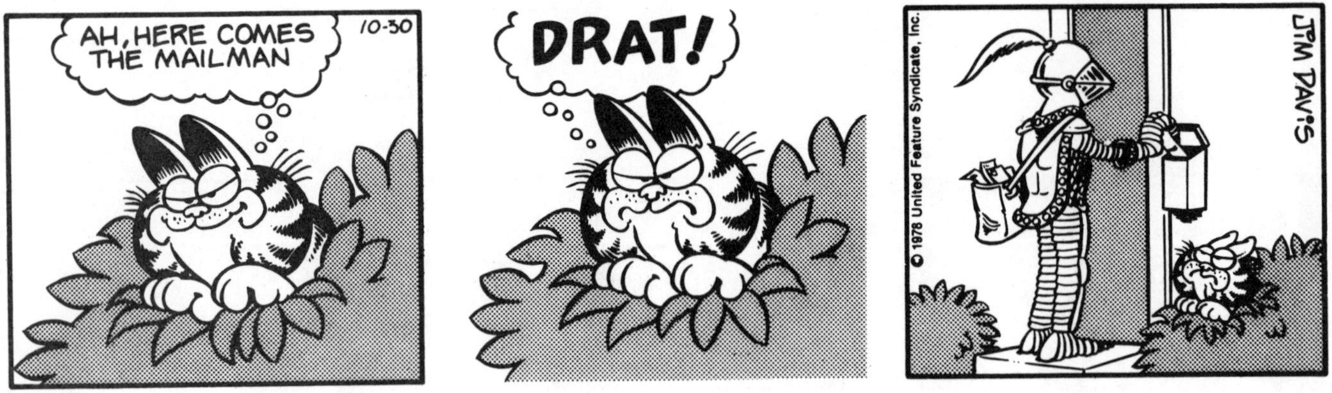
10-30
AH, HERE COMES THE MAILMAN
DRAT!
© 1978 United Feature Syndicate, Inc.
JIM DAVIS

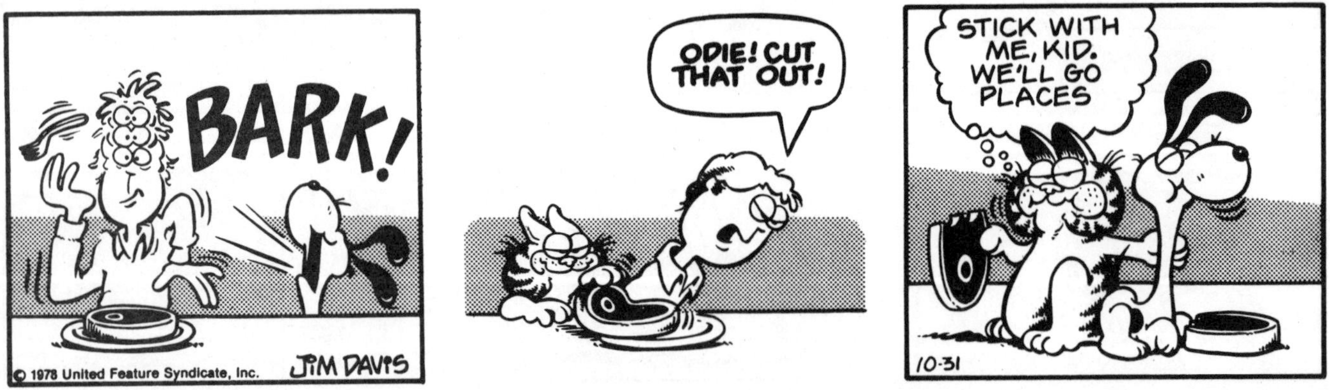
BARK!
© 1978 United Feature Syndicate, Inc.
JIM DAVIS
ODIE! CUT THAT OUT!
STICK WITH ME, KID. WE'LL GO PLACES
10-31

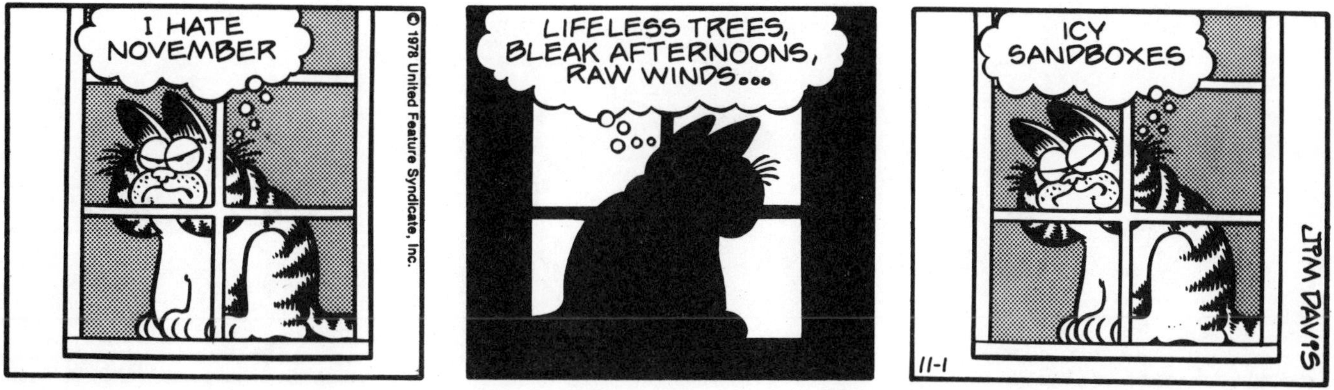
I HATE NOVEMBER
© 1978 United Feature Syndicate, Inc.
LIFELESS TREES, BLEAK AFTERNOONS, RAW WINDS...
ICY SANDBOXES
11-1
JIM DAVIS

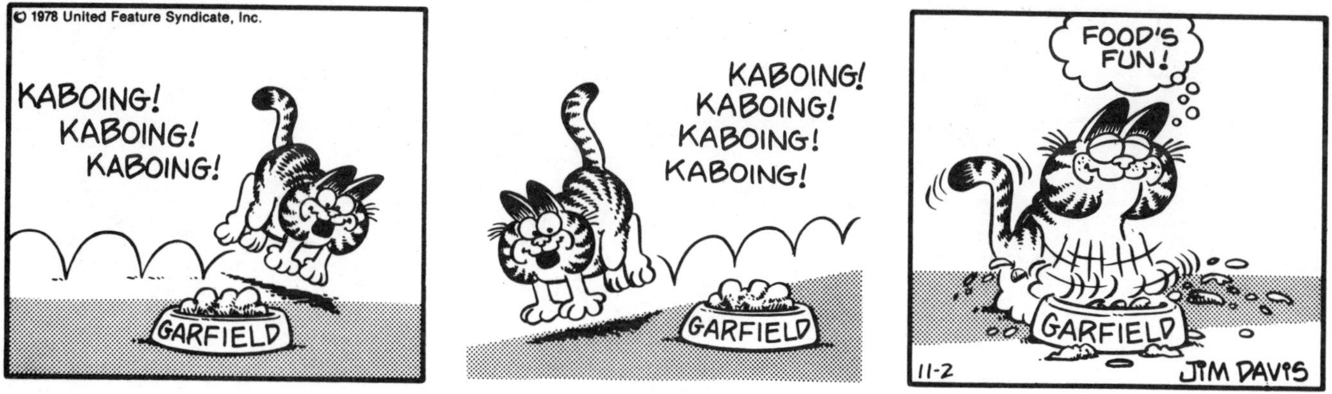
© 1978 United Feature Syndicate, Inc.
KABOING! KABOING! KABOING!
GARFIELD
KABOING! KABOING! KABOING! KABOING!
GARFIELD
FOOD'S FUN!
GARFIELD
11-2
JIM DAVIS

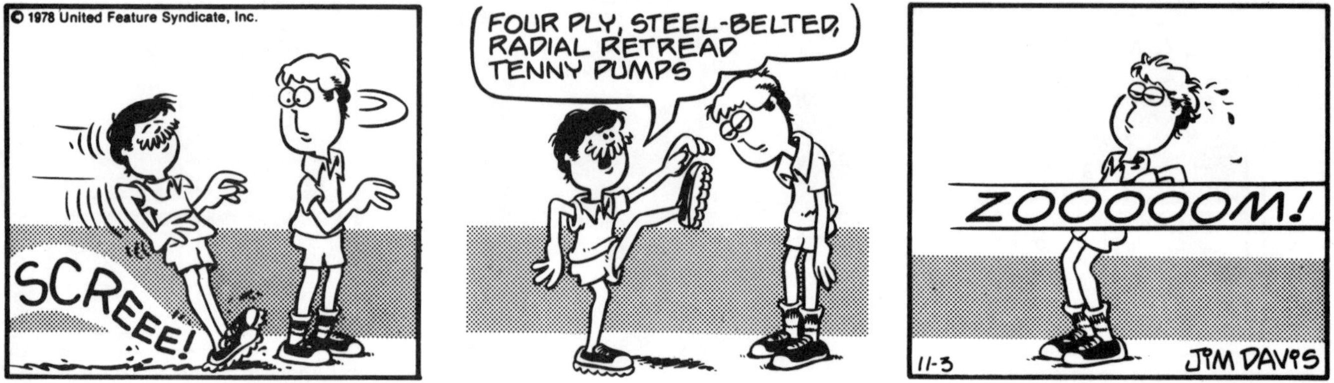
© 1978 United Feature Syndicate, Inc.
SCREEEE!
FOUR PLY, STEEL-BELTED, RADIAL RETREAD TENNY PUMPS
ZOOOOOM!
11-3
JIM DAVIS

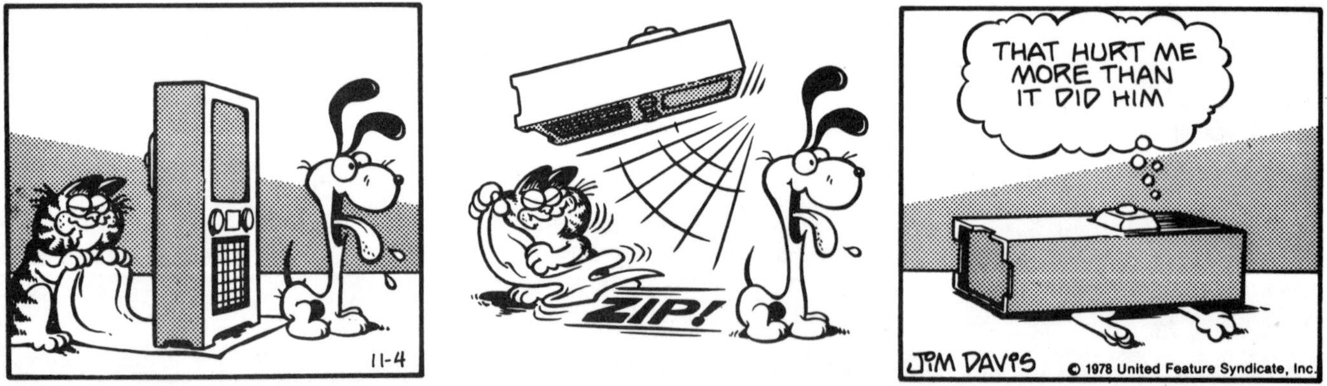
11-4
ZIP!
THAT HURT ME MORE THAN IT DID HIM
JIM DAVIS
© 1978 United Feature Syndicate, Inc.

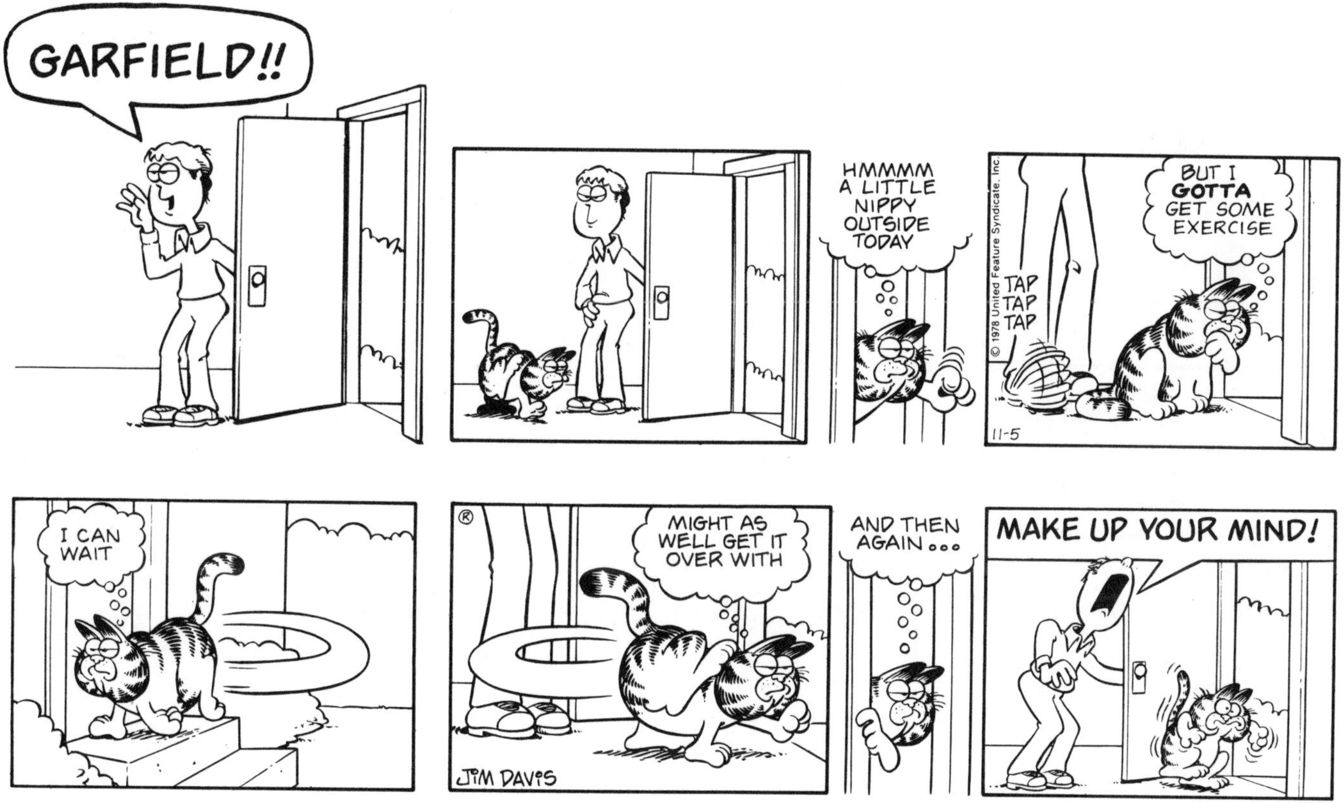
GARFIELD!!
HMMMM A LITTLE NIPPY OUTSIDE TODAY
TAP TAP TAP
BUT I GOTTA GET SOME EXERCISE
© 1978 United Feature Syndicate, Inc.
11-5
I CAN WAIT
MIGHT AS WELL GET IT OVER WITH
JIM DAVIS
AND THEN AGAIN...
MAKE UP YOUR MIND!

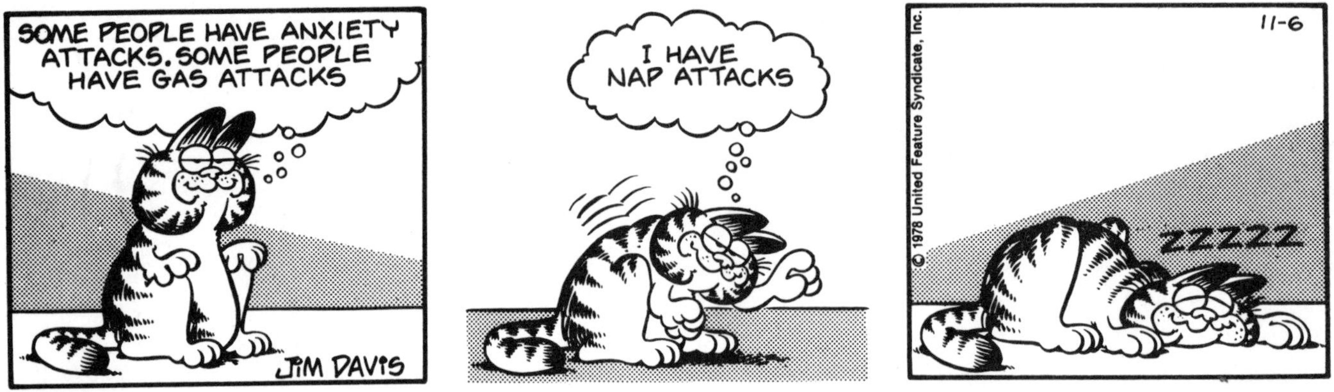
SOME PEOPLE HAVE ANXIETY ATTACKS. SOME PEOPLE HAVE GAS ATTACKS
JIM DAVIS
I HAVE NAP ATTACKS
11-6
© 1978 United Feature Syndicate, Inc.
ZZZZZ

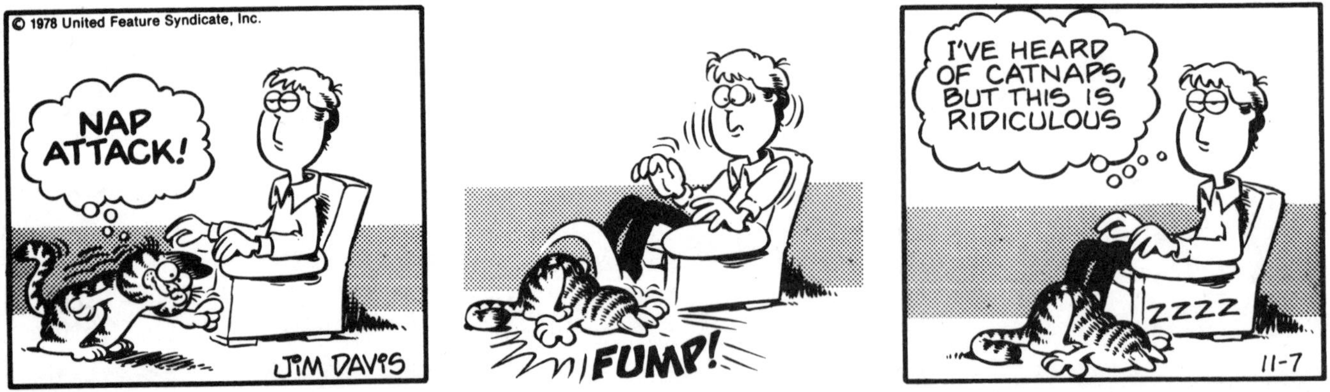
© 1978 United Feature Syndicate, Inc.
NAP ATTACK!
JIM DAVIS
FUMP!
I'VE HEARD OF CATNAPS, BUT THIS IS RIDICULOUS
ZZZZ
11-7

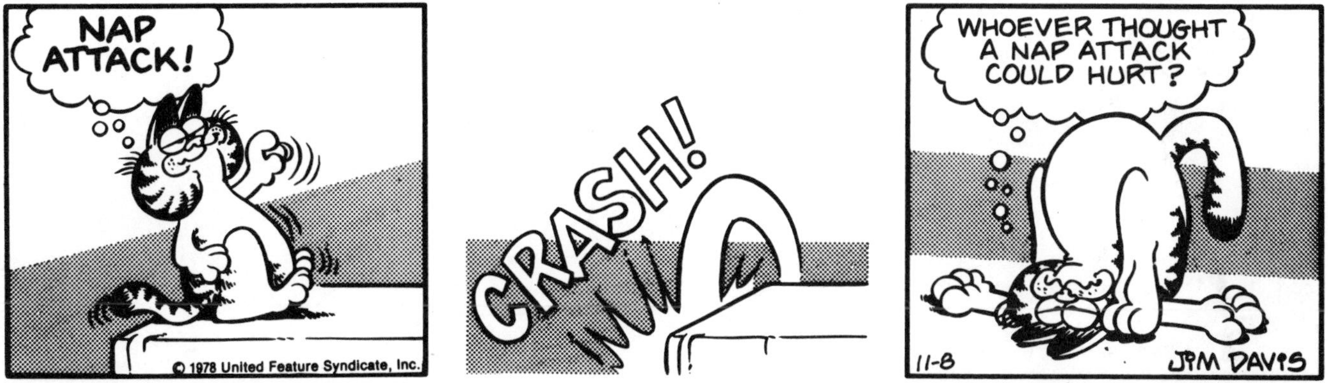
NAP ATTACK!
© 1978 United Feature Syndicate, Inc.
CRASH!
WHOEVER THOUGHT A NAP ATTACK COULD HURT?
11-8
JIM DAVIS

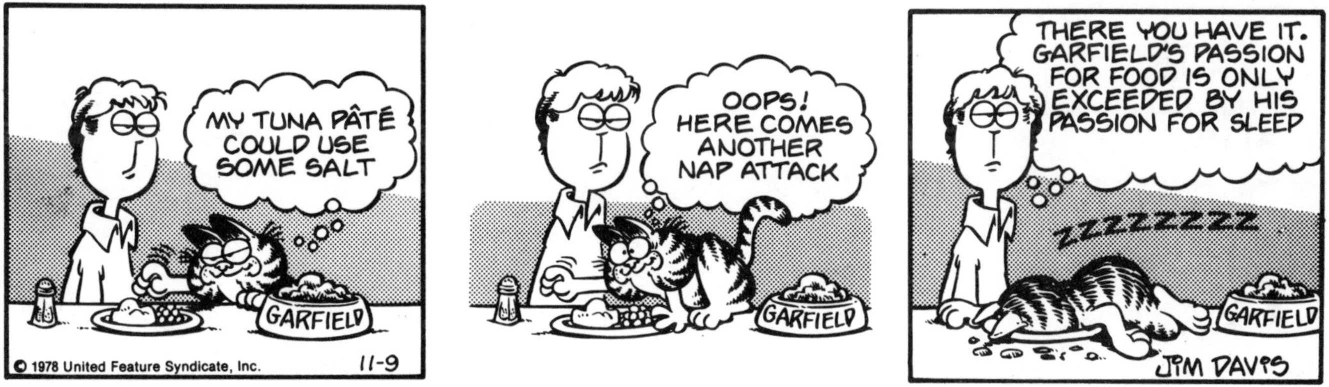
MY TUNA PÂTÉ COULD USE SOME SALT
GARFIELD
© 1978 United Feature Syndicate, Inc.
11-9
OOPS! HERE COMES ANOTHER NAP ATTACK
GARFIELD
THERE YOU HAVE IT. GARFIELD'S PASSION FOR FOOD IS ONLY EXCEEDED BY HIS PASSION FOR SLEEP
ZZZZZZZZ
GARFIELD
JIM DAVIS

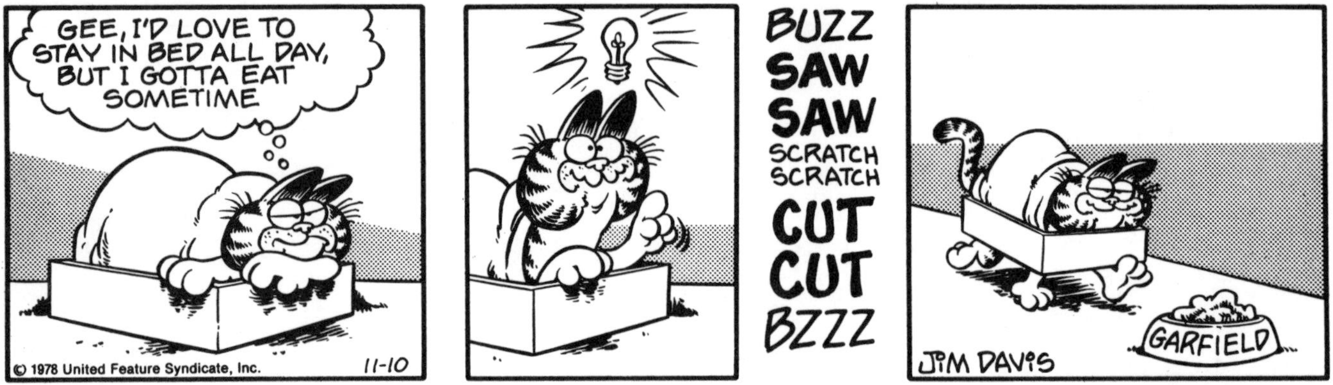
GEE, I'D LOVE TO STAY IN BED ALL DAY, BUT I GOTTA EAT SOMETIME
© 1978 United Feature Syndicate, Inc.
11-10
BUZZ
SAW
SAW
SCRATCH
SCRATCH
CUT
CUT
BZZZ
GARFIELD
JIM DAVIS

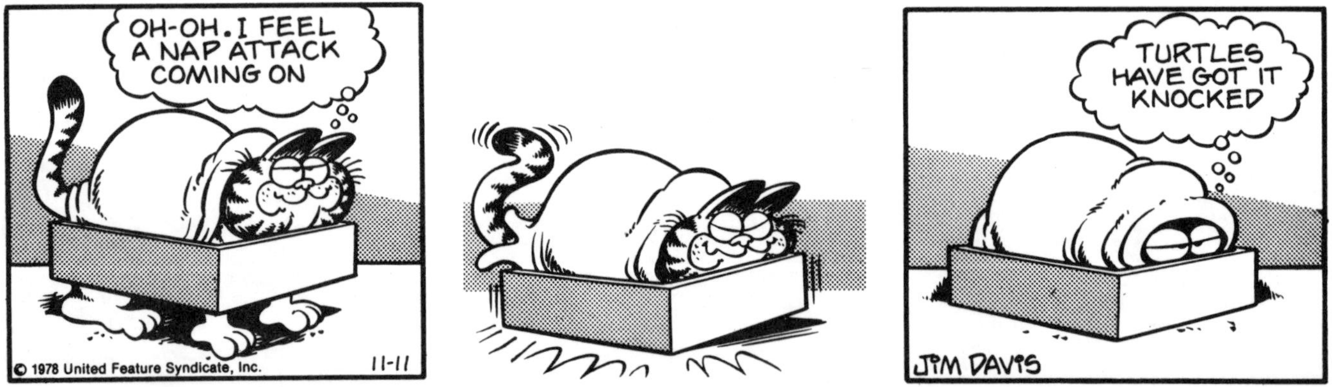
OH-OH. I FEEL A NAP ATTACK COMING ON
© 1978 United Feature Syndicate, Inc.
11-11
TURTLES HAVE GOT IT KNOCKED
JIM DAVIS

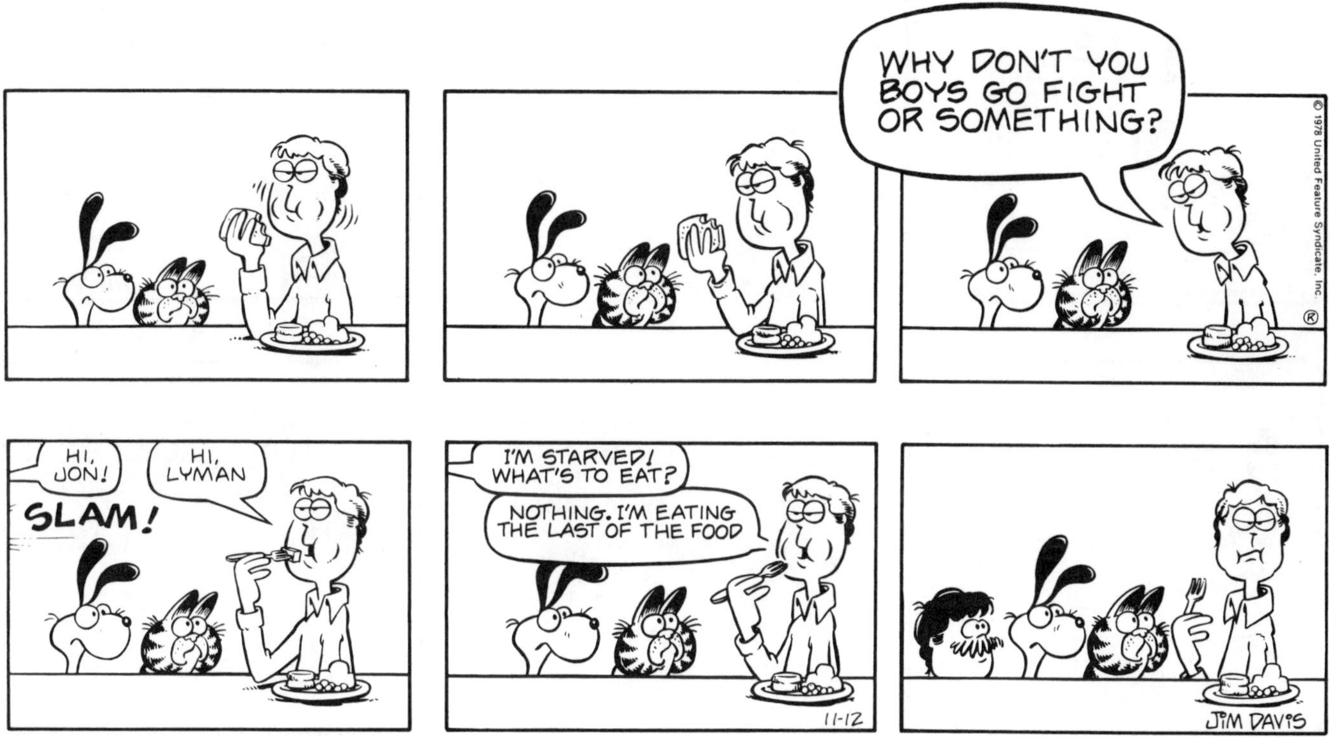
WHY DON'T YOU BOYS GO FIGHT OR SOMETHING?
© 1978 United Feature Syndicate, Inc.
HI, JON!
HI, LYMAN
SLAM!
I'M STARVED! WHAT'S TO EAT?
NOTHING. I'M EATING THE LAST OF THE FOOD
11-12
JIM DAVIS

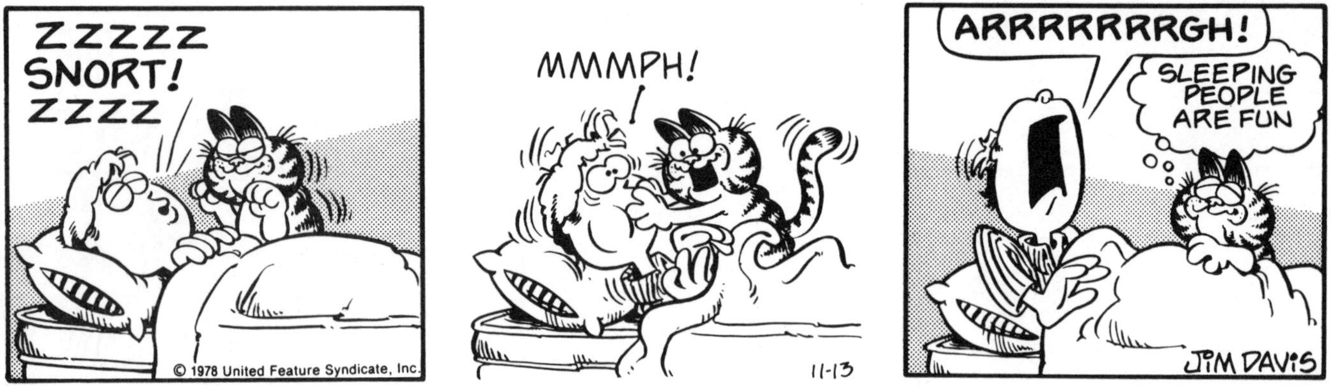
ZZZZZ SNORT! ZZZZ
© 1978 United Feature Syndicate, Inc.
MMMPH!
11-13
ARRRRRRRGH!
SLEEPING PEOPLE ARE FUN
JIM DAVIS

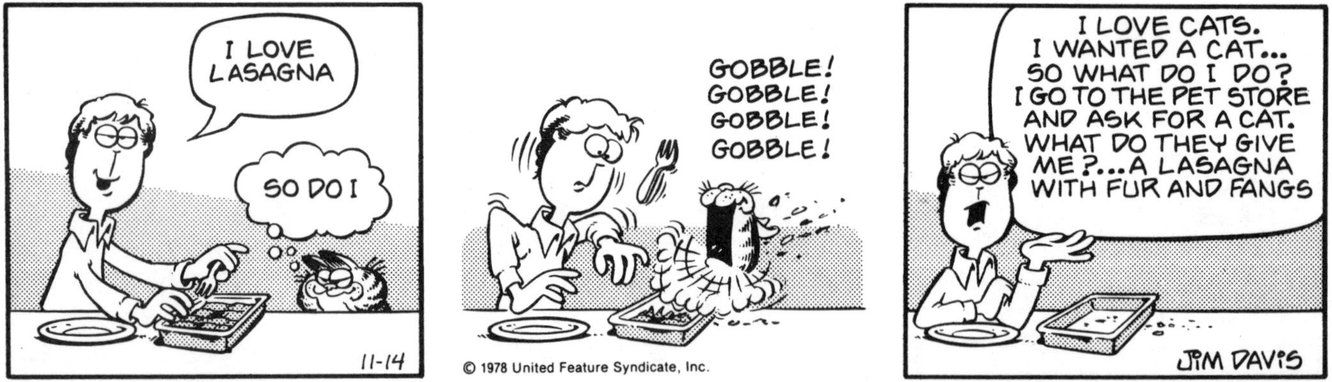
I LOVE LASAGNA
SO DO I
11-14
GOBBLE! GOBBLE! GOBBLE! GOBBLE!
© 1978 United Feature Syndicate, Inc.
I LOVE CATS. I WANTED A CAT... SO WHAT DO I DO? I GO TO THE PET STORE AND ASK FOR A CAT. WHAT DO THEY GIVE ME?...A LASAGNA WITH FUR AND FANGS
JIM DAVIS

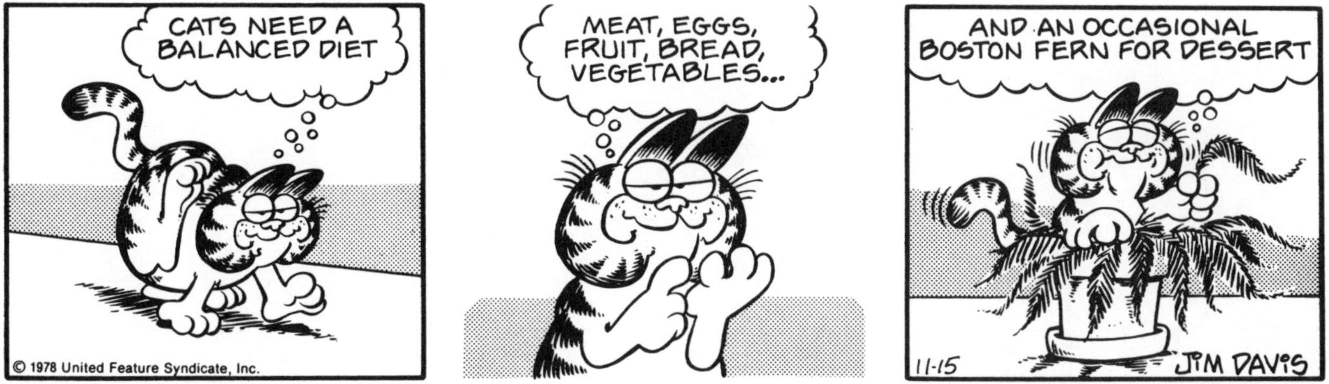
CATS NEED A BALANCED DIET
MEAT, EGGS, FRUIT, BREAD, VEGETABLES...
AND AN OCCASIONAL BOSTON FERN FOR DESSERT
© 1978 United Feature Syndicate, Inc.
11-15
JIM DAVIS

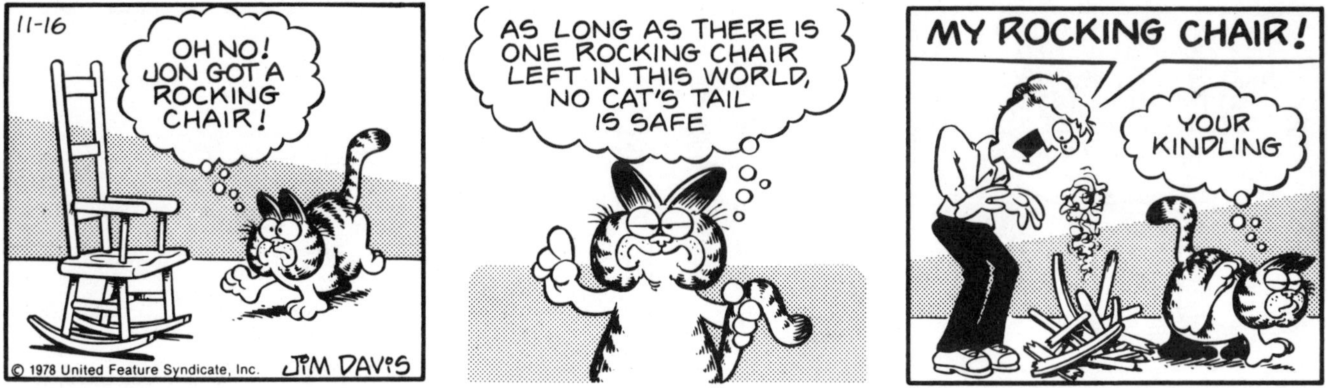
11-16
OH NO! JON GOT A ROCKING CHAIR!
AS LONG AS THERE IS ONE ROCKING CHAIR LEFT IN THIS WORLD, NO CAT'S TAIL IS SAFE
MY ROCKING CHAIR!
YOUR KINDLING
© 1978 United Feature Syndicate, Inc.
JIM DAVIS

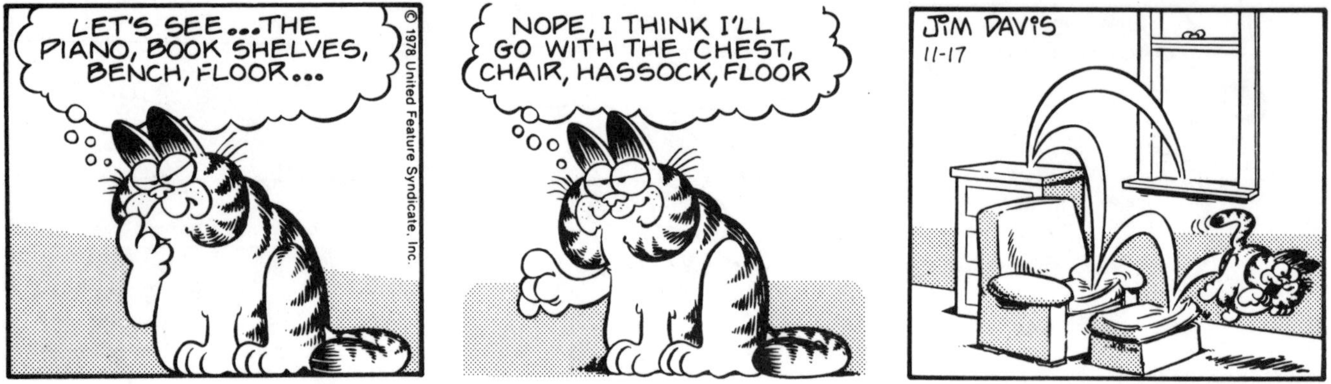
LET'S SEE...THE PIANO, BOOK SHELVES, BENCH, FLOOR...
© 1978 United Feature Syndicate, Inc.
NOPE, I THINK I'LL GO WITH THE CHEST, CHAIR, HASSOCK, FLOOR
JIM DAVIS
11-17

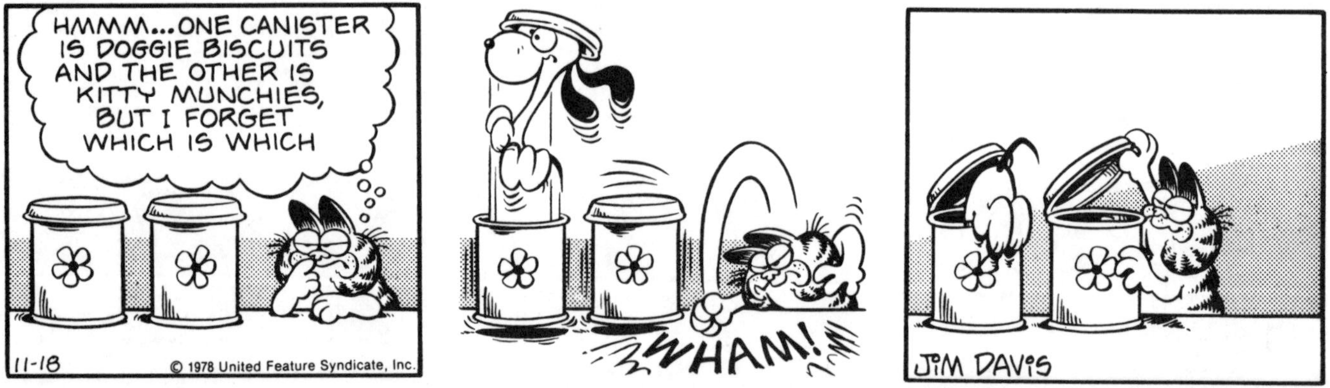
HMMM...ONE CANISTER IS DOGGIE BISCUITS AND THE OTHER IS KITTY MUNCHIES, BUT I FORGET WHICH IS WHICH
11-18
© 1978 United Feature Syndicate, Inc.
WHAM!
JIM DAVIS

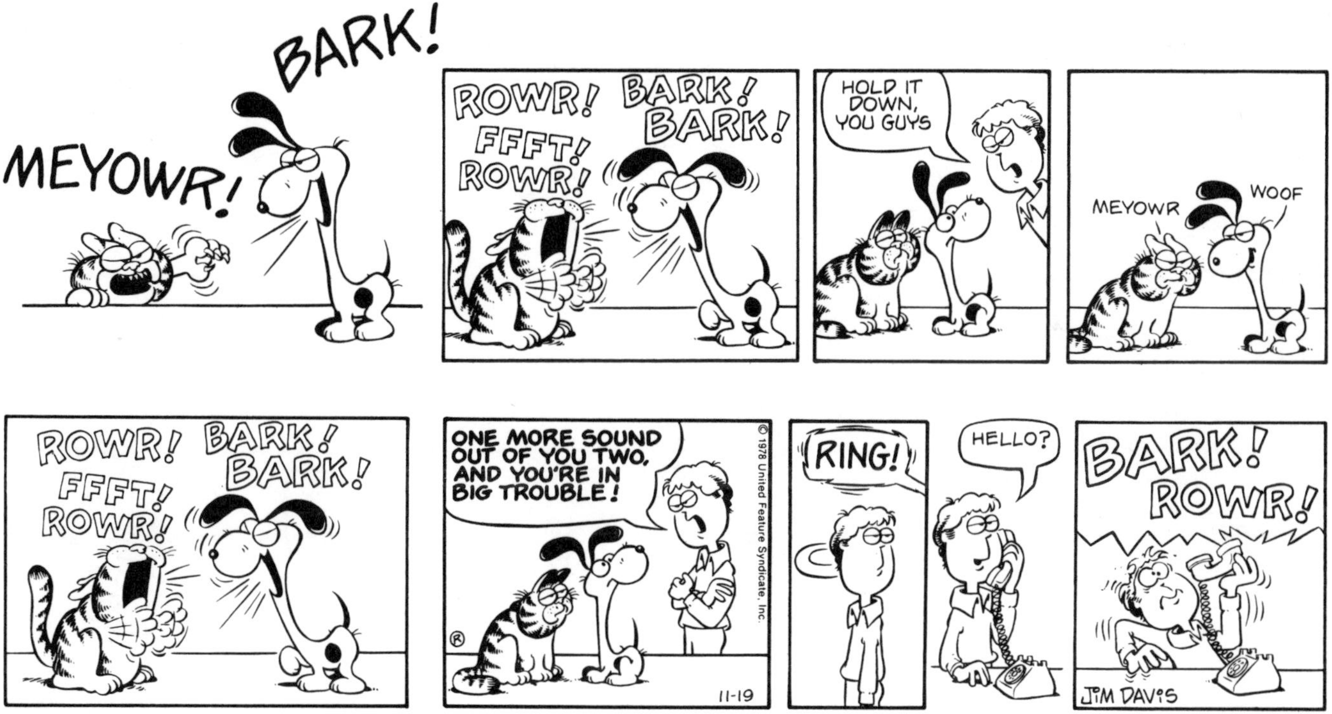
BARK!
MEYOWR!
ROWR!
FFFT!
ROWR!
BARK!
BARK!
HOLD IT DOWN, YOU GUYS
MEYOWR
WOOF
ROWR!
FFFT!
ROWR!
BARK!
BARK!
ONE MORE SOUND OUT OF YOU TWO, AND YOU'RE IN BIG TROUBLE!
© 1978 United Feature Syndicate, Inc.
11-19
RING!
HELLO?
BARK!
ROWR!
JIM DAVIS

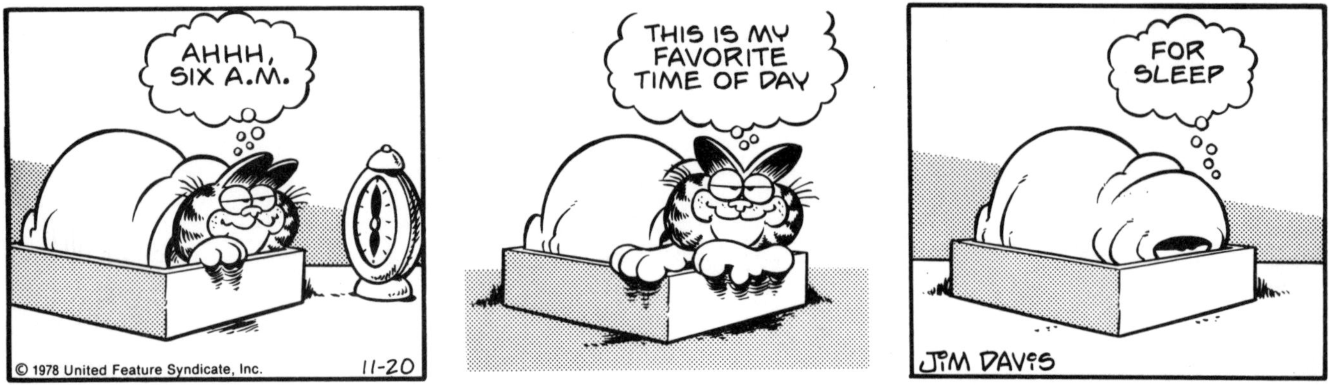
AHHH, SIX A.M.
THIS IS MY FAVORITE TIME OF DAY
FOR SLEEP
© 1978 United Feature Syndicate, Inc.
11-20
JIM DAVIS

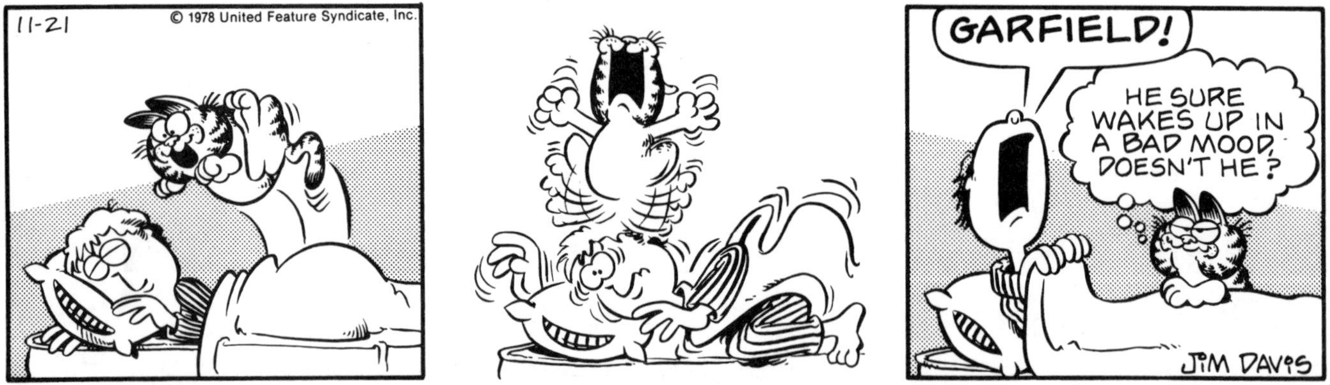
11-21
© 1978 United Feature Syndicate, Inc.
GARFIELD!
HE SURE WAKES UP IN A BAD MOOD, DOESN'T HE?
JIM DAVIS

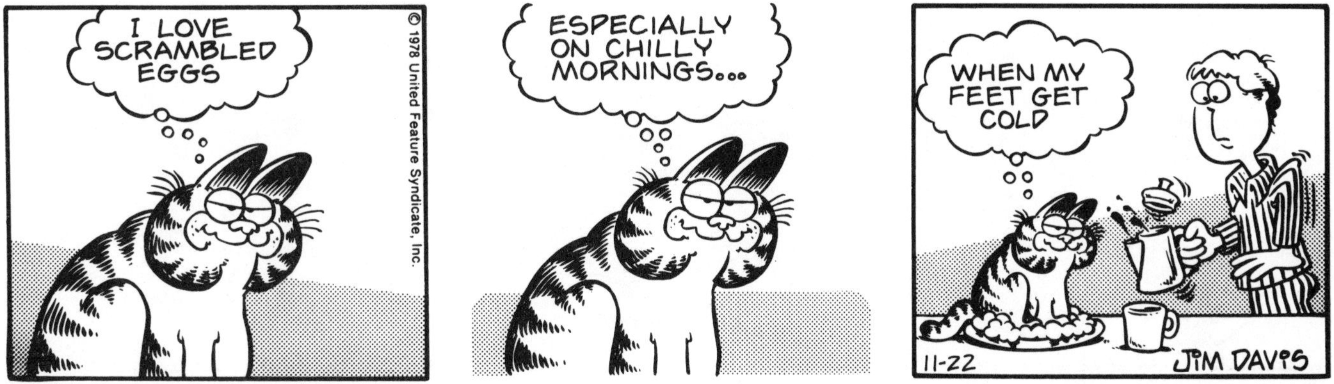
I LOVE SCRAMBLED EGGS
© 1978 United Feature Syndicate, Inc.
ESPECIALLY ON CHILLY MORNINGS...
WHEN MY FEET GET COLD
11-22
JIM DAVIS

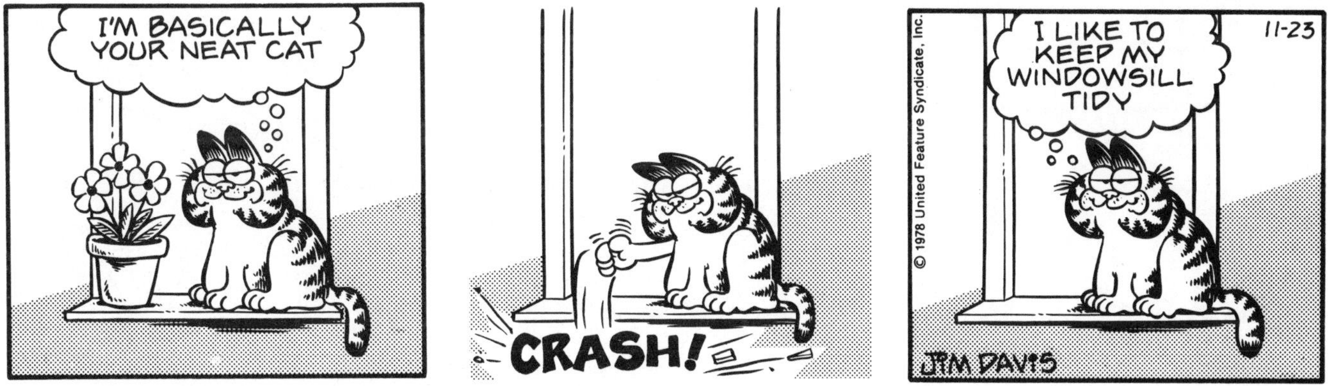
I'M BASICALLY YOUR NEAT CAT
CRASH!
© 1978 United Feature Syndicate, Inc.
I LIKE TO KEEP MY WINDOWSILL TIDY
11-23
JIM DAVIS

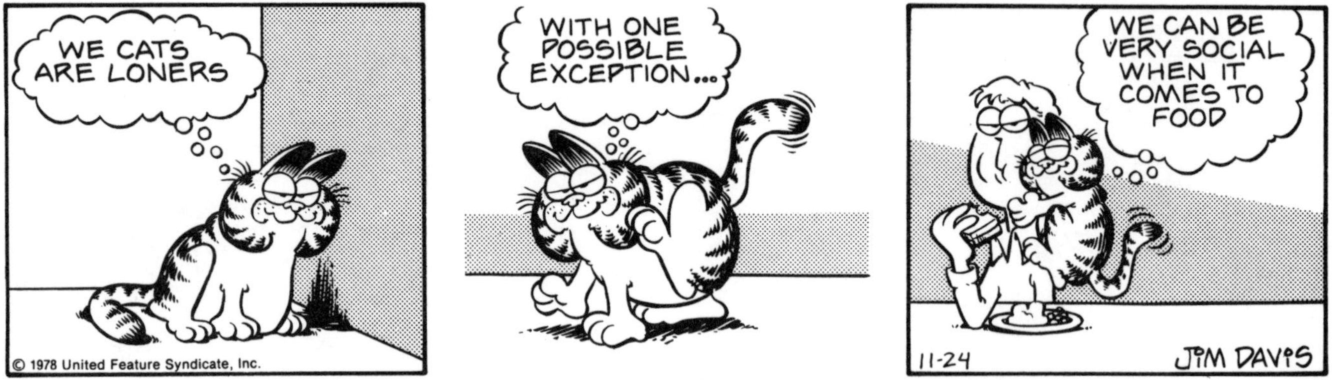
WE CATS ARE LONERS
© 1978 United Feature Syndicate, Inc.
WITH ONE POSSIBLE EXCEPTION...
WE CAN BE VERY SOCIAL WHEN IT COMES TO FOOD
11-24
JIM DAVIS

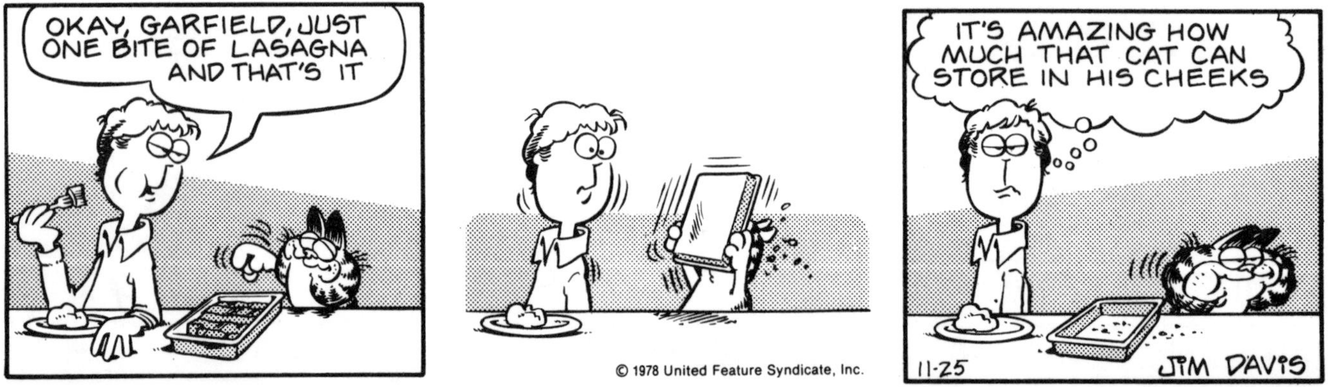
OKAY, GARFIELD, JUST ONE BITE OF LASAGNA AND THAT'S IT
© 1978 United Feature Syndicate, Inc.
IT'S AMAZING HOW MUCH THAT CAT CAN STORE IN HIS CHEEKS
11-25
JIM DAVIS

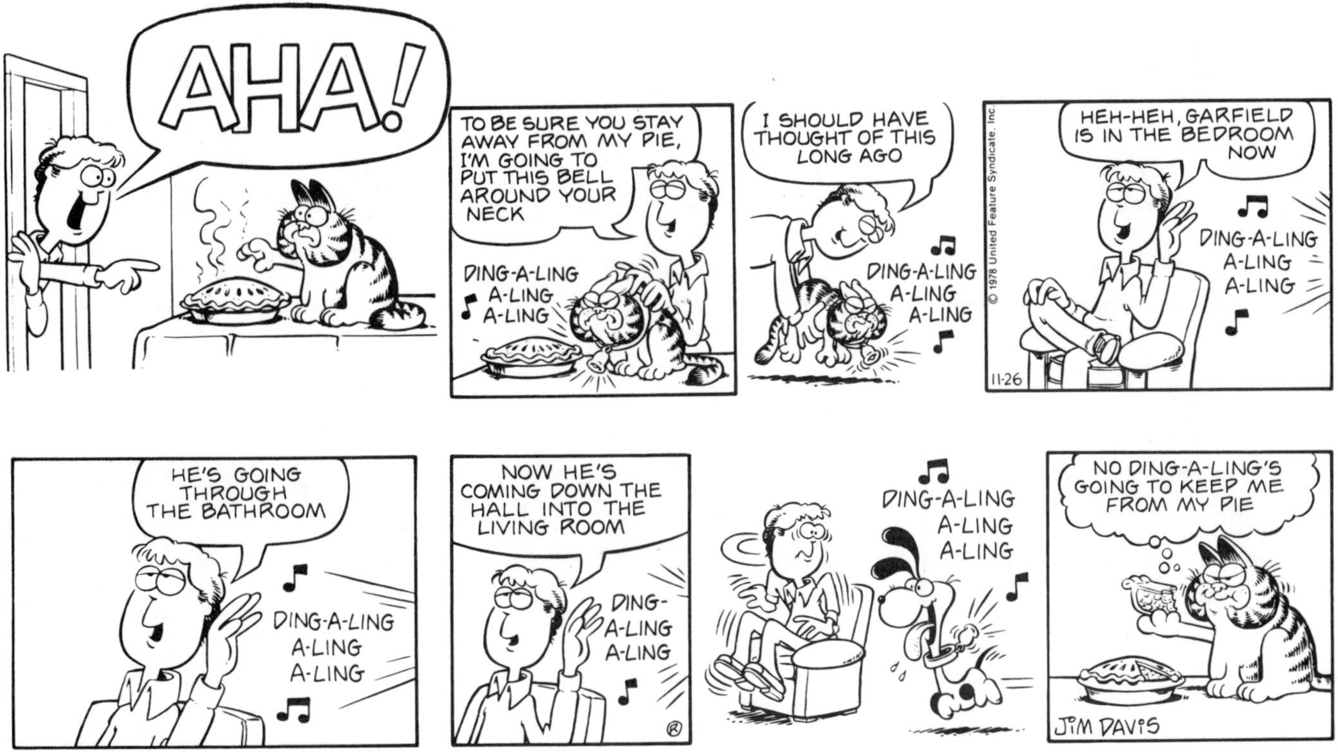
AHA!
TO BE SURE YOU STAY AWAY FROM MY PIE, I'M GOING TO PUT THIS BELL AROUND YOUR NECK
DING-A-LING A-LING A-LING
I SHOULD HAVE THOUGHT OF THIS LONG AGO
DING-A-LING A-LING A-LING
© 1978 United Feature Syndicate, Inc.
HEH-HEH, GARFIELD IS IN THE BEDROOM NOW
DING-A-LING A-LING A-LING
11-26
HE'S GOING THROUGH THE BATHROOM
DING-A-LING A-LING A-LING
NOW HE'S COMING DOWN THE HALL INTO THE LIVING ROOM
DING-A-LING A-LING
DING-A-LING A-LING A-LING
NO DING-A-LING'S GOING TO KEEP ME FROM MY PIE
JIM DAVIS

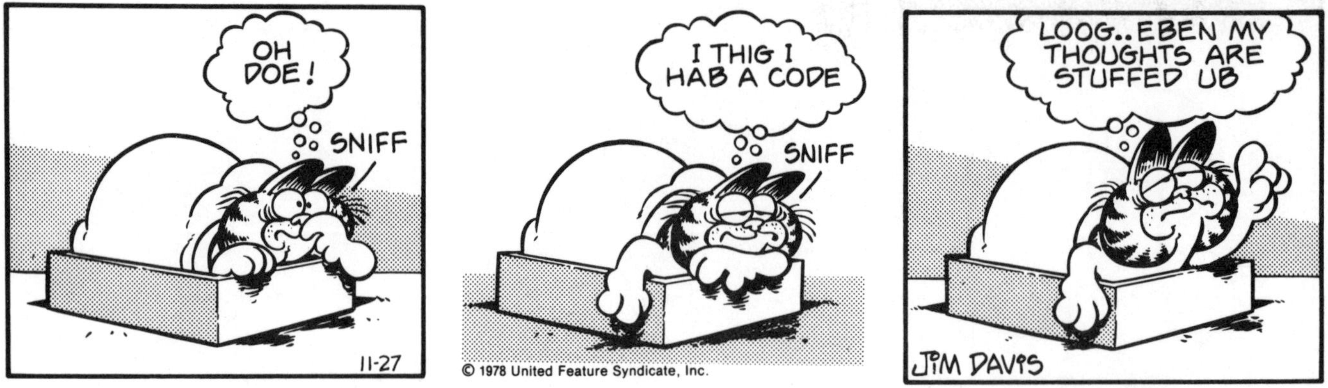
OH DOE!
SNIFF
11-27
I THIG I HAB A CODE
SNIFF
© 1978 United Feature Syndicate, Inc.
LOOG..EBEN MY THOUGHTS ARE STUFFED UB
JIM DAVIS

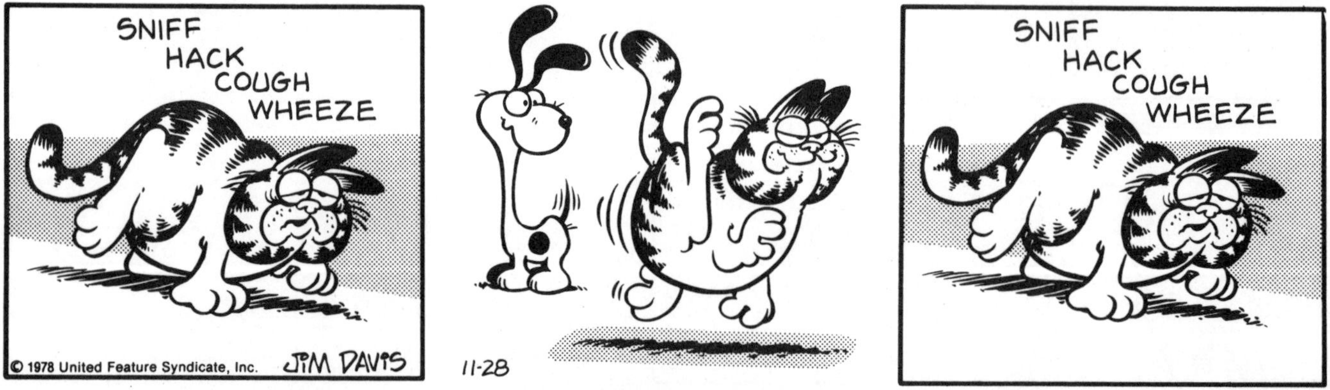
SNIFF
HACK
COUGH
WHEEZE
© 1978 United Feature Syndicate, Inc.
JIM DAVIS
11-28
SNIFF
HACK
COUGH
WHEEZE

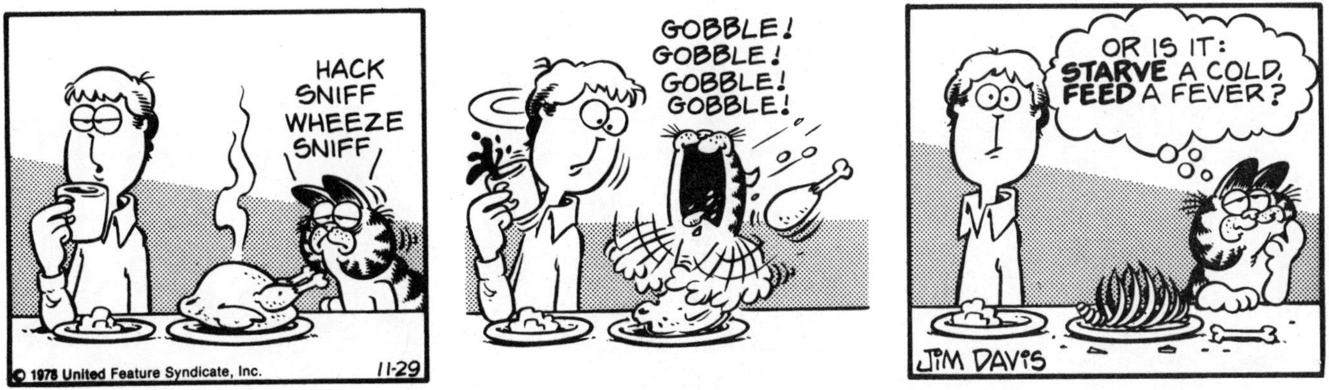
HACK
SNIFF
WHEEZE
SNIFF
GOBBLE! GOBBLE! GOBBLE! GOBBLE!
OR IS IT: STARVE A COLD, FEED A FEVER?
JIM DAVIS
© 1978 United Feature Syndicate, Inc.
11-29

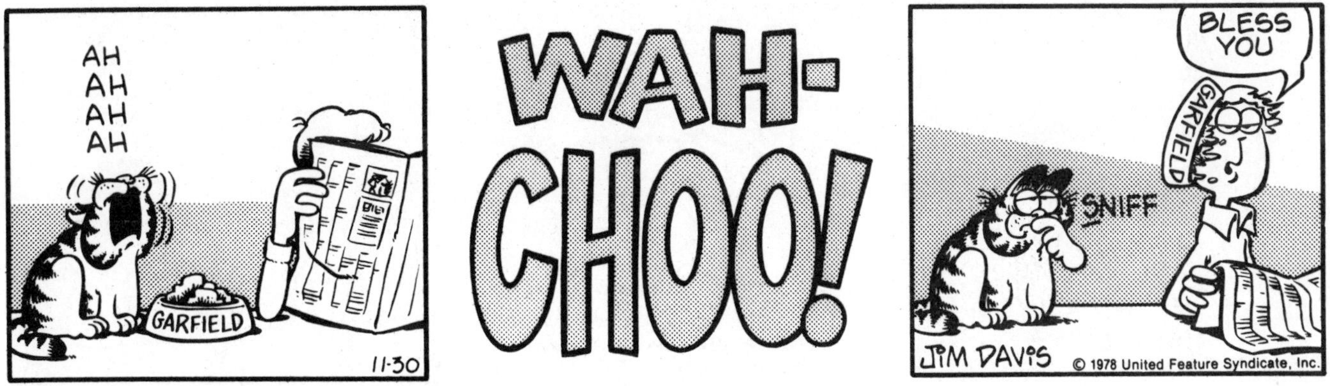
AH
AH
AH
AH
GARFIELD
11-30
WAH-CHOO!
BLESS YOU
GARFIELD
SNIFF
JIM DAVIS
© 1978 United Feature Syndicate, Inc.

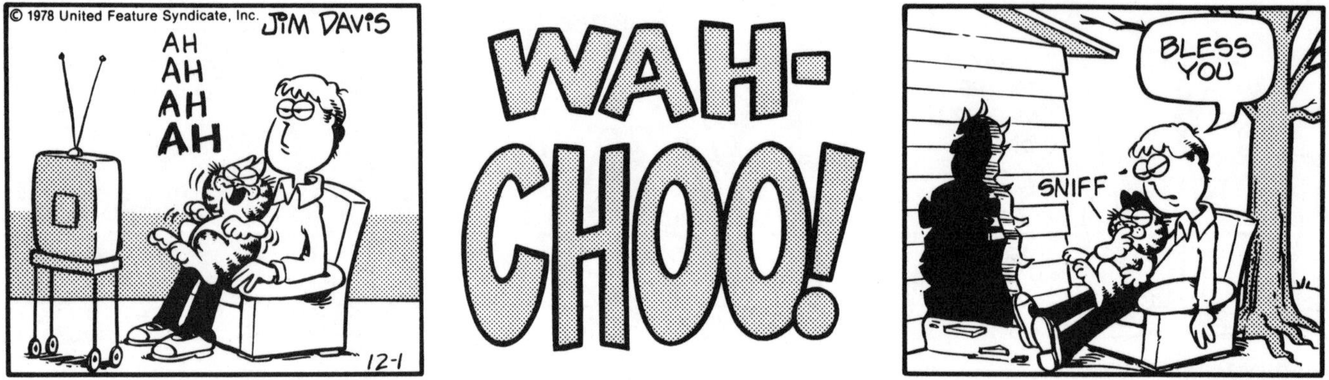
© 1978 United Feature Syndicate, Inc.
JIM DAVIS
AH
AH
AH
AH
WAH-
CHOO!
SNIFF
BLESS YOU
12-1

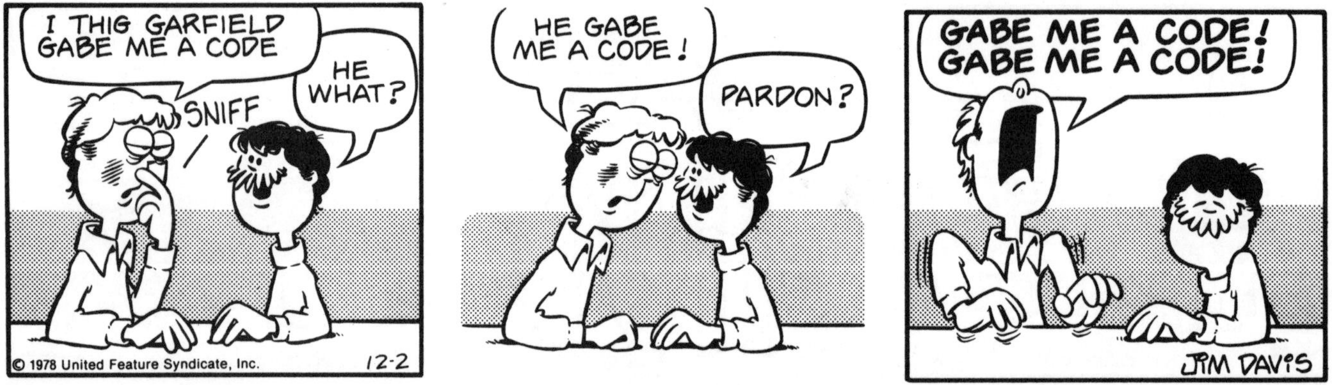
I THIG GARFIELD GABE ME A CODE
SNIFF
HE WHAT?
HE GABE ME A CODE!
PARDON?
GABE ME A CODE! GABE ME A CODE!
© 1978 United Feature Syndicate, Inc.
12-2
JIM DAVIS

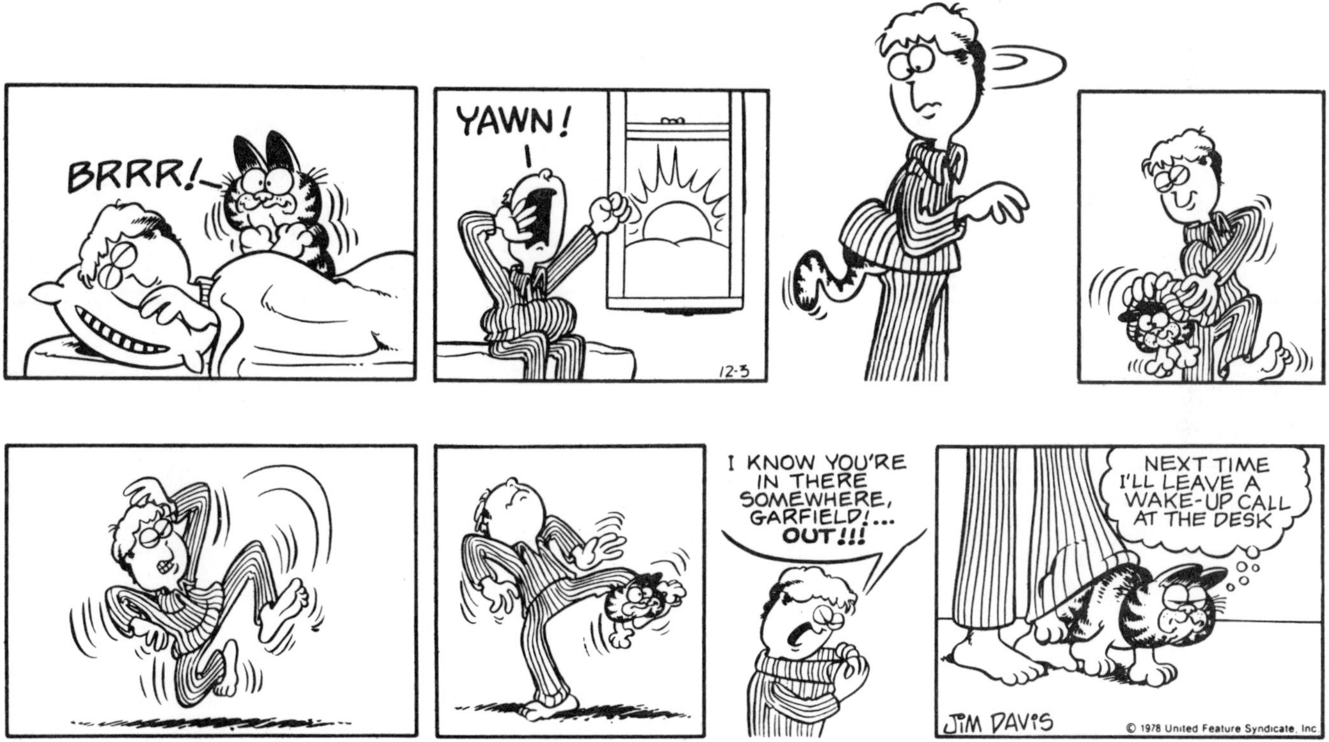

BRRR!
YAWN!
12-3
I KNOW YOU'RE IN THERE SOMEWHERE, GARFIELD!... OUT!!!
NEXT TIME I'LL LEAVE A WAKE-UP CALL AT THE DESK
JIM DAVIS
© 1978 United Feature Syndicate, Inc.

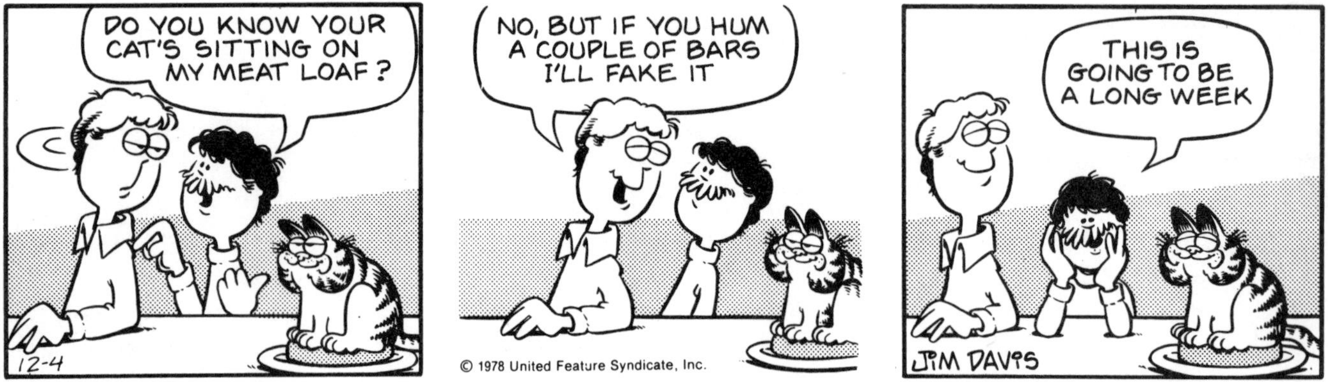
DO YOU KNOW YOUR CAT'S SITTING ON MY MEAT LOAF?
12-4
NO, BUT IF YOU HUM A COUPLE OF BARS I'LL FAKE IT
© 1978 United Feature Syndicate, Inc.
THIS IS GOING TO BE A LONG WEEK
JIM DAVIS

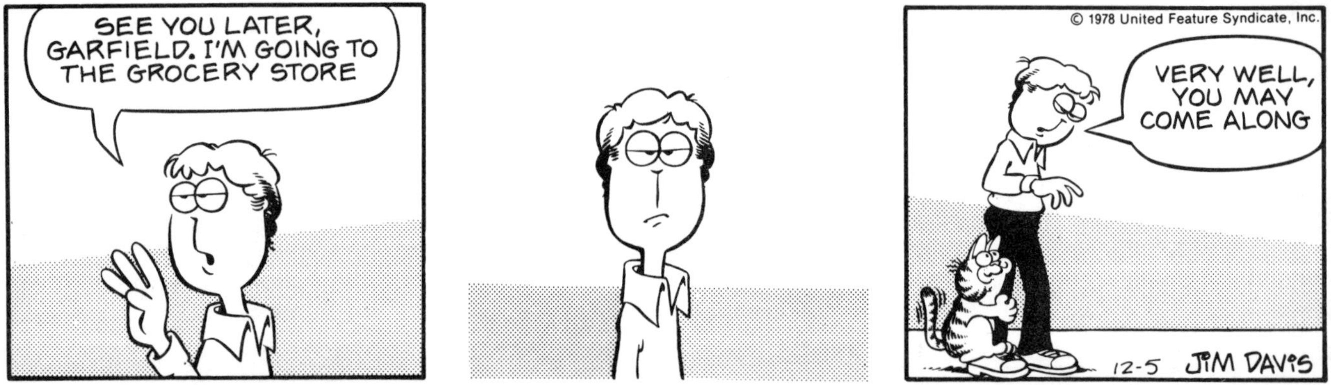
SEE YOU LATER, GARFIELD. I'M GOING TO THE GROCERY STORE
© 1978 United Feature Syndicate, Inc.
VERY WELL, YOU MAY COME ALONG
12-5
JIM DAVIS

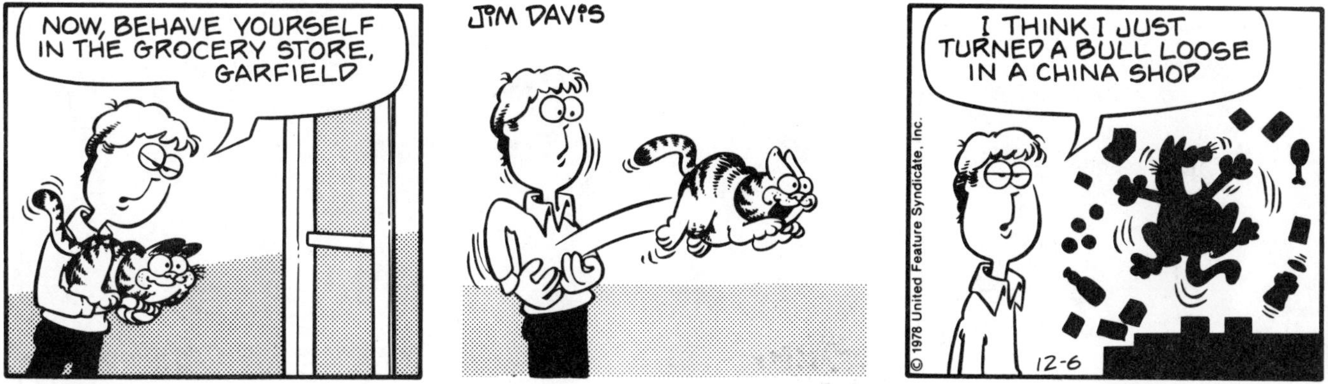
NOW, BEHAVE YOURSELF IN THE GROCERY STORE, GARFIELD
JIM DAVIS
I THINK I JUST TURNED A BULL LOOSE IN A CHINA SHOP
© 1978 United Feature Syndicate, Inc.
12-6

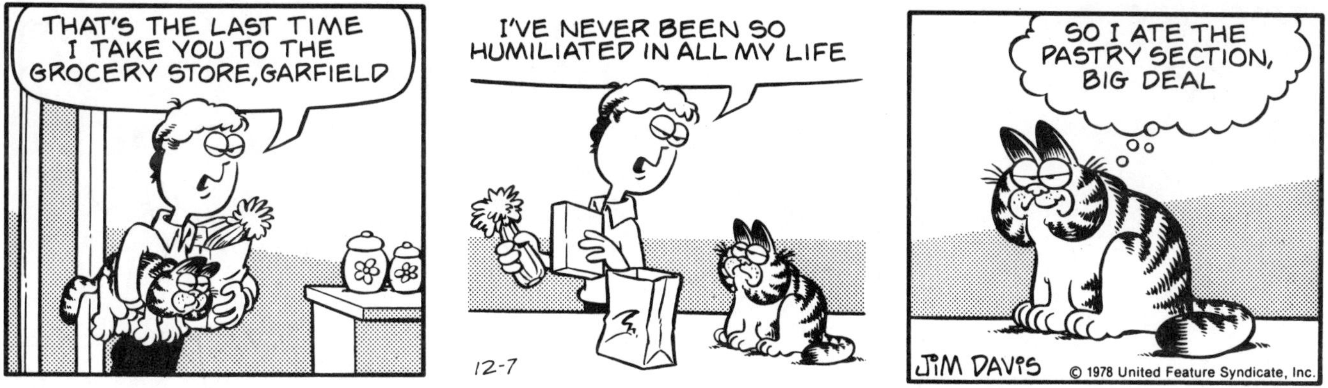
THAT'S THE LAST TIME I TAKE YOU TO THE GROCERY STORE, GARFIELD
I'VE NEVER BEEN SO HUMILIATED IN ALL MY LIFE
12-7
SO I ATE THE PASTRY SECTION, BIG DEAL
JIM DAVIS
© 1978 United Feature Syndicate, Inc.

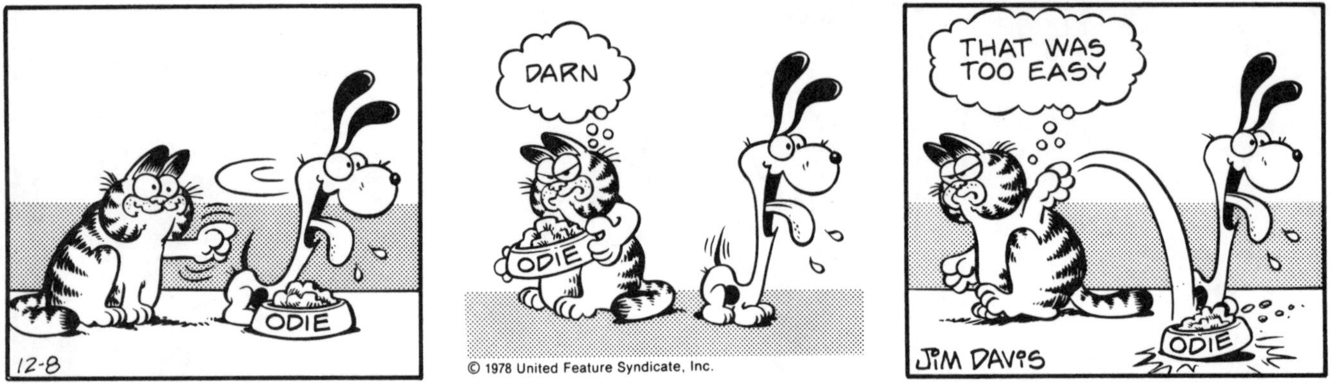

12-8
ODIE
DARN
ODIE
© 1978 United Feature Syndicate, Inc.
THAT WAS TOO EASY
ODIE
JIM DAVIS

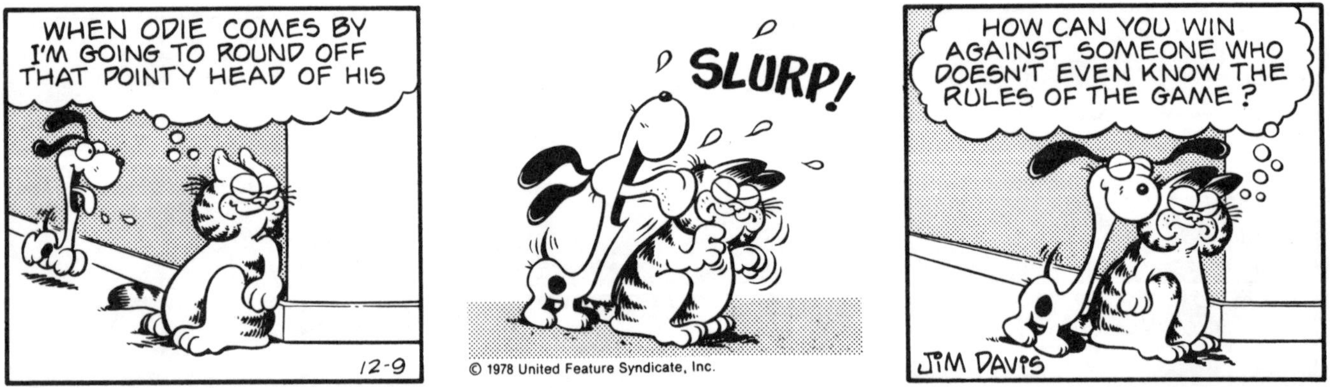

WHEN ODIE COMES BY I'M GOING TO ROUND OFF THAT POINTY HEAD OF HIS
12-9
SLURP!
© 1978 United Feature Syndicate, Inc.
HOW CAN YOU WIN AGAINST SOMEONE WHO DOESN'T EVEN KNOW THE RULES OF THE GAME?
JIM DAVIS

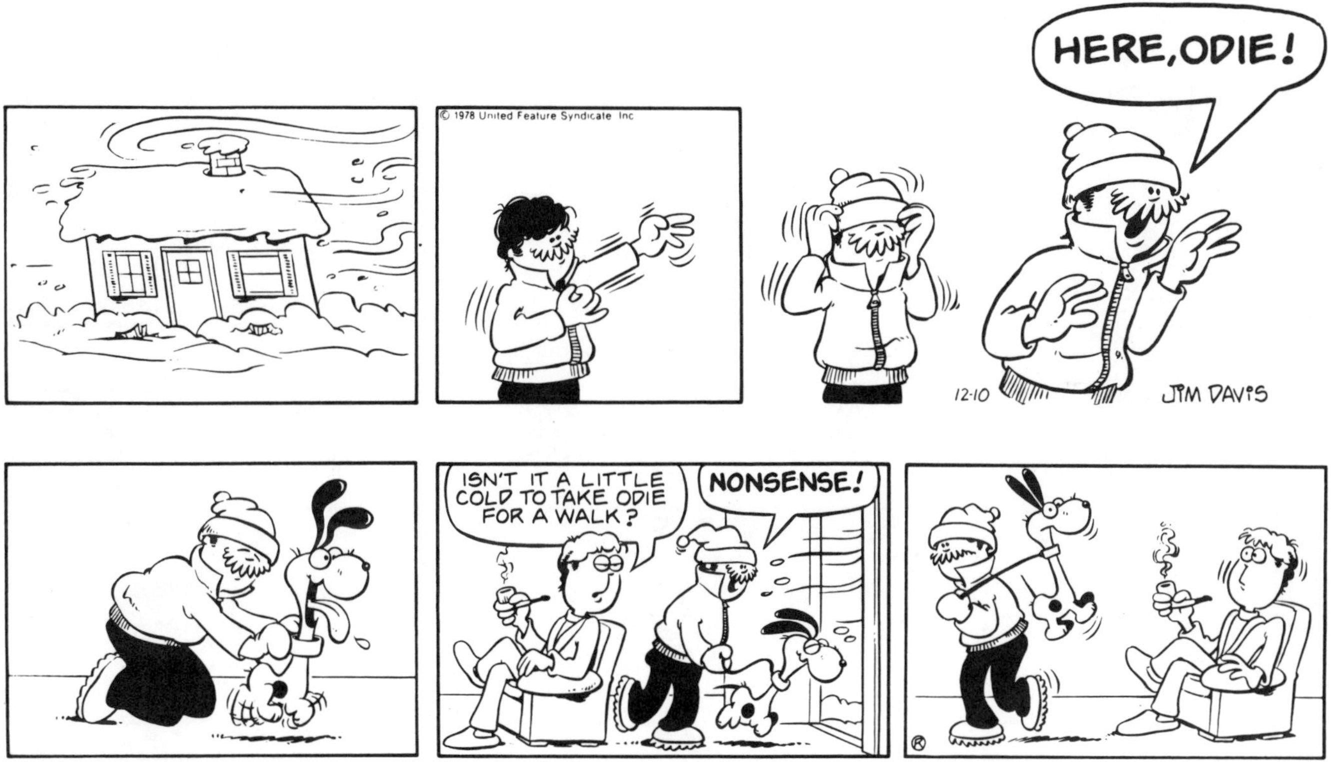

© 1978 United Feature Syndicate Inc
HERE, ODIE!
12-10
JIM DAVIS
ISN'T IT A LITTLE COLD TO TAKE ODIE FOR A WALK?
NONSENSE!

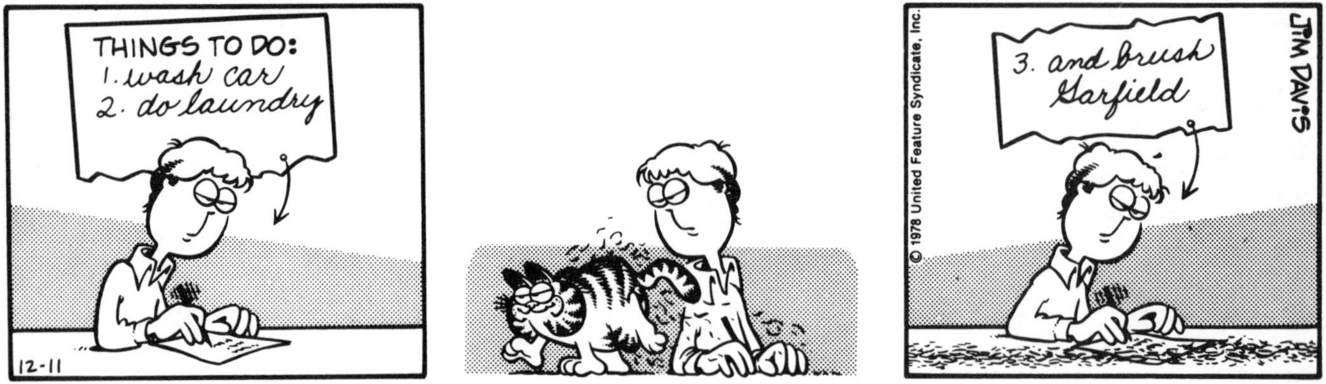
THINGS TO DO:
1. wash car
2. do laundry
12-11
© 1978 United Feature Syndicate, Inc.
3. and brush Garfield
JIM DAVIS

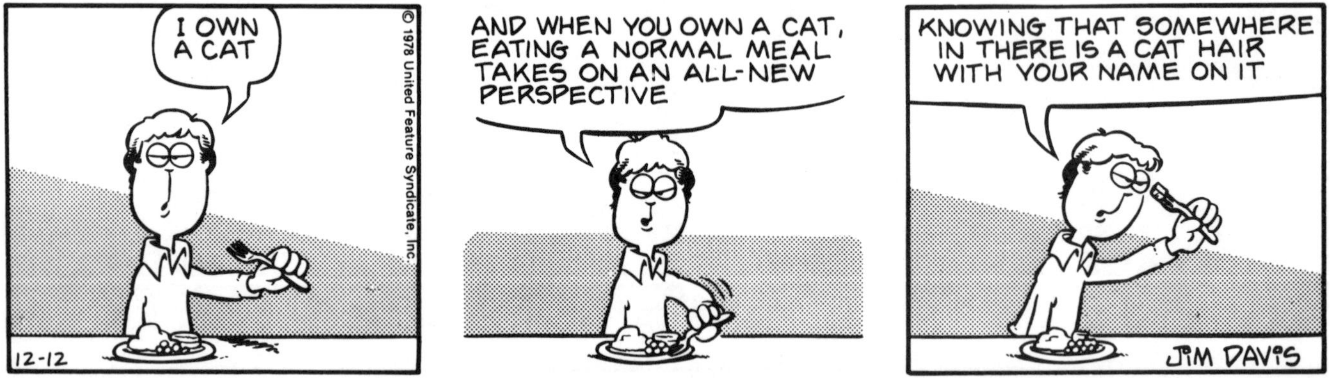
I OWN A CAT
12-12
© 1978 United Feature Syndicate, Inc.
AND WHEN YOU OWN A CAT, EATING A NORMAL MEAL TAKES ON AN ALL-NEW PERSPECTIVE
KNOWING THAT SOMEWHERE IN THERE IS A CAT HAIR WITH YOUR NAME ON IT
JIM DAVIS

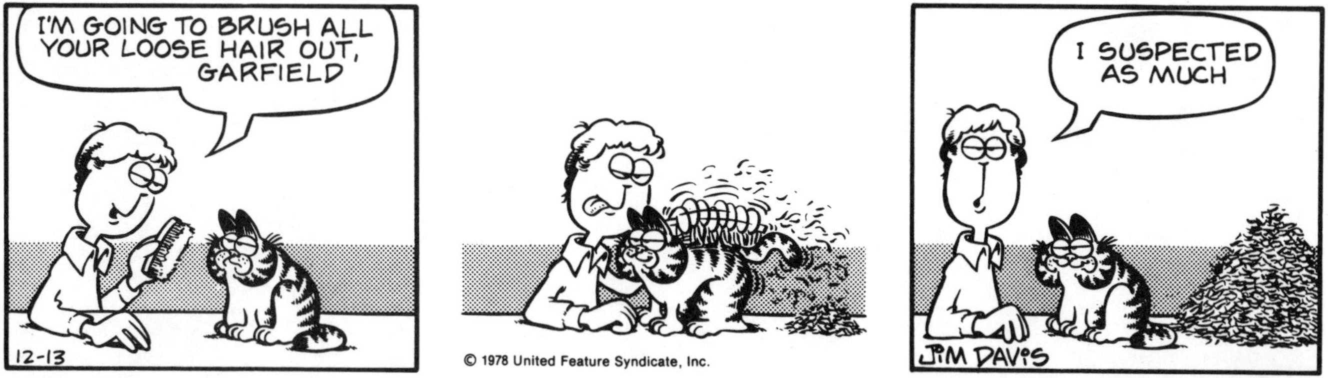
I'M GOING TO BRUSH ALL YOUR LOOSE HAIR OUT, GARFIELD
I SUSPECTED AS MUCH
12-13
JIM DAVIS

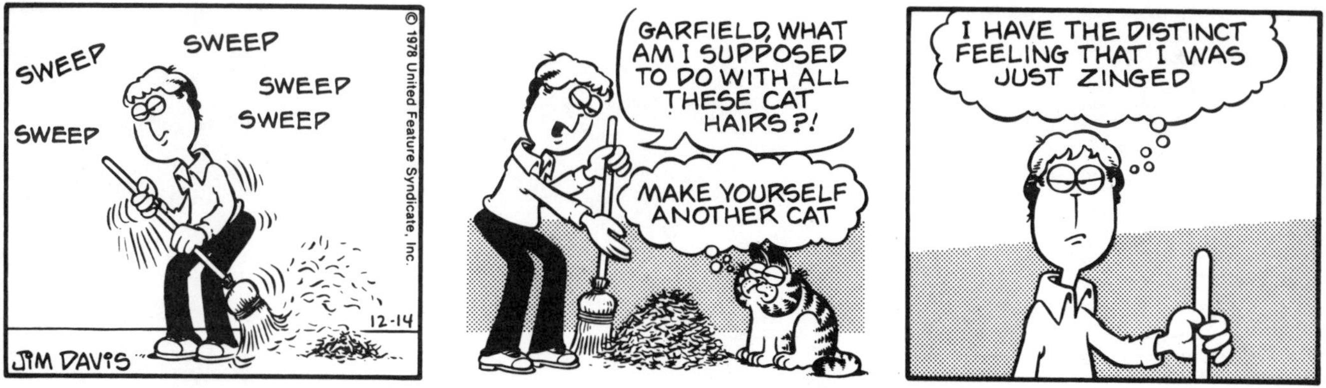
SWEEP
SWEEP
SWEEP
SWEEP
SWEEP
12-14
JIM DAVIS
GARFIELD, WHAT AM I SUPPOSED TO DO WITH ALL THESE CAT HAIRS?!
MAKE YOURSELF ANOTHER CAT
I HAVE THE DISTINCT FEELING THAT I WAS JUST ZINGED

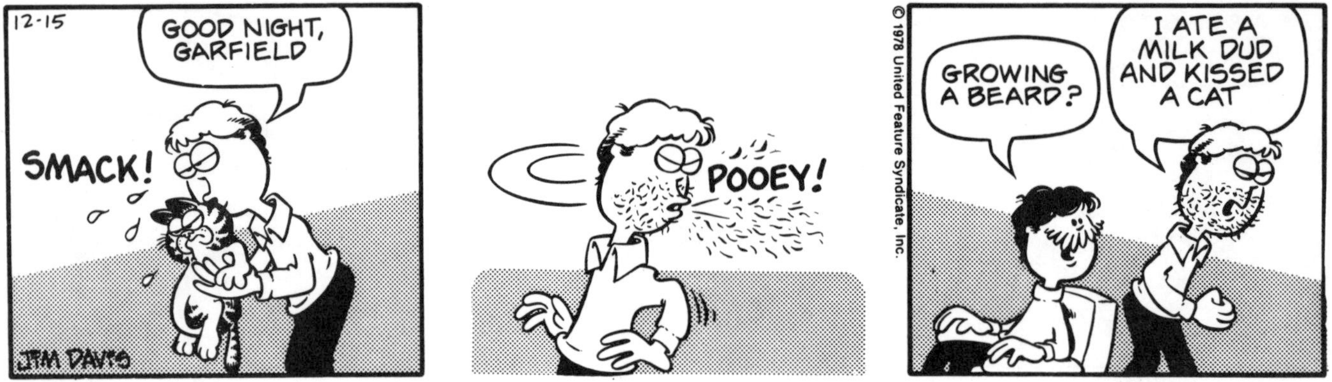
12-15
GOOD NIGHT, GARFIELD
SMACK!
JIM DAVIS
POOEY!
© 1978 United Feature Syndicate, Inc.
GROWING A BEARD?
I ATE A MILK DUD AND KISSED A CAT

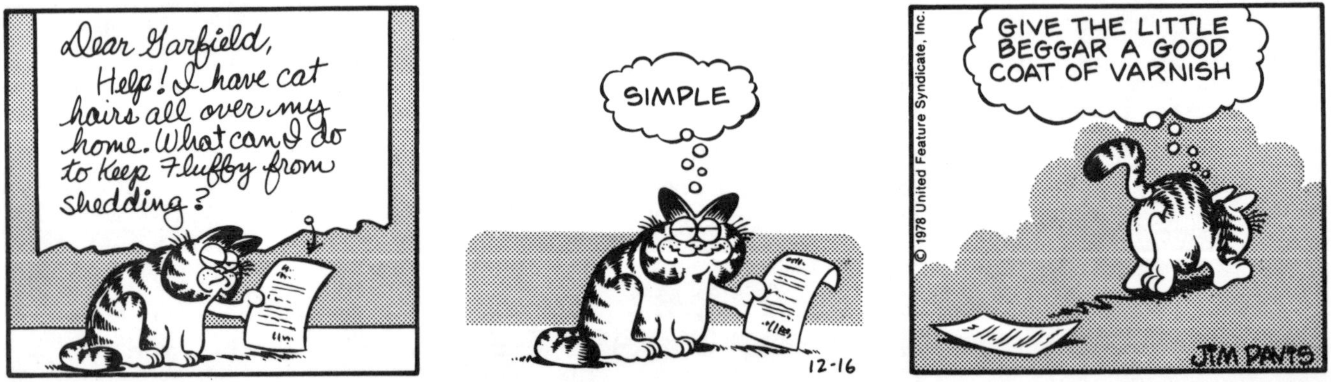
Dear Garfield,
Help! I have cat hairs all over my home. What can I do to keep Fluffy from shedding?
SIMPLE
12-16
© 1978 United Feature Syndicate, Inc.
GIVE THE LITTLE BEGGAR A GOOD COAT OF VARNISH
JIM DAVIS

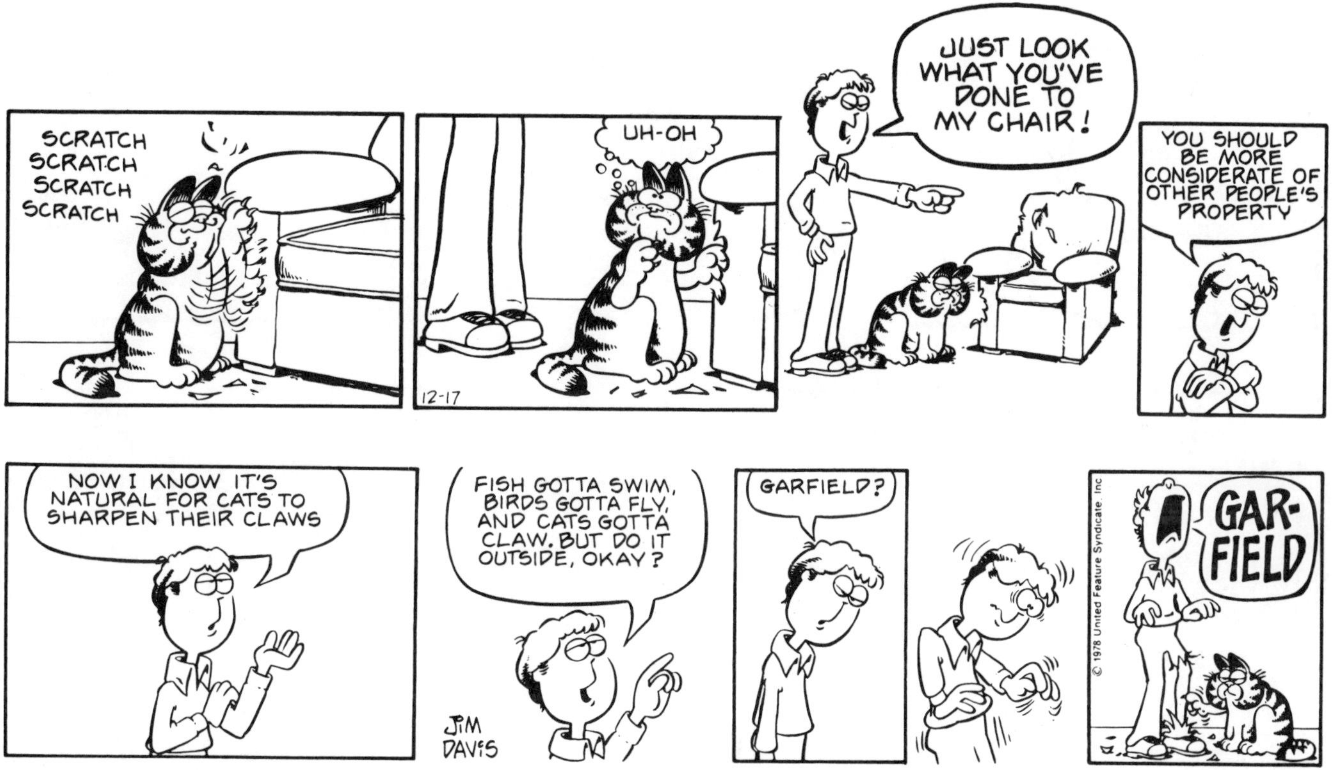
SCRATCH SCRATCH SCRATCH SCRATCH
UH-OH
12-17
JUST LOOK WHAT YOU'VE DONE TO MY CHAIR!
YOU SHOULD BE MORE CONSIDERATE OF OTHER PEOPLE'S PROPERTY
NOW I KNOW IT'S NATURAL FOR CATS TO SHARPEN THEIR CLAWS
FISH GOTTA SWIM, BIRDS GOTTA FLY, AND CATS GOTTA CLAW. BUT DO IT OUTSIDE, OKAY?
JIM DAVIS
GARFIELD?
GAR-FIELD
© 1978 United Feature Syndicate, Inc.

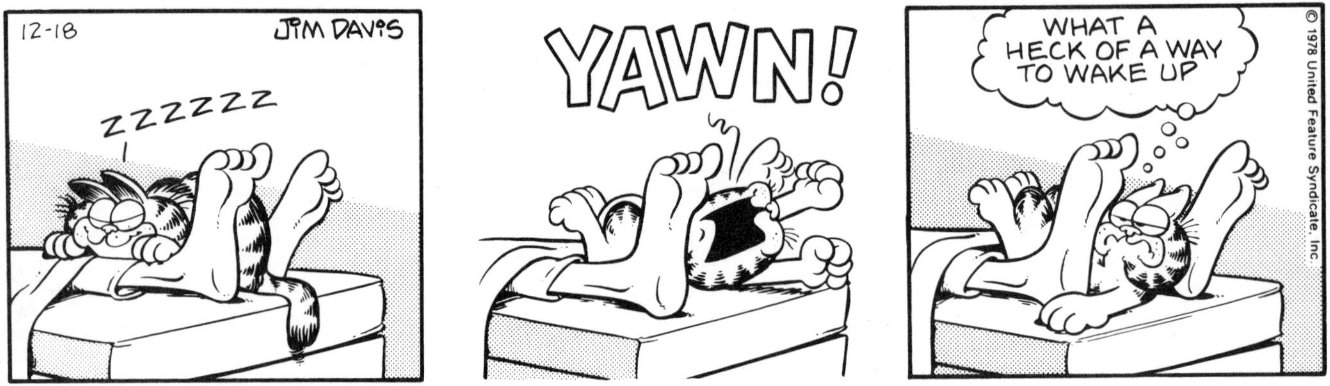
12-18
JIM DAVIS
ZZZZZZ
YAWN!
WHAT A HECK OF A WAY TO WAKE UP
© 1978 United Feature Syndicate, Inc.

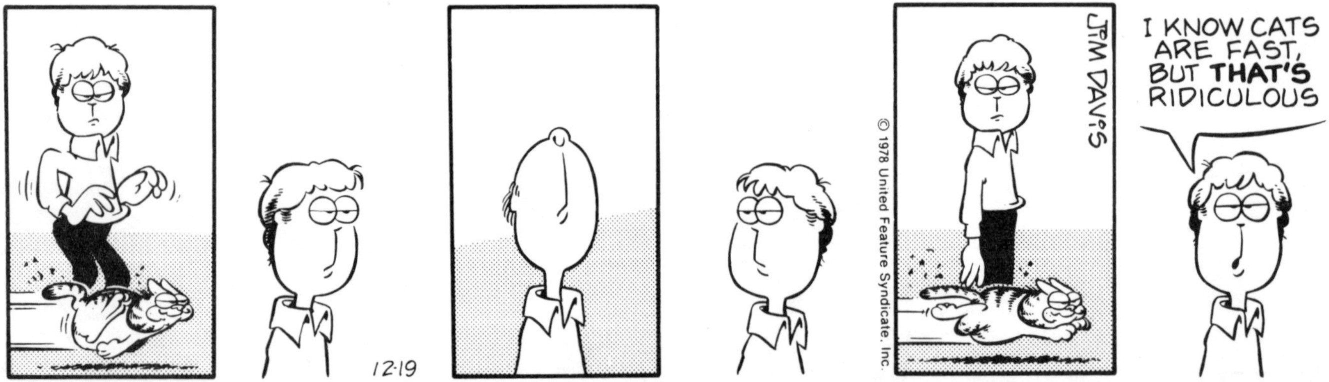
12-19
JIM DAVIS
© 1978 United Feature Syndicate, Inc.
I KNOW CATS ARE FAST, BUT **THAT'S** RIDICULOUS

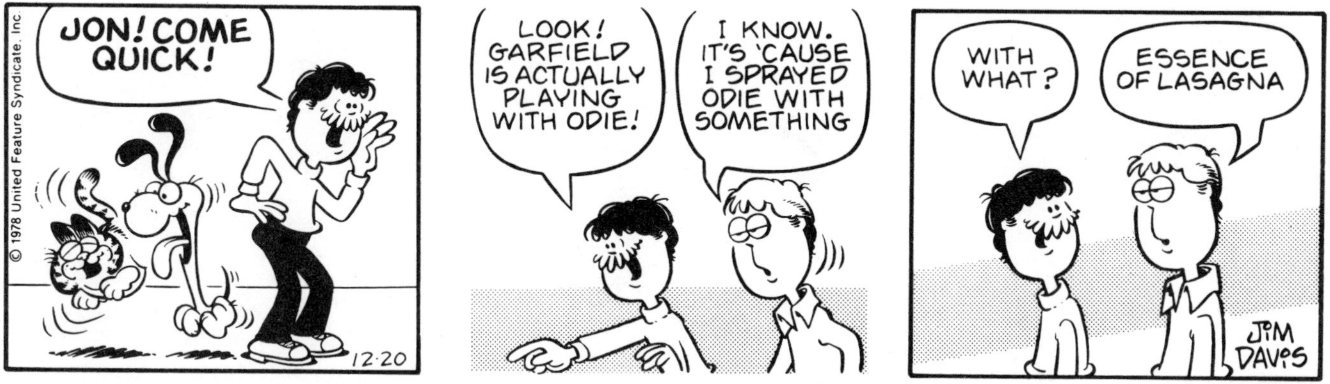
© 1978 United Feature Syndicate, Inc.
JON! COME QUICK!
12·20
LOOK! GARFIELD IS ACTUALLY PLAYING WITH ODIE!
I KNOW. IT'S 'CAUSE I SPRAYED ODIE WITH SOMETHING
WITH WHAT?
ESSENCE OF LASAGNA
JIM DAVIS

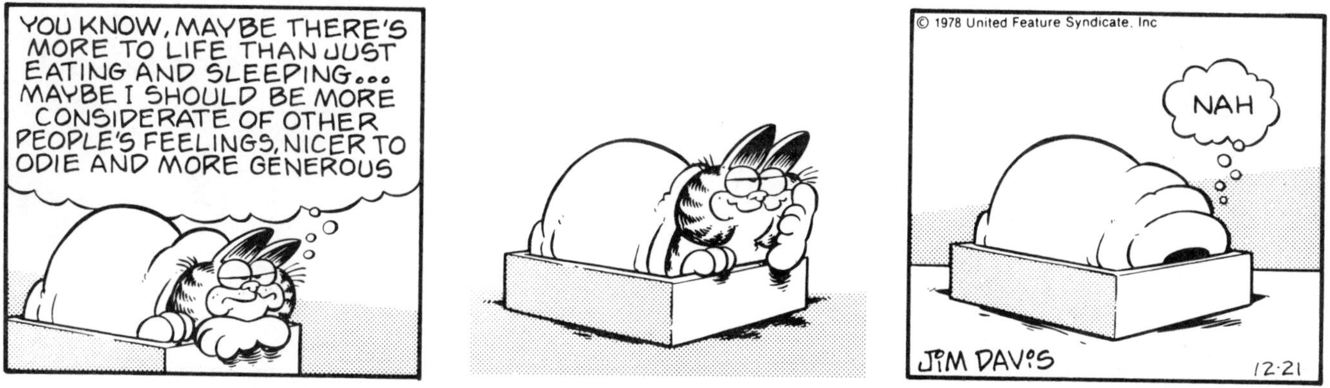
YOU KNOW, MAYBE THERE'S MORE TO LIFE THAN JUST EATING AND SLEEPING... MAYBE I SHOULD BE MORE CONSIDERATE OF OTHER PEOPLE'S FEELINGS, NICER TO ODIE AND MORE GENEROUS
© 1978 United Feature Syndicate, Inc
NAH
JIM DAVIS
12·21

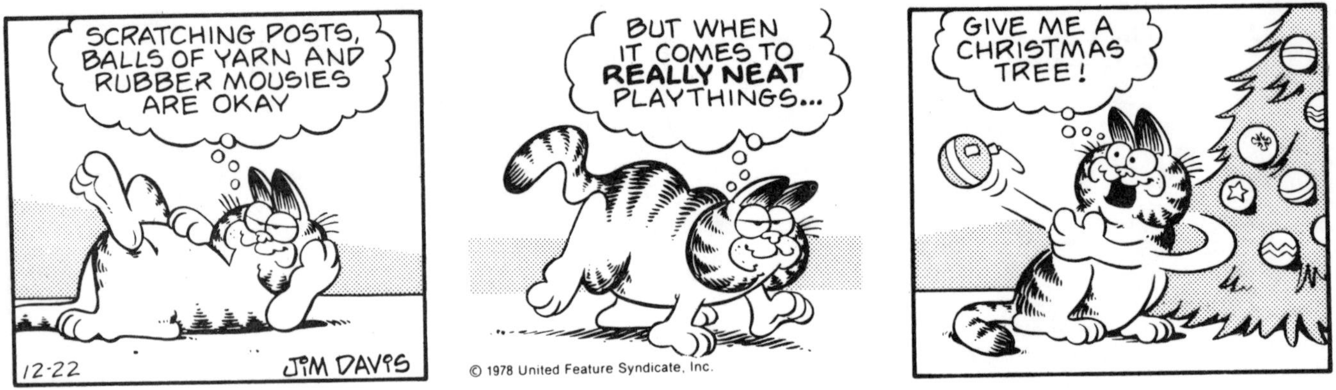
SCRATCHING POSTS, BALLS OF YARN AND RUBBER MOUSIES ARE OKAY
12-22
JIM DAVIS
BUT WHEN IT COMES TO **REALLY NEAT** PLAYTHINGS...
© 1978 United Feature Syndicate, Inc.
GIVE ME A CHRISTMAS TREE!

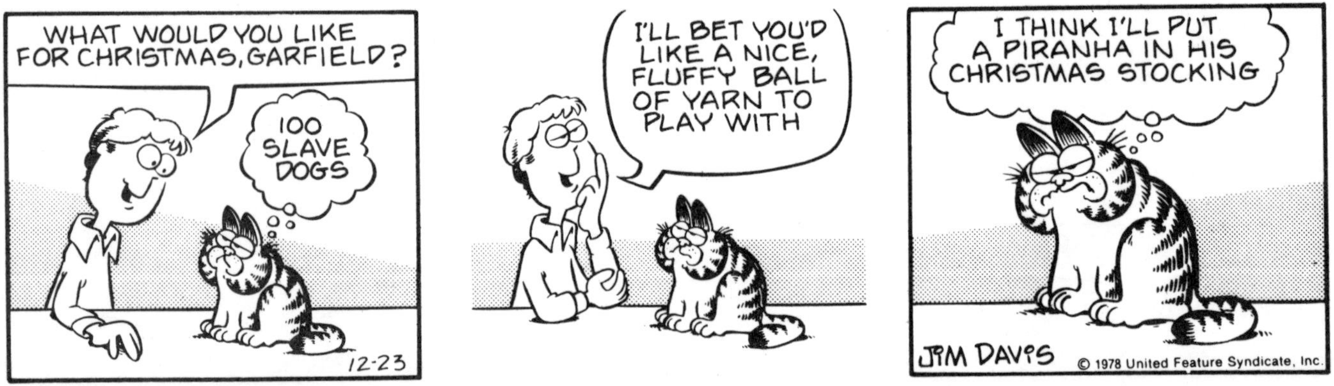
WHAT WOULD YOU LIKE FOR CHRISTMAS, GARFIELD?
100 SLAVE DOGS
12-23
I'LL BET YOU'D LIKE A NICE, FLUFFY BALL OF YARN TO PLAY WITH
I THINK I'LL PUT A PIRANHA IN HIS CHRISTMAS STOCKING
JIM DAVIS
© 1978 United Feature Syndicate, Inc.

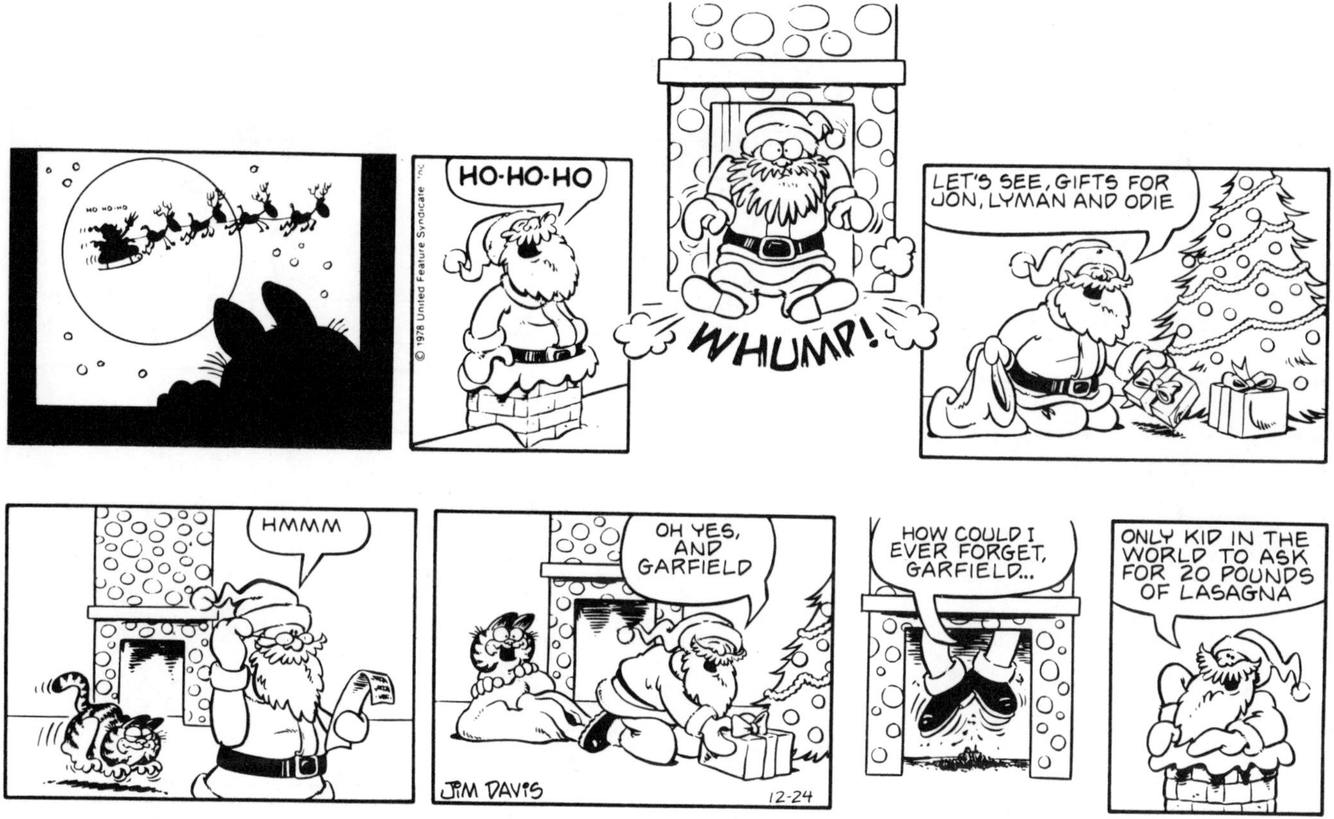
HO-HO-HO
HO-HO-HO
© 1978 United Feature Syndicate, Inc.
WHUMP!
LET'S SEE, GIFTS FOR JON, LYMAN AND ODIE
HMMM
OH YES, AND GARFIELD
JIM DAVIS
12-24
HOW COULD I EVER FORGET, GARFIELD...
ONLY KID IN THE WORLD TO ASK FOR 20 POUNDS OF LASAGNA

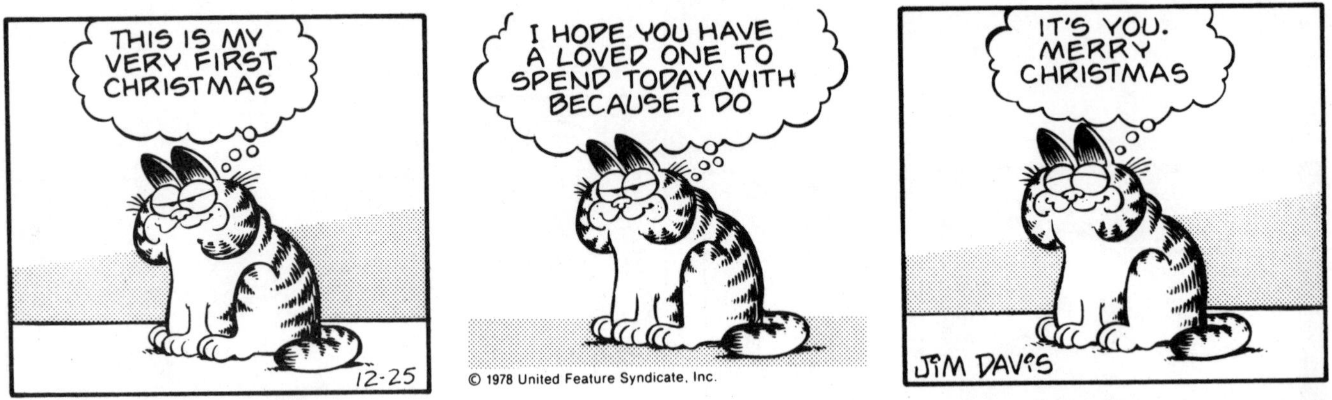
THIS IS MY VERY FIRST CHRISTMAS
12-25
I HOPE YOU HAVE A LOVED ONE TO SPEND TODAY WITH BECAUSE I DO
© 1978 United Feature Syndicate, Inc.
IT'S YOU. MERRY CHRISTMAS
JIM DAVIS

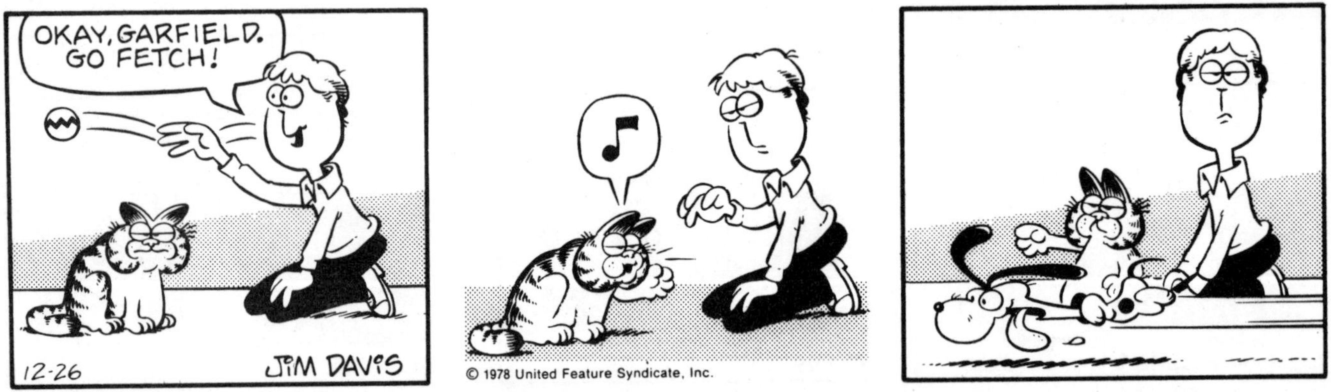
OKAY, GARFIELD. GO FETCH!
12-26
JIM DAVIS
© 1978 United Feature Syndicate, Inc.

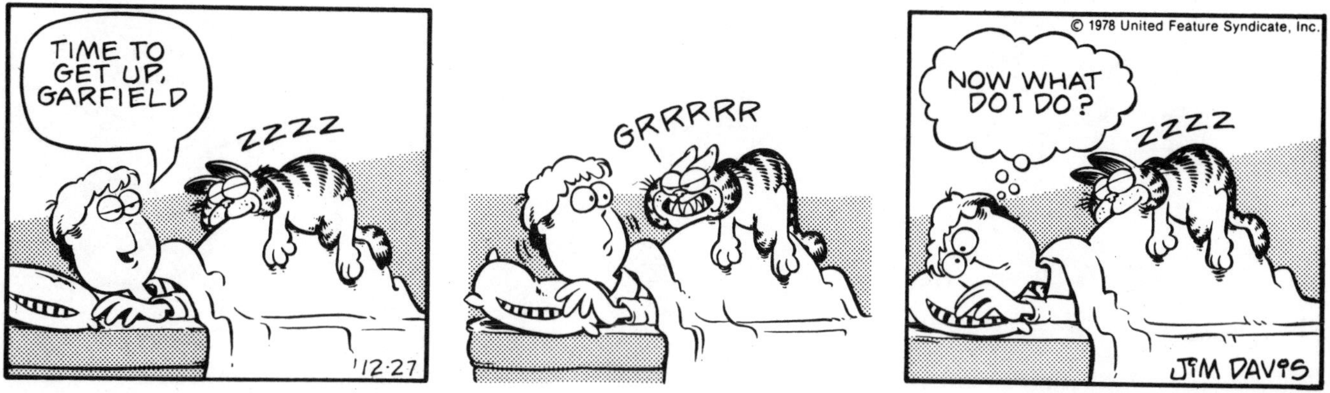
TIME TO GET UP, GARFIELD
ZZZZ
12-27
GRRRRR
© 1978 United Feature Syndicate, Inc.
NOW WHAT DO I DO?
ZZZZ
JIM DAVIS

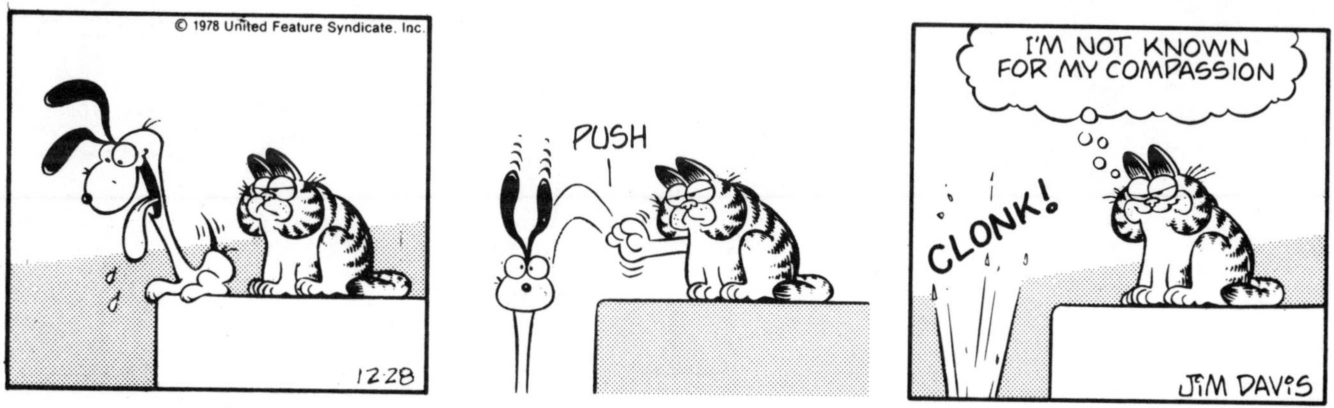
© 1978 United Feature Syndicate, Inc.
12-28
PUSH
I'M NOT KNOWN FOR MY COMPASSION
CLONK!
JIM DAVIS

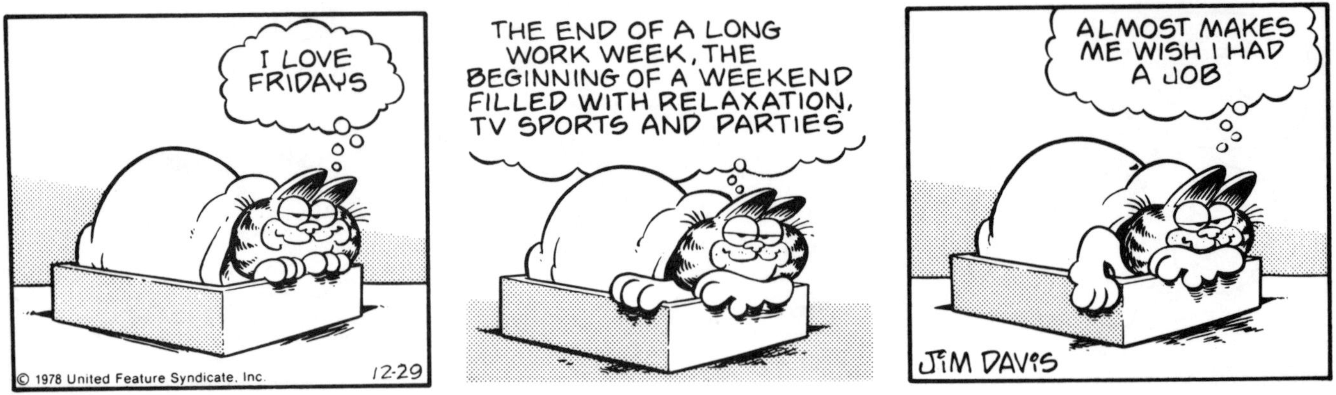
I LOVE FRIDAYS
THE END OF A LONG WORK WEEK, THE BEGINNING OF A WEEKEND FILLED WITH RELAXATION, TV SPORTS AND PARTIES
ALMOST MAKES ME WISH I HAD A JOB
© 1978 United Feature Syndicate, Inc.
12-29
JIM DAVIS

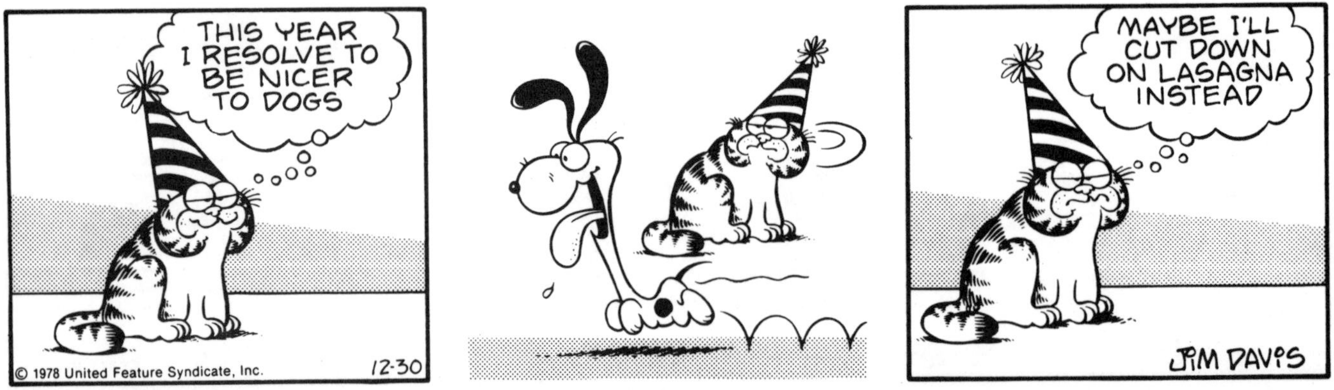
THIS YEAR I RESOLVE TO BE NICER TO DOGS
MAYBE I'LL CUT DOWN ON LASAGNA INSTEAD
© 1978 United Feature Syndicate, Inc.
12-30
JIM DAVIS

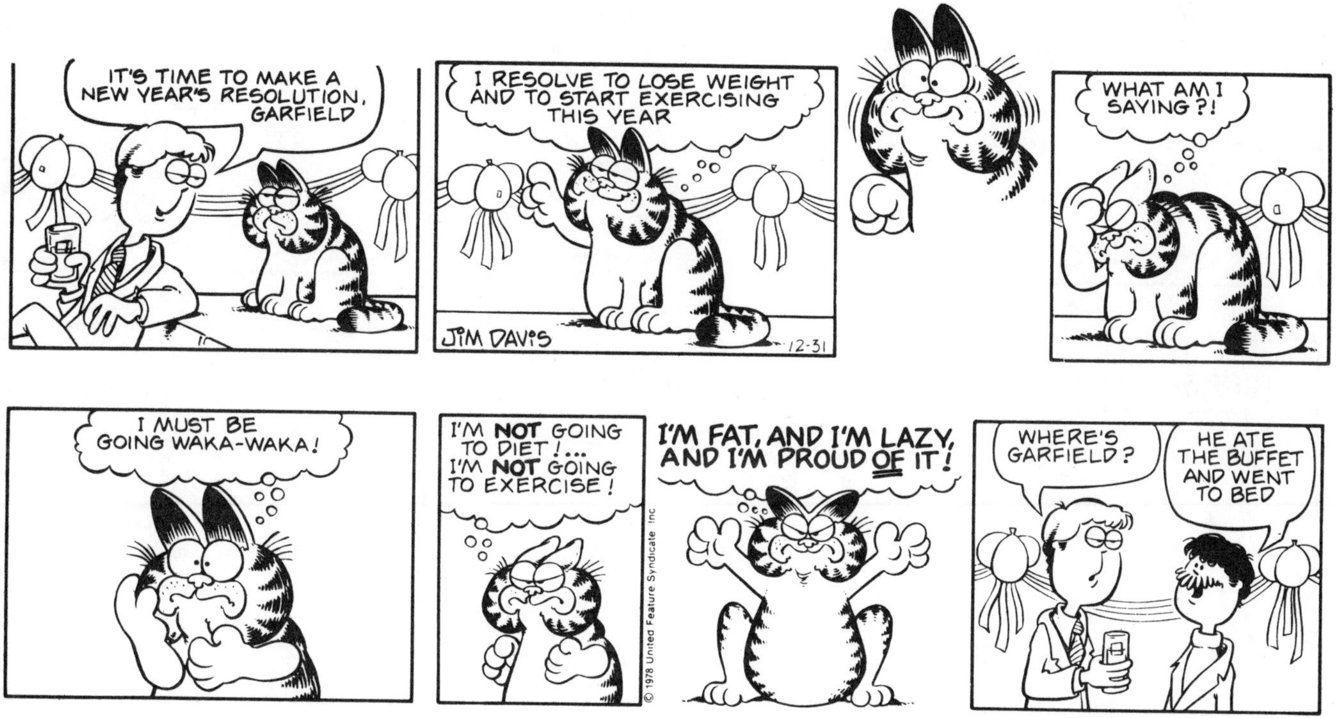
IT'S TIME TO MAKE A NEW YEAR'S RESOLUTION, GARFIELD
I RESOLVE TO LOSE WEIGHT AND TO START EXERCISING THIS YEAR
JIM DAVIS
12-31
WHAT AM I SAYING?!
I MUST BE GOING WAKA-WAKA!
I'M **NOT** GOING TO DIET!... I'M **NOT** GOING TO EXERCISE!
© 1978 United Feature Syndicate Inc
I'M FAT, AND I'M LAZY, AND I'M PROUD OF IT!
WHERE'S GARFIELD?
HE ATE THE BUFFET AND WENT TO BED

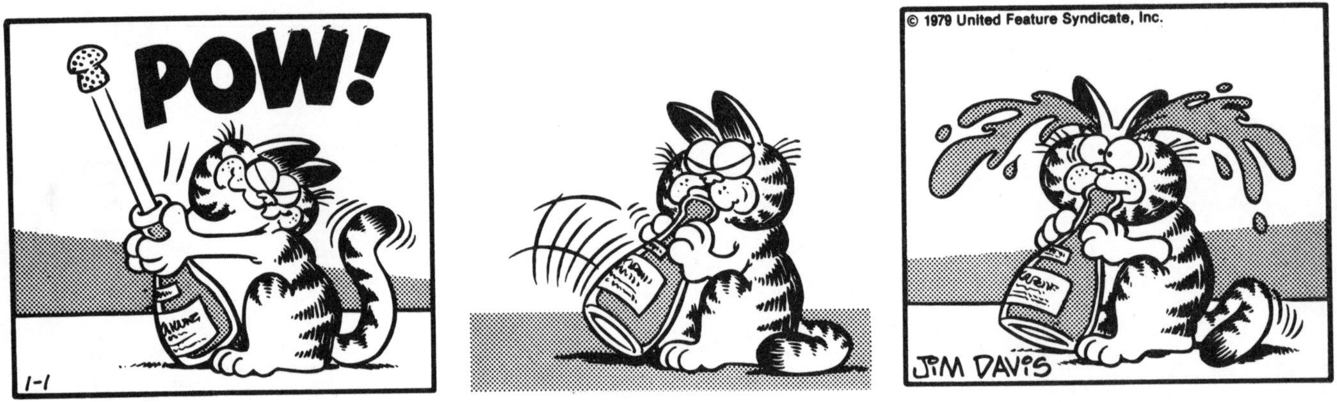
POW!
© 1979 United Feature Syndicate, Inc.
JIM DAVIS
1-1

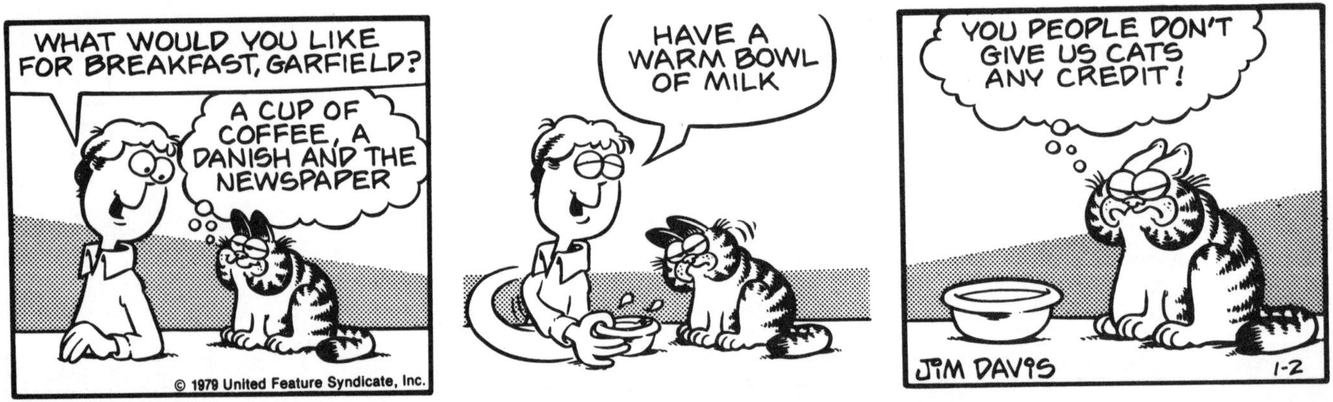
WHAT WOULD YOU LIKE FOR BREAKFAST, GARFIELD?
A CUP OF COFFEE, A DANISH AND THE NEWSPAPER
© 1979 United Feature Syndicate, Inc.
HAVE A WARM BOWL OF MILK
YOU PEOPLE DON'T GIVE US CATS ANY CREDIT!
JIM DAVIS
1-2

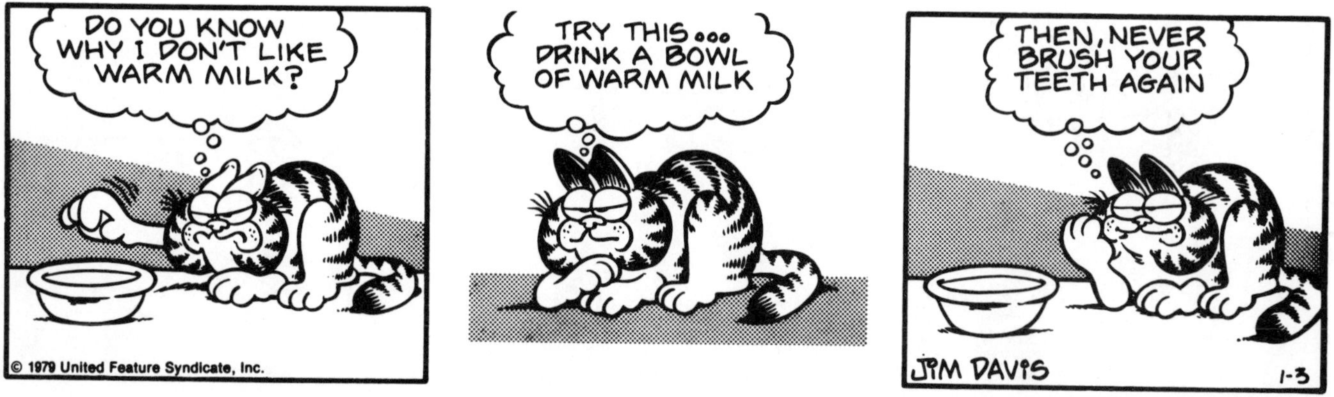
DO YOU KNOW WHY I DON'T LIKE WARM MILK?
TRY THIS... DRINK A BOWL OF WARM MILK
THEN, NEVER BRUSH YOUR TEETH AGAIN
© 1979 United Feature Syndicate, Inc.
JIM DAVIS
1-3

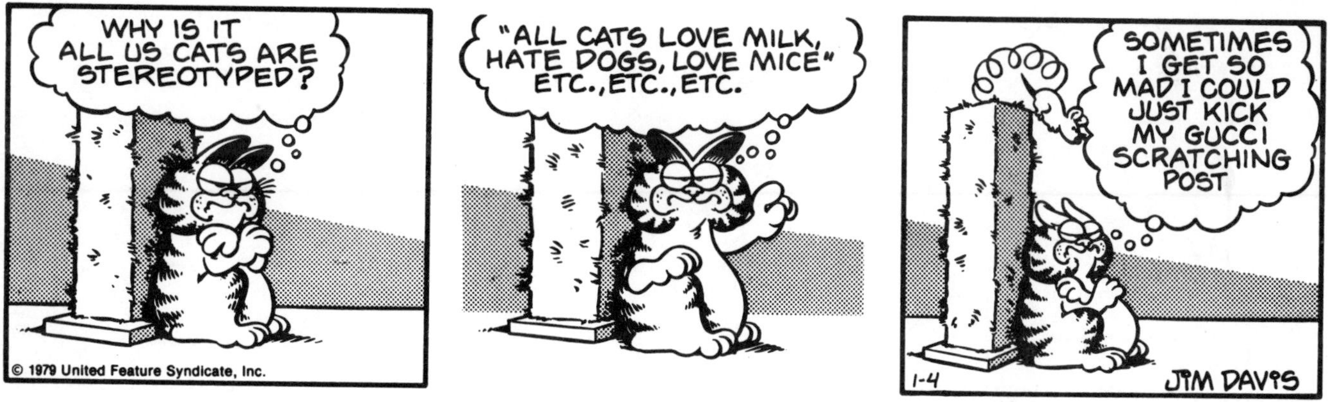
WHY IS IT ALL US CATS ARE STEREOTYPED?
"ALL CATS LOVE MILK, HATE DOGS, LOVE MICE" ETC., ETC., ETC.
SOMETIMES I GET SO MAD I COULD JUST KICK MY GUCCI SCRATCHING POST
© 1979 United Feature Syndicate, Inc.
1-4
JIM DAVIS

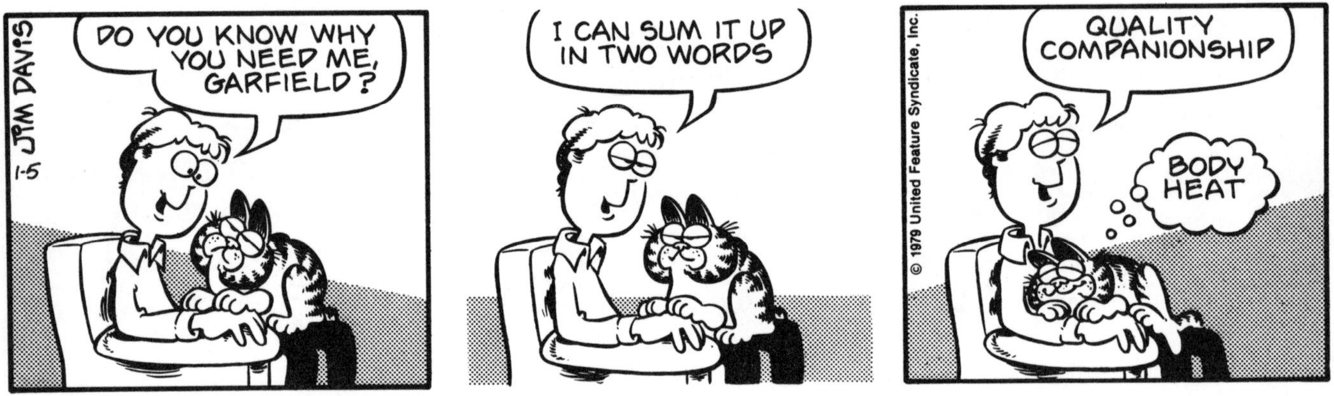
JIM DAVIS
1-5
DO YOU KNOW WHY YOU NEED ME, GARFIELD?
I CAN SUM IT UP IN TWO WORDS
© 1979 United Feature Syndicate, Inc.
QUALITY COMPANIONSHIP
BODY HEAT

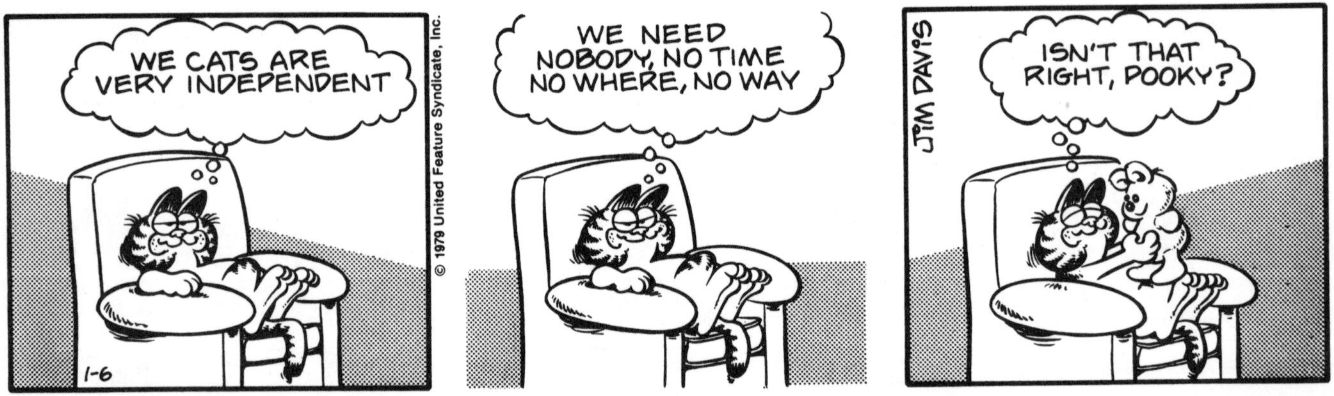
WE CATS ARE VERY INDEPENDENT
1-6
© 1979 United Feature Syndicate, Inc.
WE NEED NOBODY, NO TIME NO WHERE, NO WAY
JIM DAVIS
ISN'T THAT RIGHT, POOKY?

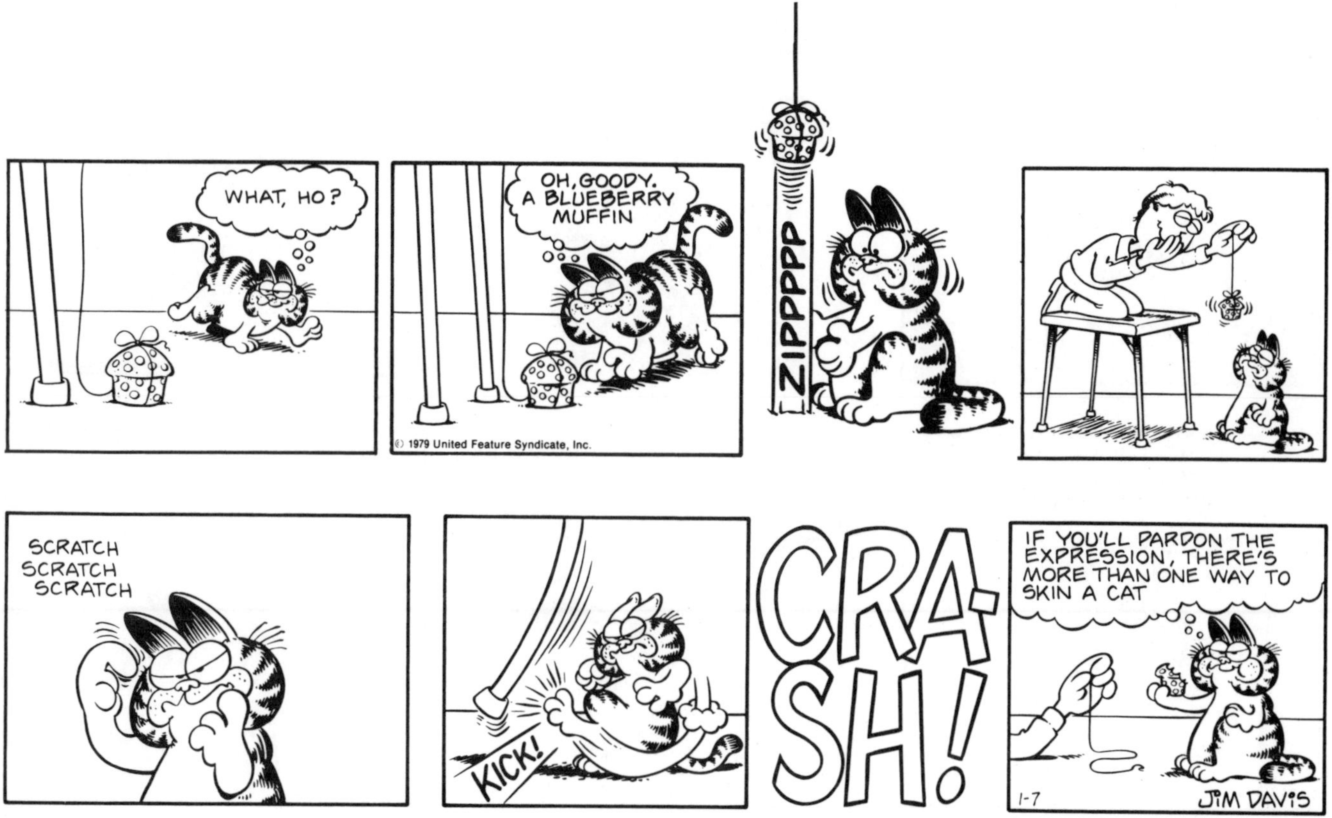
WHAT, HO?
OH, GOODY. A BLUEBERRY MUFFIN
© 1979 United Feature Syndicate, Inc.
ZIPPPPP
SCRATCH SCRATCH SCRATCH
KICK!
CRA-SH!
IF YOU'LL PARDON THE EXPRESSION, THERE'S MORE THAN ONE WAY TO SKIN A CAT
1-7
JIM DAVIS

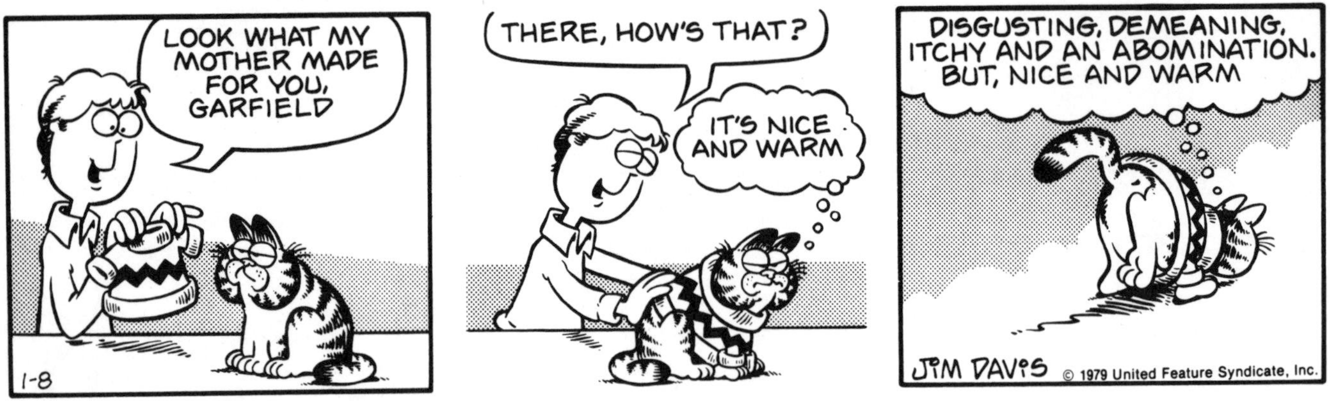
LOOK WHAT MY MOTHER MADE FOR YOU, GARFIELD
1-8
THERE, HOW'S THAT?
IT'S NICE AND WARM
DISGUSTING, DEMEANING, ITCHY AND AN ABOMINATION. BUT, NICE AND WARM
JIM DAVIS
© 1979 United Feature Syndicate, Inc.

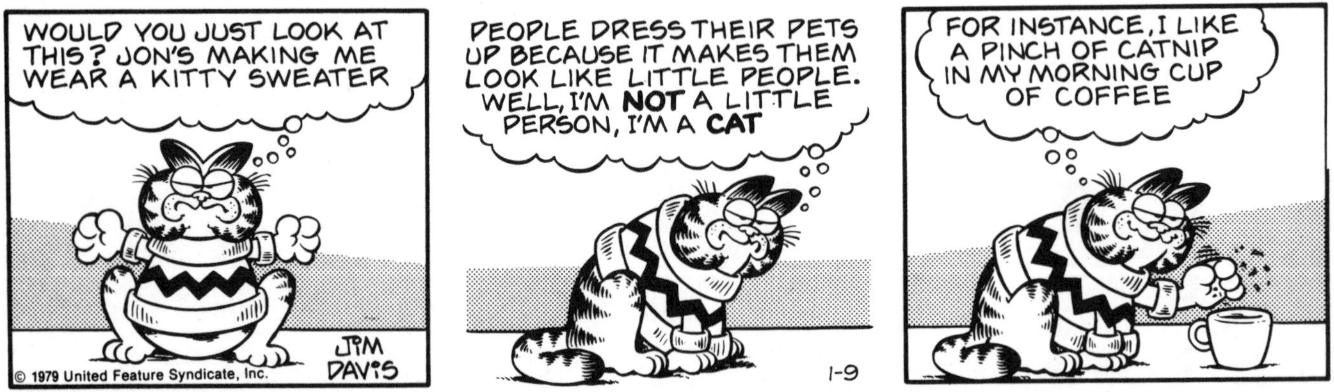
WOULD YOU JUST LOOK AT THIS? JON'S MAKING ME WEAR A KITTY SWEATER
© 1979 United Feature Syndicate, Inc.
JIM DAVIS
PEOPLE DRESS THEIR PETS UP BECAUSE IT MAKES THEM LOOK LIKE LITTLE PEOPLE. WELL, I'M **NOT** A LITTLE PERSON, I'M A **CAT**
1-9
FOR INSTANCE, I LIKE A PINCH OF CATNIP IN MY MORNING CUP OF COFFEE

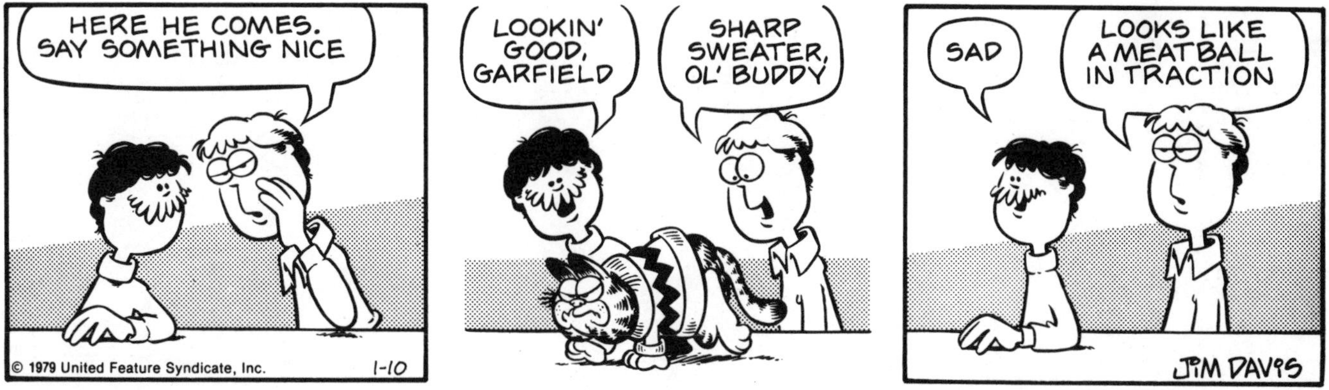
HERE HE COMES. SAY SOMETHING NICE
© 1979 United Feature Syndicate, Inc.
1-10
LOOKIN' GOOD, GARFIELD
SHARP SWEATER, OL' BUDDY
SAD
LOOKS LIKE A MEATBALL IN TRACTION
JIM DAVIS

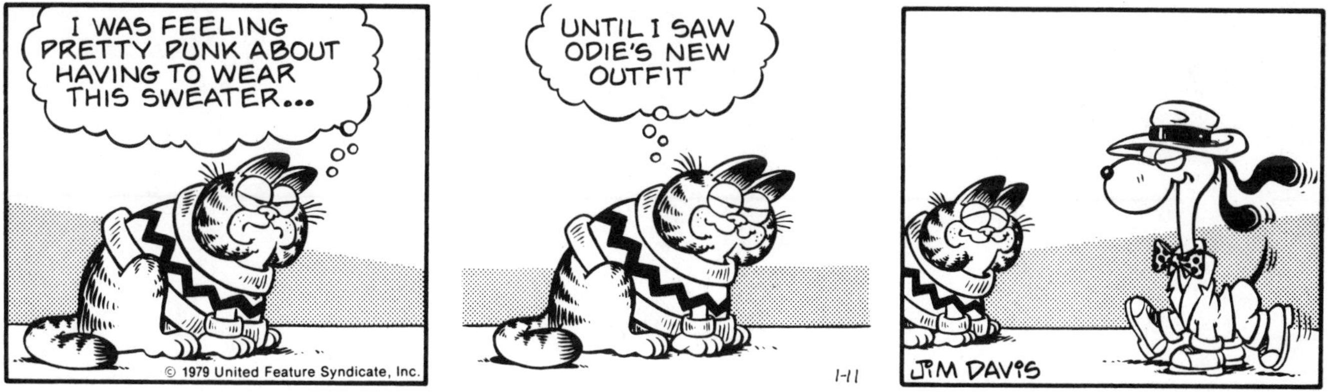
I WAS FEELING PRETTY PUNK ABOUT HAVING TO WEAR THIS SWEATER...
© 1979 United Feature Syndicate, Inc.
UNTIL I SAW ODIE'S NEW OUTFIT
1-11
JIM DAVIS

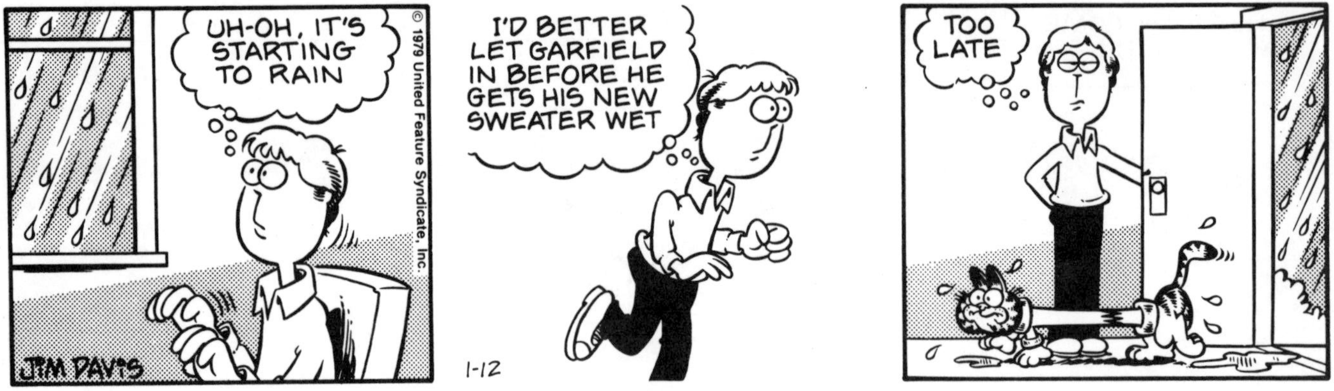
UH-OH, IT'S STARTING TO RAIN
© 1979 United Feature Syndicate, Inc.
JIM DAVIS
I'D BETTER LET GARFIELD IN BEFORE HE GETS HIS NEW SWEATER WET
1-12
TOO LATE

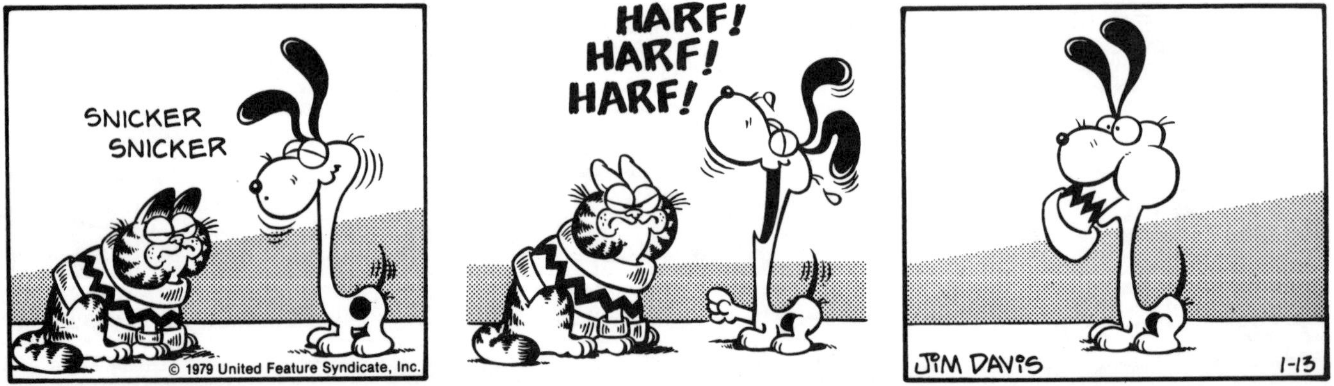
SNICKER
SNICKER
© 1979 United Feature Syndicate, Inc.
HARF!
HARF!
HARF!
JIM DAVIS
1-13

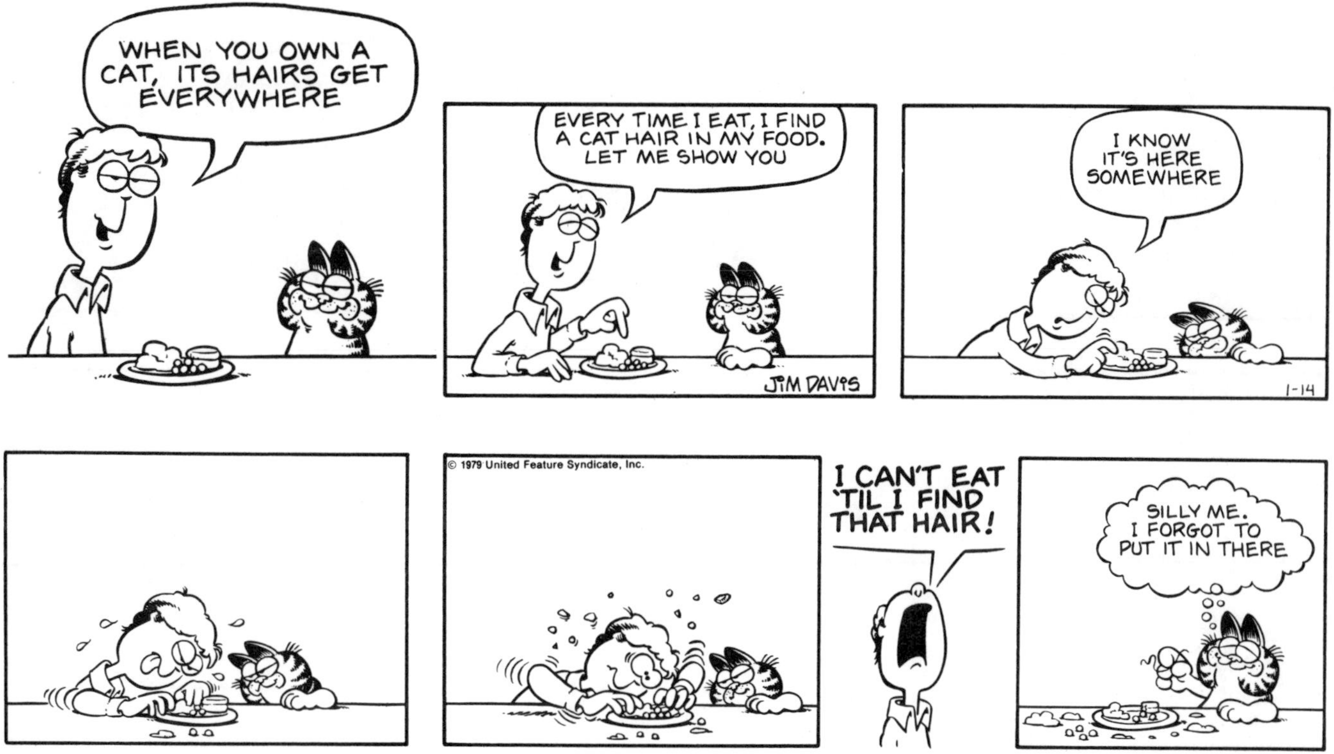
WHEN YOU OWN A CAT, ITS HAIRS GET EVERYWHERE
EVERY TIME I EAT, I FIND A CAT HAIR IN MY FOOD. LET ME SHOW YOU
JIM DAVIS
I KNOW IT'S HERE SOMEWHERE
1-14
© 1979 United Feature Syndicate, Inc.
I CAN'T EAT 'TIL I FIND THAT HAIR!
SILLY ME. I FORGOT TO PUT IT IN THERE

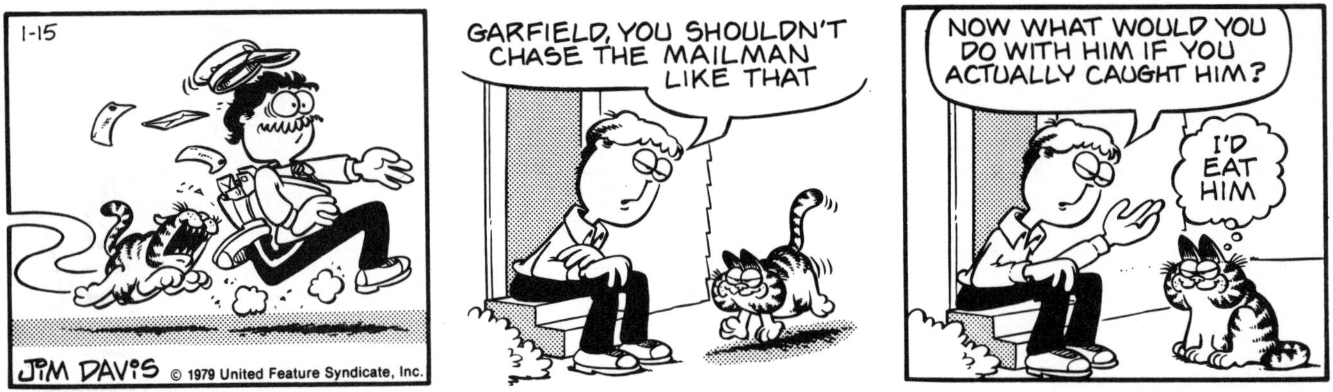
1-15
GARFIELD, YOU SHOULDN'T CHASE THE MAILMAN LIKE THAT
NOW WHAT WOULD YOU DO WITH HIM IF YOU ACTUALLY CAUGHT HIM?
I'D EAT HIM
JIM DAVIS © 1979 United Feature Syndicate, Inc.

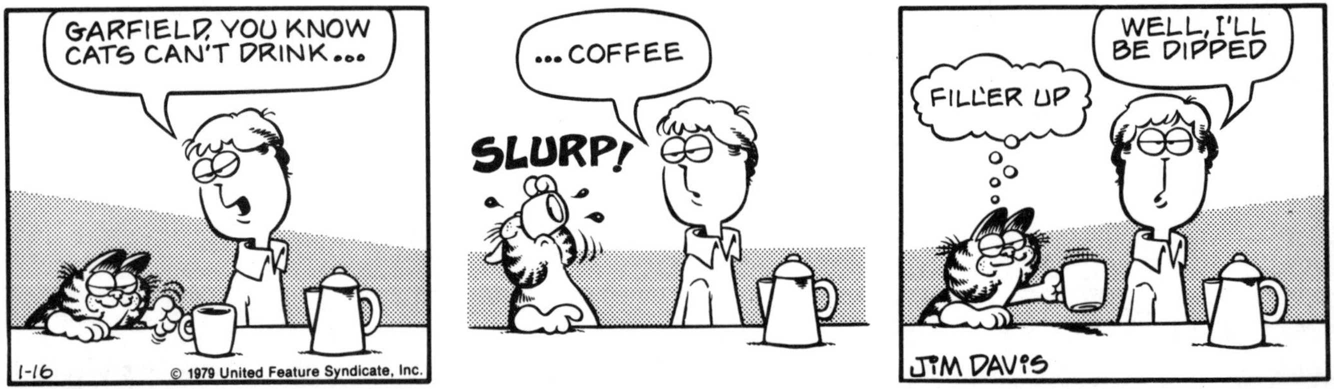
GARFIELD, YOU KNOW CATS CAN'T DRINK...
1-16 © 1979 United Feature Syndicate, Inc.
...COFFEE
SLURP!
FILL'ER UP
WELL, I'LL BE DIPPED
JIM DAVIS

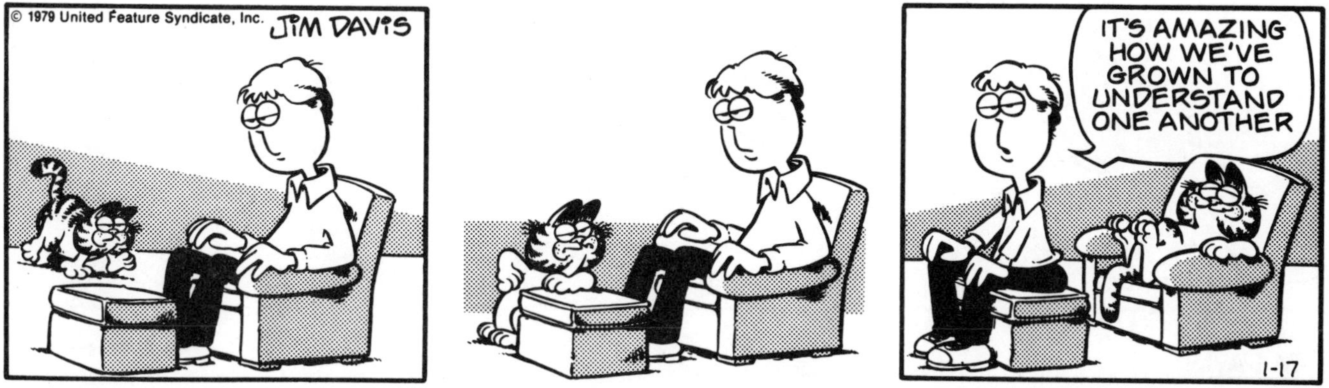
© 1979 United Feature Syndicate, Inc.
JIM DAVIS
IT'S AMAZING HOW WE'VE GROWN TO UNDERSTAND ONE ANOTHER
1-17

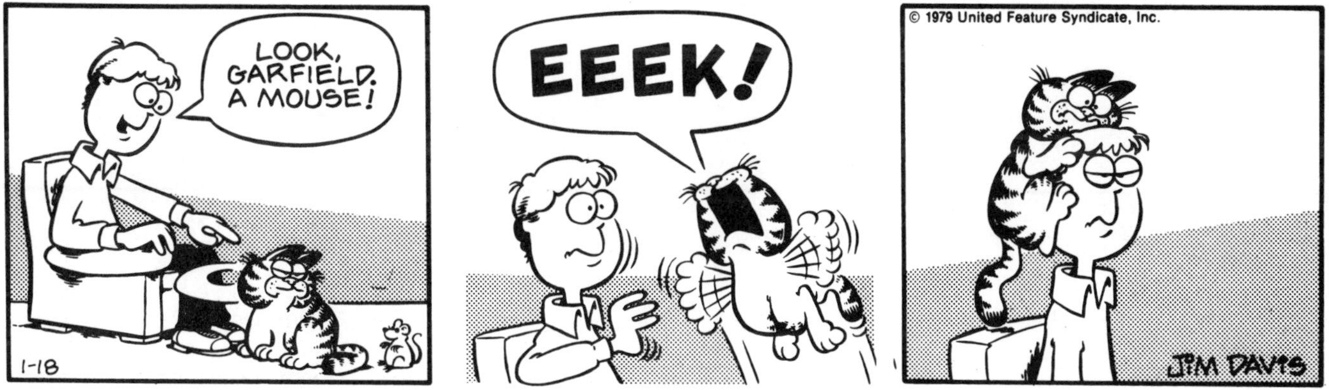
LOOK, GARFIELD. A MOUSE!
1-18
EEEK!
© 1979 United Feature Syndicate, Inc.
JIM DAVIS

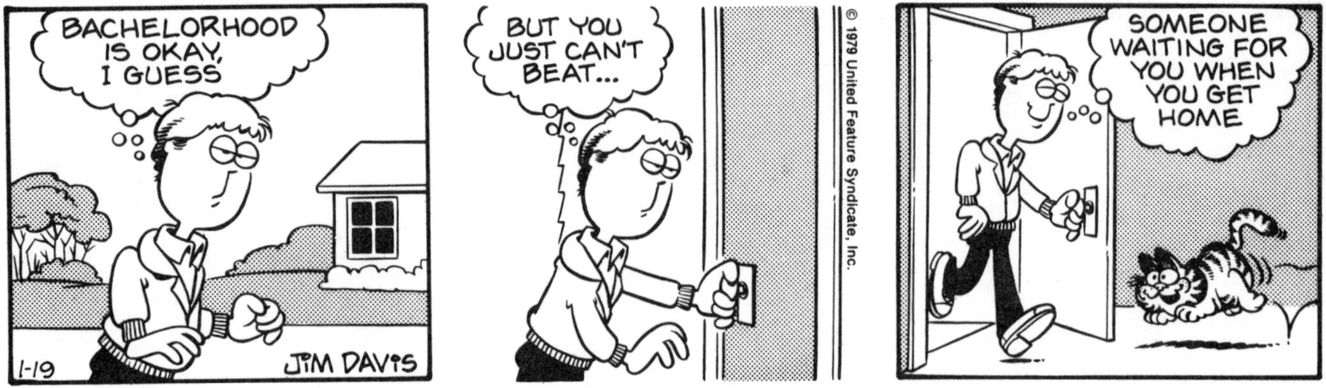
BACHELORHOOD IS OKAY, I GUESS
1-19
JIM DAVIS
BUT YOU JUST CAN'T BEAT...
© 1979 United Feature Syndicate, Inc.
SOMEONE WAITING FOR YOU WHEN YOU GET HOME

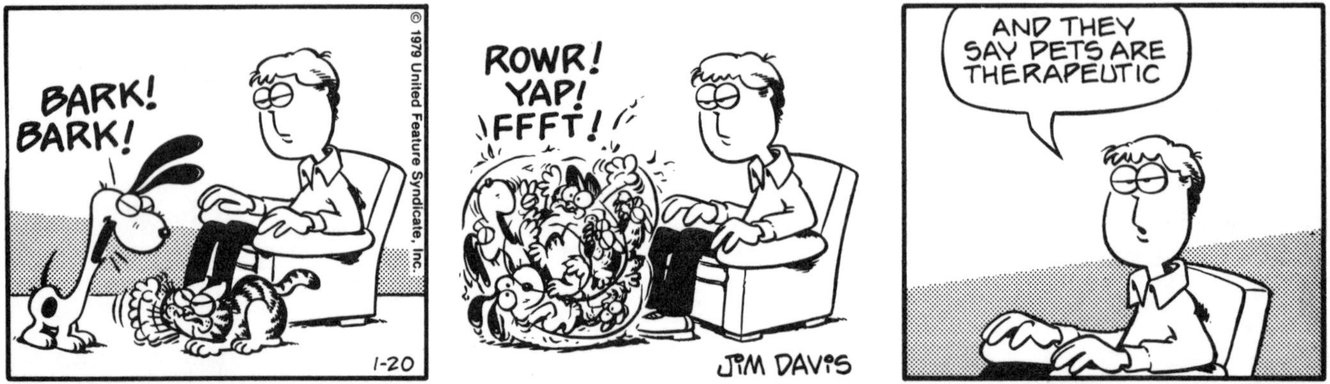
BARK! BARK!
© 1979 United Feature Syndicate, Inc.
1-20
ROWR! YAP! FFFT!
JIM DAVIS
AND THEY SAY PETS ARE THERAPEUTIC

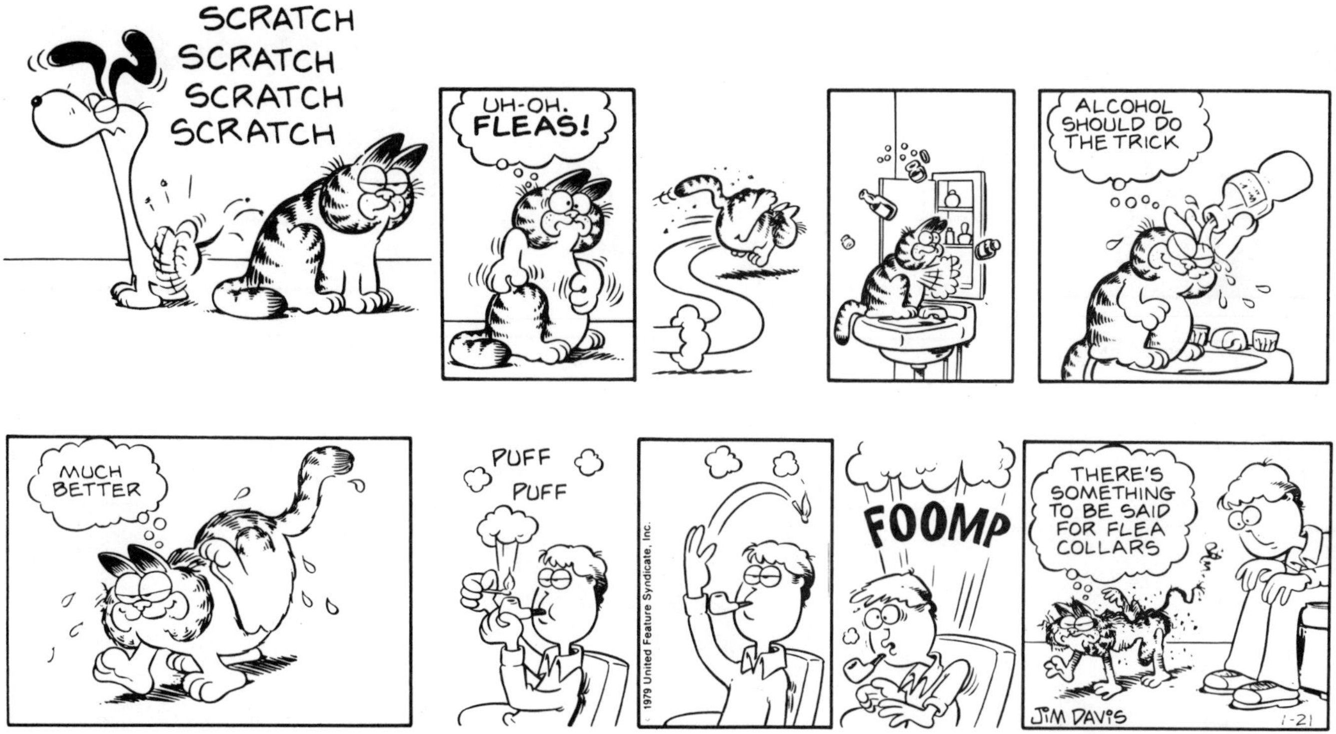
SCRATCH
SCRATCH
SCRATCH
SCRATCH
UH-OH. FLEAS!
ALCOHOL SHOULD DO THE TRICK
MUCH BETTER
PUFF
PUFF
FOOMP
THERE'S SOMETHING TO BE SAID FOR FLEA COLLARS
© 1979 United Feature Syndicate, Inc.
JIM DAVIS
1-21

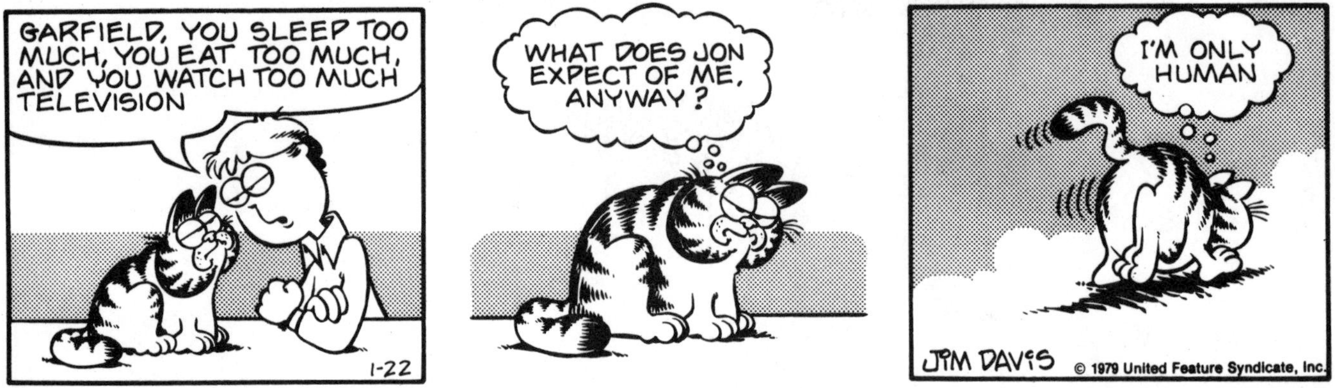
GARFIELD, YOU SLEEP TOO MUCH, YOU EAT TOO MUCH, AND YOU WATCH TOO MUCH TELEVISION
1-22
WHAT DOES JON EXPECT OF ME, ANYWAY?
I'M ONLY HUMAN
JIM DAVIS
© 1979 United Feature Syndicate, Inc.

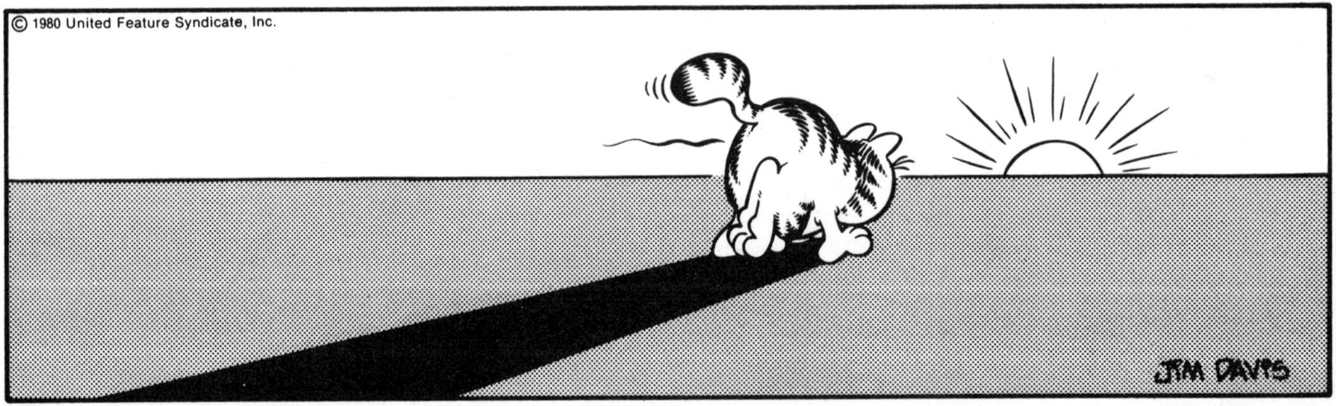
© 1980 United Feature Syndicate, Inc.
JIM DAVIS